Taylor's Guides to Gardening

Frances Tenenbaum, Editor

HOUGHTON MIFFLIN COMPANY
Boston · New York

Taylor's Guide to Shade Gardening

Copyright © 1994 by Houghton Mifflin Company
Drawings copyright © 1994 by Steve Buchanan

Taylor's Guide is a registered trademark of Houghton Mifflin Company.

Library of Congress Cataloging-in-Publication Data
Taylor's guide to shade gardening / Frances Tenenbaum, editor ;
[drawings by Steve Buchanan].
       p.   cm. — (Taylor's guides to gardening)
   Includes index.
   ISBN 0-395-65165-4
   1. Gardening in the shade.   2. Shade-tolerant plants.
I. Tenenbaum, Frances.   II. Taylor's encyclopedia of gardening.
III. Title: Guide to shade gardening.   IV. Series.
SB434.7.T4   1994   93-17635
635.9′54 — dc20   CIP

Printed and bound in Hong Kong

DNP 10 9 8 7 6 5 4

Cover photograph by Joanne Pavia
Drawings by Steve Buchanan

Contents

Contributors

Nancy Beaubaire, author of the essay on pests and diseases, is the editor of *Fine Gardening* magazine. She has a master's degree in horticulture from Purdue University and is an experienced practitioner of environmentally sound approaches to gardening and landscaping. She wrote about the organic control of pests and diseases in *Taylor's Guide to Natural Gardening.*

Steve Buchanan did the illustrations for this book, as he has for other volumes in the Taylor's Guide series. He specializes in natural history subjects. His work has appeared in *Horticulture, Garden Design, Fine Gardening,* the *New York Times,* and several books.

Rosalie Davis worked as an editor and writer for *Horticulture* magazine for ten years. She wrote the plant encyclopedia for this guide. In addition, she is the author of the essay "Shade: A Kind of Light."

Sydney Eddison's Connecticut garden has been featured on the PBS television series "The Victory Garden" and in the pages of the *New York Times.* She is the author of many magazine articles and two books, *A Patchwork Garden* and *A Passion for Daylilies.* In this guide, she tells how to grow plants successfully in shade.

Judy Glattstein, a widely published garden writer and lecturer, is the author of *Garden Design with Foliage.* She was guest editor and a contributor to the Brooklyn Botanic Garden handbooks, *Gardener's World of Bulbs* and *Plants for Problem Places.* She teaches courses at the New York Botanical Garden and the Institute for Ecosystem Studies. She wrote the essay on foliage plants for shade for this book.

Pamela Harper, author of *Designing with Perennials,* wrote the essay on perennials for this guide. She has been gardening, writing, and photographing plants since she moved here from England twenty-five years ago. Many of the pictures in this and other Taylor's Guides are hers.

Peter Loewer is the author and illustrator of dozens of books and articles on gardening, including *The Evening Garden* and *Tough Plants for Tough Places.* After many years of gardening in New York State, he recently moved to North Carolina. He is the author of the essay on shade gardening in the South.

Mary Ann McGourty, author of the essay on ground covers, is the owner, with her husband, Fred, of Hillside Gardens, a nursery in Norfolk, Connecticut. They specialize in uncommon perennials and also design perennial borders for clients in several states. She was the major contributor to *Taylor's Guide to Ground Covers, Vines and Grasses.*

Warren Schultz, author of the essay on lawns, is a former editor-in-chief of *National Gardening Magazine* and author of *The Chemical-Free Lawn,* published by Rodale Press. He wrote about lawns for *Taylor's Guide to Garden Techniques.*

George Waters, author of the introductory essay on the pleasures of shade, is the editor of *Pacific Horticulture,* one of our most distinguished gardening magazines. He was born and educated in England, where, as an avid gardener, he helped found the Garden History Society. He moved to California in 1972, and four years later helped launch *Pacific Horticulture* to provide gardeners in the summer-dry Western states with their own publication.

Mobee Weinstein, a member of the staff of the New York Botanical Garden, initiated a fern herbarium at the Garden and was primarily responsible for the fern collection. She is a past president of the New York chapter of the American Fern Society and the author, in this guide, of the essay "Ferns."

Linda Yang wrote the essay on city gardens for this guide. She is author of *The City Gardener's Handbook: From Balcony to Backyard* from which this essay has been adapted. Since 1979 she has been a garden writer for the *New York Times* and her articles appear in many other periodicals. She was guest editor for the Brooklyn Botanic Garden handbook *Town and City Gardener.* Her own patch of earth is in New York City, about five blocks from Rockefeller Center.

Hardiness Zone Map

ZONE 1	BELOW	−50° F	
ZONE 2	−50° TO −40°		
ZONE 3	−40° TO −30°		
ZONE 4	−30° TO −20°		
ZONE 5	−20° TO −10°		
ZONE 6	−10° TO 0°		
ZONE 7	0° TO 10°		
ZONE 8	10° TO 20°		
ZONE 9	20° TO 30°		
ZONE 10	30° TO 40°		
ZONE 11	ABOVE 40°		

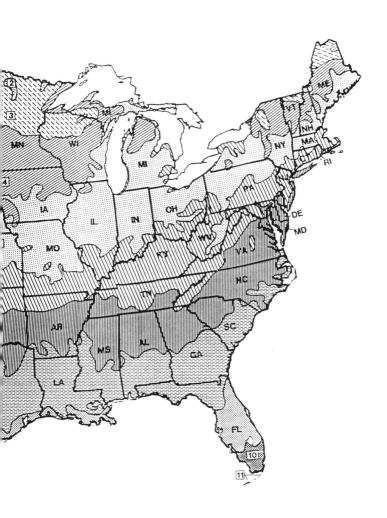

The Pleasures of Shade

GEORGE WATERS

I have sometimes asked myself why we need books with titles like *Gardening in the Shade, Shade Gardening,* and the like. Every garden has some shade cast by buildings or by trees; they also have sunny areas, but if there is a book called *Gardening in the Sun,* I have yet to find it. Is it that shade is seen as extraordinary, even as something to be avoided in the garden when possible? A neighbor once asked me to remove a tree that threw shade onto his plot. He had no trees of his own, and would rather have seen mine gone than make use of its shade for plants that prefer it. I know of others whose first task in a new garden is to fell every tree within reach.

Perhaps the subconscious is at work and shade is felt to be unwholesome because of some childhood dread. Most of us deep down link shade with unsavory characters, fears of the night, and death. Poets must share the blame for this: Blunden with his "death's shadow at the door," Brooke with his "shade and loneliness and mire," and Milton with his "beckoning shadows dire."

Poets have been too ready to praise sunlight, as well; having told us that shade is a blight they compound the felony by persuading us that everything bright is good. This is far from the truth, and the sun-worshiping population is learning the folly of its annual dash to the beach as the ozone lets through more and more of those awful ultraviolet rays.

We heliophobes appreciate shade in the garden and where it is not provided by tree or building hastily repair the deficiency with arbors, trellises, and quick-growing plants. George Schenk, in *The Complete Shade Gardener,* has shown us how valuable shade is for its contribution to the beauty of the garden, and to the well-being of the gardener. When doctors assure us that wide-brimmed hats and high-potency sunscreen help protect us from the sun's harmful rays, shady gardens are no longer merely a delight, they are a necessity.

Truth is that shady areas in the garden are more useful than places where sunlight is unremitting. So many plants have evolved sheltered from sunlight, or partially so, that even a short list of them brought into the garden will use up the shade from every wall and fence, every tree and bush, every post and rock. In the end you will be bringing in extra rocks to provide more shady places for little plants you can't do without.

The difficulty, if difficulty there be, has less to do with shade than with what commonly comes with it. Soil in the shade of trees is often full of roots, and in summer is desiccated from the tree's need for water. Soil near buildings may be shaded not only from sun but from rain, as well. Concrete, brick, and stone are porous and draw water from soil, which then evaporates on the air, further reducing moisture for plants near the foundations of buildings. Shade is sometimes blamed when lack of moisture is the culprit. But when the truth is known, gardeners learn to exploit the situation and grow unusual plants that would not flourish elsewhere in their gardens. There are plants, some early crocuses for example, that are dormant in summer and abhor moisture while resting. They are happiest near a deciduous tree whose bare branches permit winter rains to reach the roots and whose late leafing allows spring sunlight to warm their leaves and flower buds.

Pittosporums are at home in shady places and will make the most of dry soil; Japanese anemones flourish to such a degree in the shade that many gardeners withhold water to check their spread; the little wild cyclamens and some narcissuses and irises are also at home in shady places and dryish soil, and the list goes on. There are usually several ways of planting such places; success comes from experiment, but no plant will survive soil that is permanently dry. Beneath stone or concrete paving, 2 or 3 feet from a wall, plants often find a cool, moist reservoir in which roots luxuriate away from the dry soil they were placed in. Many old gardeners have learned to relocate languishing plants near a paved path and expect immediate improvement. Reversing the procedure — laying pavement where roots are in need of succor — may be the answer to a plant's prayer.

Ornamental gardens answer our need for a private world of fantasy, a secret place, enclosed and protected. In these gardens, shade is the object, not the objection. The last word in such private hideaways is, I suppose, the Victorian grotto, where ferns cover walls of rocks and shells and ivy tendrils curl about the ears of wan marble busts. Few of us now enjoy such lugubrious inventions, but we learn from them of the powerful effect upon lively imaginations which can be achieved with few resources. Any garden, however small, can be provided with a green enclosure in which books may be read, letters written, and dreams nourished, surrounded by some of the loveliest and most satisfactory of plants — those distinguished for their leaves. Not only ferns — although among them alone the variety of patterns challenges the ingenuity of the most ambitious garden designer — but primulas, hostas, smilacinas, liriopes, epimediums, correas, impatiens, ajugas, ivies, hydrangeas, monstera, ruscus, and many others will share shade, and have leaves that set off the delicacy of ferns in arrangements that please throughout the season. Many bring the fleeting glory of flowers, too, and some are scented. With them we can undo the wrongs of poets, relish shade in the garden, and furnish it gloriously.

Shade: A Kind of Light

ROSALIE DAVIS

Like leaning daffodils, gardeners favor light. The aphorism, "I Count None but Sunny Hours," once common on sundials, still sums up our worship of the great star's warming rays. But sun burns as often as it bronzes; we value settlements graced by mature plantings because shade protects plants, people, and dwellings from too much of a good thing.

As gardeners and their plantings age, shade becomes more welcome and more abundant. The gardener with some shade who combines the right plant with smart culture and appropriate design probably works a richer canvas than one who paints in unrelenting glare. Even Mediterraneans like *Iris pallida* benefit from a little shade; their blooms last longer and their glaucous leaves don't scorch and brown as easily. Plants with variegated foliage, so suited to highlighting the shadowy side of a planting, seldom perform as well in sun. Seedlings and transplants need shade while they establish themselves.

Nevertheless, few plants require shade. They need adequate light to grow, bloom, and reproduce. Many garden varieties have been bred in sunny nurseries and greenhouses; over the years hybridizers have inadvertently selected plants which prefer sun and culled out shade-lovers. While a little shade makes us more comfortable and often delays and extends bloom time, a paucity of light can result in fewer flowers, leggy plants, and leaves that lack substance and texture. Plants demand more or less light, according to species, cultivar, and age, as well as the other conditions which characterize a given site: available moisture, the direction of light and the nature of the objects casting the shadows, as well as climate and soil quality. Happily, a few hours of direct sun, filtered light, or indirect light suffices for many plants if conditions are otherwise favorable. After all, shade is not the opposite of full sun; midnight is. Shade is a kind of light.

As such it changes constantly. Natural light varies with latitude (your geographical location in relation to the equator), season, and time of day. Weather and topography interfere with light, changing the way vegetation grows. So, before remaking your landscape or acquiring a new inventory of plants, it makes sense to establish how much and what kind of shade you have — and where, and when.

Books on alternative energy show how to tally your solar potential by charting the paths of altitude and azimuth angles across your yard throughout the year. Good exercise, no doubt, for agriculturists and architects who wisely try to use all available foot-candles of light. But most amateurs trying to succeed with ornamentals won't need to involve themselves with compass and calculator to improve their understanding of the intensity, duration, and existing patterns of light and shadow in their yards and gardens. A few simple truths from earth science, observation, and rational design would serve as well.

Latitude

This book will be most useful for North Americans who garden in a temperate climate, corresponding approximately to zones 4 to 8 (on the United States Department of Agriculture's hardiness map). These lands experience more seasonal variation in light, as well as heat, than climatic extremes nearer the Arctic Circle to the north or the Tropic of Cancer toward the south. Because the earth is round and its orbit stationary, lands at the equator receive the shortest and strongest rays of sun. The farther one gets from the middle of the globe, the longer and weaker are the sun's rays. In this hemisphere, therefore, the further south you live, the more light and heat your garden will receive (and the longer your growing season will be).

Seasonal Changes

As we revolve around the sun each year, light shifts with the seasons because the earth is slightly tilted on its axis. Shade gardeners know this means that sunlight effectively moves north in winter and spring, and south in summer and autumn, when shadows grow longer and the days grow shorter. At the winter solstice in late December, the shortest day of the year, the sun reaches its southernmost point and is furthest from the North American garden. Then it reverses course, progressing closer north throughout the snowiest, coldest, but always lengthening days of winter.

As the sun moves toward us, it climbs higher and higher on the horizon, each day falling at a more and more direct — therefore sunnier — angle. The advancing sun reaches the halfway point at the spring equinox in March (and on its retreat, in September) and its annual zenith at the time of the summer solstice in late June. On that longest day the sun has reached its northernmost limit; it will climb no closer. Shadows are at their shortest and shade will never be more welcome. From that point, the cycle renews: the sunlight retreats, moving south and away; the angle of light slackens; the days grow shorter and eventually cooler.

Although the sun is the same distance from us at the autumnal equinox in September as it is at the vernal equinox in March, spring and fall in the shady garden differ. In spring, the ground tends to be cool and damp, and still-bare deciduous trees allow considerable sunlight. In autumn, the same spot may be much warmer, drier, and until leaf-fall, shadier.

Owing to the low profile of the sun, the average house casts a long, cold shadow on a north-facing back yard for most of the winter, but the same spot in summer — even in a higher latitude — may receive significant early and late light. Such a place is better for a small flowering tree, such as a kousa dogwood, than a full-size conifer, like a Norway spruce, which would shade the place even more. A deciduous specimen would admit light on the darkest days of the year and provide a welcome tent of shade in high summer.

Morning Sun and Afternoon Shade

Whatever the season, the sun rises in the east and sets in the west. It reaches its daily climax at noon (1 P.M. during daylight-saving time), when it is due south and its rays are overhead. Like spring and fall, morning and afternoon sun correspond numerically, but there the similarity ends. While the angle of the sun at 11 A.M. may be the same as it is at 1 P.M., early and late light speak different languages.

Morning is the spring of the day. Plants are full of moisture, the air is cool and damp, and light is a welcome tonic. The eastern side of a house, wall, tree, hedge, or slope, therefore, shelters plantings during the heat of the day from excessive moisture loss that would occur if they were exposed on the western side of the same feature. (Chiefly, plants lose water through simple evaporational cooling besides their own processes of transpiration and respiration.)

Afternoon, on the other hand, is more like autumn. It is warmer and drier. As the sun begins its afternoon decline, its angle may weaken, but the decrease in humidity and increase in heat that usually accompany it cause plants to need more and more water, until, with evening, the day begins to cool off. By afternoon, unfortunately, much water in the soil's surface, in plant tissue, and in the air has been used. Typically, everything warms up and continues losing moisture, placing plants under greater and greater stress.

Plants on a western exposure receive shade in the morning when they are best able to tolerate full sun, and are exposed to sun late in the day when they would most benefit from shade. It is no wonder that grapevines and gardeners alike welcome an afternoon rain in summer to bring cooling cloud cover and invigorating moisture back to earth. And a southern or western site exposed to midday sun can be as much of a problem in winter in cold climates, especially for broad-leaved evergreens, as in summer in warm climates.

Nature solves such problems in interesting ways. The leaves of American beech saplings, for example, persist through winter to shade the juvenile bark from winter sunscald. Young plants of all species typically are found in the shadow of older growth. Gardeners must rely more on sensible selection, siting, design, and culture.

Exposure

Given the daily and seasonal patterns of sunlight, it is no surprise that the compass orientation of a site — whether it faces east, west, north, or south — matters so much. Naturally, in every garden in the northern hemisphere, the southern exposure will always prove the lightest and warmest because that is the origin of sunlight. At any given latitude in most of the contiguous forty-eight states, therefore, light is most intense on a southern exposure, at noon, on an unclouded midsummer's day. An umbrella of deciduous trees on the sunny, southern side of your garden is more likely to expand your choices of what you can grow than to limit them. Incidentally, it also keeps paint from peeling, clapboards from cracking, and children from sunburning.

If shade is most welcome and most needed on the southern exposure, the opposite is true for the northern. And topography alone creates oblique shade on a north-facing slope, because the sun comes from the south. In the South, where intense sunlight often limits a gardener's choices, northern slopes tend to be preferred locations. In the North, southern exposures may offer welcome sun and light to many plants in the shorter, cooler growing season.

Even on a small scale, orientation is significant. The western side of a sugar maple turns red in autumn before the eastern side of the same tree. It is nice to have a whole house to shade an east-facing mixed border, but if your best location is a western side yard, a wall or fence on that side of a planting may provide enough shade to protect plants and conserve moisture in the soil. In such a microclimate, even a little shade may prolong the flowering of lilies, preserve a cool root-run for clematis in summer, and moderate the fluctuations of temperature that can play havoc with marginally hardy perennials in winter.

Shade gardeners must always keep in mind that any direct eastern, western, northern, or southern exposure may be problematic, depending on the limitations of the individual site and requirements of plants you are trying to grow. While eastern light is generally ideal for the majority of traditional garden plants, if that side of your garden is a microclimate exposed to wind, sea spray, dust, car exhaust, or road salt, far fewer plants will thrive.

Climate

Climate influences how much sun any given plant can take, how much shade it would prefer. A cloudy day is always a shady day, and good for transplanting and prolonging bloom. Similarly, in a so-called "English" climate, typified by frequent fog, high humidity, and less variation in temperature, such as the Pacific Northwest and parts of the coastal Atlantic states experience, plants need more sun. In the sere, cloudless environs of eastern Colorado, even notorious sun-soakers like roses, water lilies, cacti, and succulents would enjoy a patch of shade in the middle of the day. In fact, the more variation in temperature that your region has, the more shade will be needed to modify the damage extreme heat and cold do to plants.

And wherever wind and storms habitually batter a garden, understory plantings will appreciate the additional mechanical buffer that shade trees, hedges, and artificial windbreaks provide. Every region of the country has its own peculiarities of climate that the wise shade gardener needs to study. The evergreen magnolia that enjoys six hours of sun in Boston might settle for three in Charleston. From Washington, D.C. (located in zone 7) south, three hours of direct sun between 11:30 A.M. and 4 P.M. is generally considered full sun, enough for almost any garden ornamental you might wish to grow. In these regions, most gardeners need shade at noon when intense sunlight can restrict a landscaper's choices as fully as the boreal cold and darkness of zone 3.

Categories of Shade

Armed with this basic information about the variables of light and shade, you will probably find it worthwhile to study the habits of sunlight in your own beds and borders over the course of a year. You will want to see how things look when leaves are out and when they are gone, in winter when shadows are long and long-lasting, and in summer when they are short and fleeting. Then try to describe these areas in traditional shade gardening terms. The larger the garden, of course, the more types of shade it will boast and the more choices you, as a gardener, will have.

There are several time-honored categories that characterize in the broadest terms the type of shade a given area receives: part, light, full, and dense shade. Assigning your beds and borders these labels should be to the shade gardener what the value drawing is to the art student: an exercise in assigning to gradations of light and shadow fixed positive or negative values. In the following descriptions, it is assumed that conditions are otherwise good, that is, capable of sustaining a variety of plants. The exception is the dense and dry category, which is challenging, but not hopeless.

Wherever you live, these classifications will prove most useful in selecting and siting plants if you accept them as one early step in evaluating the shade in your own garden. At best, these relative terms have been in use long enough to have an accepted meaning among shade gardeners. At their weakest, these categories may limit description to the quantity of light a place receives, when another factor — notably moisture — might actually spell the difference between success or failure of a given plant.

Part Shade

Most gardeners would like to have a spot in their garden that is partly shaded. Also called semi- or half-shade, part shade makes for the sunniest sort of shade garden, an area which alternates between full sun and full shade. Preferably, the area is shaded during midday and afternoon and is open and sunnier during the cooler, more humid, morning hours. Exactly how many hours varies enormously, but at least a few hours of direct sun are desirable. Better to have more in cooler northern and foggier climates and less in hotter southern or bright Mediterranean locales.

An example would be a border on the eastern side of a house which receives direct sun until midday and progressively more shade throughout the afternoon when the shadow of the building would protect it. Other man-made structures that provide half-shade might be a pergola, a fence of spaced pickets, or a lathhouse. To the benefit of plants in its shadow, any of these would approximately halve available sun. The boards in these constructions should run north to south, not east to west.

The yard that receives morning light and afternoon shade allows for a wealth of plants. Here would prosper billowing thickets of shrubs for year-round interest; luxuriant mixed borders for endless seasonal interest; cutting gardens; a world of hostas and lilies; and fine lawns of fescues, perennial rye, and shade-loving cultivars of Kentucky blue.

In such an arena, one can experiment with a surprising number of plants too often reserved for sun, such as choice annuals, spring and summer bulbs, herbs, foliage plants, ornamental grasses, dwarf conifers, and rock-garden subjects, provided you have a good four to six hours of full sun every day. With fewer hours, gardeners will move toward the shadier palette of plants that thrive in light shade.

Light Shade

Light shade offers an ideal compromise between human comfort and horticultural promise. Also called dappled or moving shade, light shade lies between part shade and full shade. Here, the sun never seems far away and in fact is not so much blocked as it is filtered, typically by the translucent screen of deciduous trees such as black locust, which has an airy canopy of small leaves. Preferably, species should also be deep-rooted and thus compatible with understory plants — smaller trees, shrubs, and herbaceous plants. Shallow-rooted trees like maples and sycamore rob the soil of moisture and nutrients.

Deciduous trees which have a denser canopy of leaves, such as tulip poplars, may be limbed up to produce that enhanced atmosphere known as high shade, that sine qua non of shade gardening under which plants enjoy good air circulation and adequate sun as well as protection from the intense light of noon. In late fall, winter, and early spring when these trees are bare, the lightly shaded area will still be desirable, being then open and sunny.

Under such a radiant canopy, one can choose from that rich miscellany of garden subjects one thinks of most often in terms of shade gardening: choice ground covers, ferns, and woodland wildflowers. Here would also flourish certain small specimen trees such as stewartia and kousa dogwoods; broad-leaved evergreens like camellia, mahonia, *Ilex,* and rhododendrons; shade-tolerant deciduous shrubs like viburnum; many foliage plants; some cool-growing annuals, perennials, bedding plants, and summer-blooming bulbs. Many subjects from the partly shaded garden that grow in only a few hours of direct sun, such as garden foxgloves and hardy geraniums, also thrive in an abundance of indirect and filtered light.

Full Shade

Full shade suggests a garden that is nearly always in substantial shade during the growing season. However, the shade is not that gloomy perpetual kind created by many tall buildings, mature evergreens, or usurping shade trees which are either too dense, too low, or too greedy. Other conditions are good: air moves freely to discourage fungi, and the soil is fertile, well-drained, and moisture-retentive during dry spells. Plants are protected from soil-packing foot traffic, drying winds, animals, flooding, and other environmental stresses. A fairly open area on a northern exposure, an expansive yard surrounded by a perimeter of mature trees, or the ground under spreading, high-limbed old shade trees (such as white oak) or under a glade of arborescent rhododendrons are a few examples.

Though more limited than the earlier categories, full shade is still conducive to the growth of a variety of worthwhile garden plants. These might include ferns, broad-leaved evergreens, a range of ground covers and foliage plants, and still a happy assortment of forest flowers and choice bedding plants like mimulus and impatiens — more than moss and ivy, anyway! Here is where the true shade-lovers live.

Wherever even a limited amount of daylight shines, horticultural opportunities exist if other conditions are good. Variegated ivy and climbing hydrangea would thrive on the walls of a north-facing city courtyard, and urns of caladium and begonia on its floor. Wild ginger, lady ferns, and violets would make a dark and bright tapestry among ferns in quite heavy shade.

Look to nature; there are many plants which evolved at the margin of wood and meadow, on northern and eastern slopes, in the dappled clearings under old-growth hardwood trees, even on the piney floor of softwood forests — wherever a bit of sun comes through there will be flowers. Pachysandra and impatiens do not spell the limits of the shady vocabulary; they are but several of a multitude of useful and beautiful plants.

Dense and Difficult

Critical in all your observations in evaluating shade has been to consider the object making the shadow. Ground under shallow-rooted deciduous trees like maples or low-branching beeches; near tall, mature hedges; or under needled evergreens is seldom promising because it is poor and dry as well as dark. Some trees, like black walnuts, cause additional problems because they produce chemicals which inhibit the growth of other plants. You may be able to limb up, thin, or remove offending trees, but mature deciduous trees that we treasure for privacy or the fruits they bear but that create too much or too dry a shade present the gardener with a difficult choice.

Experimentation is usually worthwhile. The cooling shadows of a white pine might appeal to us on a late afternoon in July, but the roots of the tree would doubtless compete too vigorously for water, and the acidity of fallen needles causes other soil problems. Limbing up such lone sentinels is a hideous solution; you can probably upgrade the soil or water creatively. Perhaps you can thread soaker hoses under the mulch, enough to grow a nice mix of epimediums, woodland wildflowers, and ericaceous evergreen ground covers.

A plant's tolerance for shade is but one index in a complex matrix of cultural requirements and preferences. Dense shade challenges the most experienced gardener, often because the impediment to gardening in the shade is not a lack of light, but a lack of other amenities. The perpetual shade behind a three-story house in a congested neighborhood is a gloom where few green plants would thrive.

There may be enough light for bird's-foot violet, but, like many deeply shaded areas next to artificial structures, drainage has been improved in order to preserve foundation walls and so forth — to the detriment of the soil. There may be alkaline construction rubble as well. Rain leaders that periodically flood such spots hardly make up for the near-desert conditions that prevail in drier weather.

You can deploy that cadre of relentless ground covers that veterans know will grow where nothing else will. Plants like English ivy, pachysandra, goutweed, and lilies-of-the-valley thrive practically anywhere in zones 4 to 9. Even under Norway maples some of the carpet-forming sedums such as *S. kamtschaticum* and *spurium* will grow, without their usual problems of invasiveness. In older brick-walled neighborhoods of East Coast cities one sees plants like these growing between walks and walls, garden plants struggling and succeeding in exceedingly harsh microclimates.

The Joy of Shade

The more one gardens in shade, the more one appreciates the creature comforts and pleasures it offers. Shade gives critical protection to new plantings and broad-leaved evergreens, but its advantages do not end there. Its sheltering umbrella protects us from sunburn and heat. The green cathedral of deciduous trees disarms and transmutes the light of the longest days into a luminous, warm atmosphere. In shade, our eyes behold the color, form, and texture of a garden, of its blossoms, architecture, and leaves with easy clarity and delight. Pictures come out better.

With good sense and artistry, any exposure can be turned to advantage. An espaliered fruit tree may bloom ahead of schedule in a western location, while on the east it will have fewer fruits which ripen later, if at all. That shady northern ell at the back of the house may be too dark for all but ivy and impatiens, but it is a welcome oasis in summer, a place for two chairs, a table, and good company.

Shade gardeners can deploy the architectural lines of ferns and the color and texture of foliage to work as design substitutes for blossoms. The use of color counts; whites and yellows will illuminate a shady spot while violets and purples may get lost.

Don't depend on plants alone. Redesign, as well as better selection and culture, is always worth considering. Structures painted white reflect more sun. Replacing a solid fence with spaced pickets will double the light and air. Paths and paving schemes can usually be improved. The worst shade may be the best place for a pleasing pattern of paving bricks or tiles, a neat bed of gravel or bluestone chips, stepping stones of wood or slate, a cushion of moss, a hammock, or the setting for a sculpture.

Many ordinary garden objects will light up and soften a cold corner. Examples include a handsome metal watering can, a pot of well-grown foliage, an empty urn, a stack of algae-covered clay pots, a wheelbarrow so worn out it's antique, and so forth. Anything you like to look at — except, perhaps, a sundial.

How to Garden in the Shade

SYDNEY EDDISON

Most of what a gardener needs to know about shade can be determined by looking. Study the site at different times of day and different times of year to determine when and where the shadows fall and for how long. And do not count on memory alone — make notes. In addition to exposure, and the degree and duration of light reduction, consider the following: the climate and hardiness zone of your region and the depth, fertility, and structure of the soil. Understanding your specific conditions will guide you in making an appropriate choice of plants. How well they will grow will depend on careful preparation of the soil and proper care after they are planted.

Because shade gardening is a frustratingly inexact science, understanding the problems is more important than following exact rules. Very few plants demand complete shade. Even ferns, which are generally presumed to be shade-lovers, actually prefer open woodland where they receive a generous amount of light. Similarly, many of our woody ornamentals like rhododendrons, azaleas, mountain laurels, and witch hazels are edge-of-the forest plants. All flower more profusely where they receive ample light. There are, of course, virtually indestructible plants that tolerate both full sun and dense shade, but even these worthies refuse to flower in unrelieved darkness.

Because amount and duration of light is the first consideration in shade gardening, it helps to have a clear picture of the most frequently encountered types of shade: dense shade, light or dappled shade, and half or partial shade. (For more on this, see "Shade: A Kind of Light," p. 4.)

Trees with thick canopies of large, overlapping leaves growing cheek by jowl in a woodland setting create dense shade. Rays of sunlight may pierce the gloom in occasional shafts, but otherwise the forest floor lies in deep shadow throughout the day. The average gardener is not equipped to remedy this situation without professional help. Tree work should be performed by a licensed and insured arborist. However, selective removal of a few trees and limbing up those that remain will admit enough light to suit many woodland plants and shade-tolerant ornamentals. Limbing up simply means taking off the lower branches of a tree, and sometimes, if the trees are not too close together, this alone will do the trick. A city garden entirely surrounded by the walls of tall buildings also usually falls into the category of dense shade.

Growing plants in a thicket of birches or locusts requires no heroic measures. Trees like these with small leaves or feathery, compound leaves offer only fitful resistance to light penetration. The slightest breeze parts their delicate foliage, alternately admitting light and casting fleeting shadows. The result is dappled shade in which innumerable plants thrive.

The third type, half or partial shade, is found in every garden. The eastern façade of a residence whose long dimension runs from north to south receives half a day of sun and half a day of shade. A house oriented in the opposite direction — from east to west — casts a fairly consistent band of shade on the north side, while the south side basks in sun for much of the day.

Man-made light barriers, apart from reducing the level of illumination, present few problems for the shade gardener. One exception is the presence of construction waste in the soil adjacent to buildings. Not only is the rubble an inhospitable growing medium, it usually contains chunks of sheetrock and mortar. Both contain lime which is anathema to shade-loving ericaceous plants like rhododendrons, azaleas, *Pieris japonica,* and other favorite broad-leaved evergreens. In order to safely grow these plants, the offending debris must be excavated and replaced with good, humus-rich loam (see **Soil**).

Trees: Living Light Barriers

Shade can also be produced by topography and by living plants. The flat landscape of the prairie offers no escape from the sun, while the western mountains and the hills and valleys of the northeast either trap the sun or exclude it, depending on the exposure and time of day. Plants, especially trees, are one of the most common light barriers in the garden. They are also one of the least understood elements in shade gardening. Recognizing their growth habits and cultural requirements is the first step toward gardening beneath them in a way that is mutually satisfactory.

Contrary to one of our cherished notions, most trees do not grow like carrots. Instead of driving a long, earth-penetrating tap root into the ground, they spread out a far-reaching network of roots in the top 18 inches of soil. This shallow arrangement of roots is poignantly displayed when a big tree is uprooted in a wind storm, exposing a huge pancake of roots and earth, standing on edge at the base of the trunk. The original extent of this root mass was probably far greater than meets the eye.

Tree roots extend far beyond the drip-line (the perimeter of the area beneath the branches). Deep cultivation of the soil under trees — even at some distance from the bole — can result in damage to the roots. In the documented case of one stately copper beech, a trench dug 12 feet from the trunk caused injuries to the roots severe enough to kill the tree. Nor is it a good idea to substantially alter the soil level within the drip-line. Roots require oxygen which they extract from spaces between the soil granules. An added layer of dense soil or fill can compact the air spaces, causing suffocation. However, these cautions being respected, it is possible to garden under most trees. Beeches, red maples, and Norway maples are exceptions. Their webs of exposed roots are so extensive and competitive that lesser plants give up the unequal struggle for water and nutrients.

Large trees with heavy foliage present shade gardeners with the greatest challenge. A solid dome of leaves acts like an umbrella, effectively shedding water and keeping the soil under the tree dry. As nutrients in the soil must be dissolved in water before they can be taken up by plant roots, understory vegetation is at a disadvantage. One maxim has it that plantings beneath maples, or other trees with dense canopies and extensive root systems, should receive twice the recommended amount of fertilizer — one application for the herbaceous plants and one for the tree. While it is true that the yearly application of a complete fertilizer produces lusher plants, it is not strictly necessary. Soil covered with an organic mulch is self-sustaining. However, the maxim definitely applies to water. A mature maple can transpire hundreds of gallons of water a day, which it gives off as vapor through its porous leaves. This water is drawn up by the roots from the surrounding soil, leaving the supply depleted.

Nature: The Role Model

Gardeners who want to plant beneath trees could do worse than study the layered look of a woodland, taking heart from nature's lessons and following her example. Trees do not grow by themselves in open spaces, they coexist with understory shrubs and carpets of weeds and wildflowers. And despite the competition for moisture and nutrients, this association benefits all of the plants. The fallen leaves of deciduous trees and discarded needles of evergreens provide a loose, organic mulch for the shrubs and herbaceous plants. They, in turn, keep the tree roots cool and shaded and contribute their own organic waste to the rich brew of woodland soil.

Translating this example to the garden, a lawn tree will be healthier and happier standing in a bed of shade-tolerant plants than alone surrounded by shorn grass. Trees employed as lawn specimens are at best a contradiction in terms, and at worst an endangered species. Their lives are threatened every week by mower blades or the savage strokes of a string trimmer. It only takes one whack with a string trimmer to effectively girdle a young tree. Gardening under trees is a matter of finding a balance in the natural contest for survival between the dominant woody specimens and the plants at their feet.

Water

Water is usually the chief bone of contention between trees and the plants growing beneath them. Plants in full growth are largely made up of water, but they lose moisture very rapidly in the summer months, and the supply has to be constantly replenished. Rain alone is often insufficient to fulfill their needs. In the relatively cool Northeast, an inch of rain a week during the growing season is the indispensable minimum. Shrubs and herbaceous plants growing under thirsty trees, like maples and tulip trees, require 2 inches of water a week. Even that amount would be hopelessly inadequate in the hot South where high temperatures evaporate moisture in the twinkling of an eye. Fickle nature all too often fails to deliver the requisite amount of rain, and gardeners are called upon to make up the deficit. By all means, water your shade plantings if you can. In some parts of the country restrictions make it impossible, in which case soil improvement and mulch are critical.

Good soil and mulch are the shade gardener's secret weapons. Fortunately, soil is one element in the physical environment of the garden over which the gardener has almost complete control. This is not to say that it is easy to replace heavy clay or barren, sandy soil with porous loam, but it is possible to improve the texture, drainage, and fertility of any soil with the liberal addition of organic matter. The vast majority of garden plants, especially shade dwellers, rejoice in rich, friable, well-drained loam endowed with a spongelike capacity to hold water. Plants growing beneath trees *demand* such soil, particularly in the absence of irrigation.

Soil

Loam is a mixture of clay particles, sand, and organic matter. Organic matter is nothing more than decayed animal and vegetable residues; the decaying residues act as a sponge, storing water until plants need it. Ultimately, countless microscopic inhabitants of the soil recycle the organic wastes into humic acid — the dark, sticky by-product of decay — which is the substance that gives healthy soil its rich deep color and its characteristic structure. Humic acid binds mineral particles together in units of different sizes, leaving open spaces in between to hold the water and air that are vital to plants. Ideal soil is composed half of solids — sand and silt glued together with humic acid — and half of water and air (20 percent water and 30 percent air). Providing a reasonable facsimile of this mix for the shade garden can be done by analyzing the existing soil and amending it as necessary.

How do you tell what your soil needs? It is surprising how much can be determined simply by exercising the senses. Observe the color of the earth. Shades of gray, yellow, or tan suggest that organic matter is in short supply. Look for earthworms. They only inhabit moist, humus-rich soils and are therefore a welcome sight. Moreover, as they stitch their way up and down through the soil layers, they distribute decomposed animal and vegetable wastes to the barren subsoil and aerate the whole complex mixture.

Next, feel the soil. A pinch rubbed between the fingers tells something about its structural composition. If it feels grainy, it contains a high proportion of sand. Sandy soils have their virtues. The sharp, irregular mineral crystals hold open air pockets, lightening the texture and offering little resistance to delicate feeder roots. Sandy soils also provide good drainage.

On the other hand, they may dry out too quickly and lack fertility. Heavy clay soil is composed of tiny, closely packed mineral particles and is silky to the touch. The slick surface is slow to absorb water, but once the water has filtered down into the minute spaces between particles, it evaporates gradually. However, when it finally does dry out, clay soil is as hard and impenetrable as a shard of pottery.

In either case, the addition of organic matter will improve the soil and provide a more suitable environment for shade plants. If the existing soil is sandy, working in compost, peat moss, decomposing leaves, rotted manure or the locally available equivalent will bind the sand particles together and slow down the escape of valuable moisture. If the soil is dense and silty the organic matter will lighten the texture, ease the way for plant roots, and improve drainage. Moisture retention and good drainage appear to be incompatible requirements, but plant roots need air almost as much as they need water. If every space between the solid particles of earth is filled with water, the plants will literally suffocate, being unable to take in the necessary oxygen. (Anyone who has ever suffered from a bad head cold knows the feeling!) If the waterlogged condition persists over a period of time, the plant roots will rot.

Improving the soil quality is only half the battle. The earth at the base of large trees is full of roots. If it is not practical to dig down, the soil must be built up instead. The additional soil can be contained by a single course of large rocks or a low wall of some other durable material. A few inches of loam does not constitute a threat to the tree. Instead, the tree's roots will take full advantage of this layer of light, humus-laden soil, and in time, additional compost will be needed to refurbish the soil for the benefit of the other plants.

Planting

An 8-inch layer of good, moisture-retentive soil is ample for most perennials. For a ground cover like periwinkle or pachysandra, 4 inches is adequate. To plant shrubs, a hole of the proper depth needs to be excavated among the tree roots — cutting off a few roots with sharp lopping shears will not harm a healthy, mature tree. Shrubs, like trees, have roots that reach out horizontally, not vertically. The planting hole need not be excessively deep, but for field-grown shrubs that arrive with their roots enclosed in burlap, the holes should be at least twice as wide as the root balls. As a rule of thumb, shrubs should be planted with the tops of their root balls at the same level as the surrounding ground.

Once the soil is prepared and suitable plants have been

chosen for the degree of shade provided by the tree or trees overhead, the rest is straightforward. The soil should be damp at planting time, but not wet. Like shrubs that come with an earth ball, container-grown perennials should be planted so that the soil in which the plant is growing is level with the top of the soil in the bed. Rooted cuttings of pachysandra and slips of other ground covers should be planted with a bit of the stem, just above the roots, under the soil. It is important to water immediately after planting and to keep the bed moist. If enough sun reaches the plants to cause wilting, erect a temporary shade. The sun barrier can be as crude as an old sheet propped up on stakes so that the material will not touch the plants or as sophisticated as specially constructed wooden frames with lath slats. The slats admit light but temper the heat of the sun and act as a wind break. Wind greatly accelerates evaporation.

Mulch

When the newly planted bed has been carefully watered, it is ready for a 4-inch layer of organic mulch. Mulch does more for the plants, the soil, and the gardener than any horticultural product on the market, and it is the least expensive. In the Northeast, autumn leaves are free for the raking. Instead, they are carted off by the ton to landfills. Why every town in New England does not harvest this valuable crop, run the leaves through a shredder, bag them, and *sell* them to eager gardeners remains a mystery. Other sources of organic substances suitable as mulch include pine needles, pine bark, straw, ground corn cobs, buckwheat hulls, and wood chips.

Mulch, by definition, is any material spread on the ground to retain moisture. Derived from the German word *molsch*, meaning soft or beginning to decay, the term and the technique have been in use since the seventeenth century. Nature, of course, has been employing the practice since the arrival on earth of green plants, seasonally covering the bare earth with living matter which ultimately dies and decays, thus recycling nutrients for the next generation of plants and animals.

While the primary function of mulch is to conserve water in the soil, it also prevents erosion, protects shallow roots, and contributes to the general health and well-being of the garden. In addition, a layer of mulch discourages the germination of weed seeds, thereby saving the gardener time and trouble. And in the heat of summer, it reduces the soil temperature. Recently conducted experiments in the Midwest proved that mulched soil stayed almost 15 degrees cooler than soil exposed to the sun. Beneath the layer of mulch, the temperature varied only a few degrees between day and night readings, while open soil showed a range of 25 degrees between the maximum and minimum temperatures.

Maintaining a consistent temperature is also the function of a winter mulch. On a sunny winter day the temperature can rise well above freezing, and that night fall to 10 degrees. It is these temperature fluctuations that can cause damage to living plant tissue. Providing shade prevents the soil from being warmed by the sun and subsequently exposed to extreme cold. Maintaining a relatively even soil temperature also tempers the ill effects of cyclical freezing and thawing. At freezing temperatures, open soil rises up in a honeycomb of ice, dragging shallow-rooted plants out of the ground. When the ice melts, the plants are left high and dry with their roots exposed.

The materials used as a summer mulch can be topped up to serve during the winter months, or the entire bed can be covered with evergreen boughs. There are two schools of thought about the best time to apply a winter mulch. One is that early application — in October in the Northeast — postpones dormancy and therefore gives plants more time to grow. The other school withholds the mulch until just before the first hard freeze on the theory that new growth should not be encouraged in case of frost injury. In the opinion of this Connecticut gardener, it is six of one and half a dozen of the other. However, early mulching is advisable if the planting has been done in the fall. Prolonging the growing season helps recently installed plants to become better established.

Maintenance

A shade garden could not be easier or less demanding to maintain. The sun is a friend of weeds, whereas a well-mulched garden in the shade is virtually weed-free. That leaves watering in the summer and covering the plants with evergreen boughs for the winter as the only chores. Otherwise, the garden is self-sufficient. A shady garden is truly restful because it asks so little of the gardener. In the words of poet Theodosia Garrison,

> The kindliest thing God ever made,
> His hand of very healing laid
> Upon a fevered world, is shade.

Flowers for Shade

PAMELA HARPER

Gardeners often ask, "What can I grow in the shade?" If the shaded spot in question has morning sun or good indirect light, and if the soil is reasonably free of competition from the roots of trees, this isn't necessarily a handicap. There are many flowers that thrive in shade.

Perennials for Morning Light

Many garden perennials find morning sun and afternoon shade perfect. Spring is rich with possibilities. Varying with climate, early bloomers might include masses of such familiar shade-lovers as pink bergenia, with its crisp cabbagey foliage; the forget-me-not blue of *Brunnera;* and the spectrum of colors found in the columbines, *Aquilegia,* which offer fernlike leaves as well to the border or rock garden. The great tribe of *Pulmonarias,* the lungworts, are well suited to part shade; their handsome leaves act as a ground cover after flowers go by. *Pulmonaria angustifolia* has flowers of brilliant blue and plain green leaves. *Pulmonaria* 'Roy Davidson' has flowers of paler blue and leaves lightly spotted gray. *Pulmonaria saccharata* has large silver-dappled leaves, and a superb selection called 'Argentea' has leaves entirely silver-plated; its flowers open pink and fade to blue.

In mid- to late spring, leopard's bane, *Doronicum*, offers its yellow daisy-form blooms. This genus of stout perennials with soft, oval to heart-shaped green leaves and bright 2-inch-wide flowerheads is easy to grow in beds and borders in part to light shade. They may retire as summer's heat presses on, so plant with something that has reliable summer foliage — daylilies perhaps. Leopard's bane prefers a cool, rich, moist soil, even during dormancy. Widely grown *D. cordatum* (also sold as *D. caucasicum*) is hardy to zone 4 and grows 18 to 24 inches tall. The variety 'Spring Beauty' bears double flowers. 'Madame Mason' has a better reputation in the South, where it retains foliage better in the summer than other varieties. Leopard's bane, incidentally, is well suited for cutting.

Foxgloves, *Digitalis,* add the all too rare spirelike form to the half-shady border in early summer. They prefer a rich, moist, but well-drained soil. Longer-lived species include *D. grandiflora,* with creamy yellow bells, and the dainty, 3-foot-tall *D. lutea,* with small ivory blooms densely packed along the spike. The blooms of *D. × mertonensis,* a cross of *grandiflora* and *purpurea,* have a distinctive dark pink taffy color with freckles. Hardy to zone 5, *× mertonensis* is shorter lived and requires more frequent division than other perennial species of *Digitalis*. The biennial *D. purpurea* comes in purplish pink, paler pinks, cream, pristine white, and the enchanting selection called 'Sutton's Apricot'. Color forms come more or less true from seed.

The delicate deep salmon, pink, or white flowers and handsome leaves of *Heuchera,* coral-bells, are easy to find room for in the front of a border or even along a wall. *Heuchera americana* 'Dale's Strain' is an easy and adaptable plant with the added bonus of beautiful silver-dappled leaves. This crossed with the popular purple-leaved *Heuchera micrantha* 'Palace Purple' gave rise to *H.* 'Montrose Ruby', which has silvery patterning on purple leaves as well as the typical bell-shaped flowers. *Heuchera americana* has greenish to reddish foliage and white flowers in late spring to early summer, rising on stalks well above the 20-inch-tall foliage. 'Palace Purple' has white flowers and grows about 18 inches tall, with dark purple leaves that are red underneath. All are suited to part to light shade. These plants have dainty spikes of flowers which add an exquisite filigree to bouquets of larger, more ruffled blooms. (That hybrid of coral-bells and foamflower, *× Heucherella,* usually does better in the South than coral-bells.)

If you can emulate its wild habitat, *Silene virginica,* fire pink, will give bright touches of true red. It grows on the shady fringes of woods, usually on well-drained slopes or woodland clearings, and blooms in early summer.

Summer Bloom in Half-Shade

As the season progresses and heat and light grow more intense, gardeners find shade indeed a boon. True, a border without sun from the south or west for several hours a day will depend heavily on foliage, annuals, woody plants, and architectural features for summer interest, but there is nevertheless a choice company of shade-lovers that proffer midseason bloom.

Daylilies, *Hemerocallis,* those summer stalwarts of the border, grow well and flower adequately in half light. Yellow 'Hyperion' is widely available and long ago proved its overall worth as a plant in and out of flower. Countless other cultivars exist in a broad palette of yellow, orange, salmon, and red. Their substantial, linear foliage of medium green holds up well in heat, and their fleshy roots help these hardy perennials withstand drought and stabilize shifting soil. They are versatile plants for massing or edging, or for use in larger borders.

Vary the form and color of summer plantings with the divided deep green leaves and pink blossoms of Japanese anemones, either *Anemone* × *hybrida* or *A. vitifolia.* Other choice flowers for accent include bouncy pink or white hardy begonia, *Begonia grandis;* creamy white candles of bloom offered by the bugbanes, *Cimicifuga;* satiny yellow bells of *Kirengeshoma palmata;* and the opalescent strands of orchidlike toad lilies, *Tricyrtis.*

Where there's moist, well-drained soil as well as afternoon shade, the cardinal flower, *Lobelia cardinalis,* might bring a splash of scarlet to a green summer scene. No guarantees, because this is a choosy plant, seldom long-lived, though self-sowing where it elects to stay.

Where summers are long and hot, many perennials that accept full sun in cooler regions may do better with afternoon shade. Among these are blue-flowered monkshood, *Aconitum;* chartreuse lady's-mantle, *Alchemilla;* some campanulas and a few of the hardy geraniums, which are generally in the pink, violet, or blue range. Less well known is bear's-breech, *Acanthus.* This genus of perennials has very showy leaves — large, divided, glossy, sometimes spiny — and lupine-like spikes of flowers. Most grow 3 to 4 feet high and have white, lilac, or pale purple flowers in summer. *A. spinosus* survives winters as far north as zone 7. *A. mollis latifolius,* the most popular species, is only hardy to zone 8. As a rule, the genus enjoys part shade to light shade, needing moist shade in the southern limits of its landscape range, and well-drained soil wherever it is to succeed.

In Moist Soil

The shade gardener with good, moist, well-drained soil as well as morning light has more choices in all seasons. The curious yellow blooms of *Corydalis* could help provide bright points of yellow throughout the spring and summer. Botanically similar to their close relatives *Dicentra,* the bleeding hearts, this group of low-growing herbs has soft, ferny foliage and flowers like miniscule dessert spoons hanging in loose clusters. These at once enjoy adequate moisture and good drainage. They have a delicate texture of both blossom and leaf which is especially needed in rocky settings or small gardens.

Twelve-inch-tall *Corydalis cheilanthifolia* (zone 5 or 6) sets out its half-inch hanging blooms in late spring or early summer and is well suited for part shade. Others in the genus, notably the common *C. lutea* (zone 5) tend to be less perennial, but bloom even later and tolerate much more shade.

Other perennials needing soil that doesn't get dry include spring's well-loved cowslips, *Primula,* and many later bloomers such as astilbes; the peach-leaved bellflower, *Campanula persicifolia;* meadowsweets, *Filipendula;* meadow rues, *Thalictrum; Ligularia;* and goatsbeards, *Aruncus.* Shorter than a foot tall, little *Aruncus aethusifolius* is neat and dainty enough for the smallest garden. Native to Korea and hardy to zone 4, it has fernlike leaves and a mounding habit with delicate spires of creamy flowers in late spring to early summer, and is suitable for morning sun to light shade. Seedheads provide summer interest and may be used to good advantage in dried arrangements.

Adaptable Woodlanders for Part to Light Shade

An east-facing bed or border against a building or fence, or a spot where large but distant trees cast afternoon shade is in fact doubly blessed, for here will also grow quite a few species usually thought of as woodlanders. Freed from competition from thirsty tree roots, many flowers that evolved in the woods will do better in the half-shaded border or lightly shaded wild garden than they would in nature. Spring-blooming *Disporum,* fairy-bells, for example, falls happily into this category.

You could also add waxy, early blooming hellebores, *Hel-*

leborus; the classic spring lace of foamflowers, *Tiarella,* in pink or white; soft clumps of creeping phlox, *Phlox divaricata, P. stolonifera,* in blue, white, or pink; and Jacob's-ladder, *Polemonium reptans,* with its crisp formal leaves and blue blossoms. The large, brilliantly colored primroses sold by florists in spring seldom survive the winter. Try to find instead the Barnhaven strain of *Primula vulgaris,* with its sweet, silky flowers and crinkled leaves. You may have to grow them from seed. These are very hardy and they come in a great range of colors, single and double. As do most woodland species, these flower in spring or very early summer. In cooler regions green-and-gold, *Chrysogonum virginianum,* may continue to flower through summer. In warm regions it may take a summer rest and then repeat in autumn.

Japanese bleeding heart, *Dicentra spectabilis,* is unquestionably a spring bloomer, but the native bleeding hearts, *D. eximia, D. formosa,* and the many selections and hybrids such as 'Bountiful' and 'Luxuriant' may continue to flower through summer. Most have pink flowers but there are also beautiful white-flowered forms.

Dicentra eximia, fringed bleeding heart, grows 12 to 18 inches high, with pink flowers on foot-tall spikes for a long period in early summer, longer where summers are sufficiently cool and damp. It is shorter, with more finely divided leaves and narrower flowers, and the blooming period is generally longer than *D. spectabilis.* It is used to good advantage in naturalized shoals in light shade or woodland, or on the shores of island beds. There is also a white form, *Dicentra formosa,* the Pacific bleeding heart, which is slightly shorter but similar, and better suited to the West Coast. Both are hardy to zone 3.

Natives for Light Shade

And so to the woodland garden.

This is as close to "natural" as gardens can get, which doesn't mean that such a garden will take care of itself. If the trees are less competitive — oaks, or old orchard apples, for example — the plantsman's approach might be to grow the great range of woodlanders from our own and other lands. Plants adapted to growing under trees are usually shallow rooting, relying on the surface duff renewed each year by falling leaves and small branches. Raking and burning or carting off the leaves would defeat nature. Perhaps this style is not for the overly tidy.

Still, there is much good culture can do. Pruning off the lower branches of trees allows in more sun and air. Filling pockets around roots with soil or compost helps establish

plants and encourages them to spread out into natural colonies, so delightful under a sparse canopy of boughs.

If the trees are predominantly deciduous, with a layer of
rich, moist leaf mold underneath, you may only need to clean
out some of the underbrush to clear space for drifts of such
spring bloomers as the rue anemone, *Anemonella thalic-
troides.* This low-growing perennial with compound leaves is
a member of the buttercup family and bears white flowers in
loose clusters in mid-spring. A native of North American
woods, it prefers moist, acid soil and grows in part to moderate
shade. *Hepatica,* another perennial in the same family, has
downy little flowers early in spring. White-flowered *H. acu-
tiloba* likes neutral soil, while pink *H. americana* prefers more
acid growing conditions. All three are hardy to zone 5.

In light woods and rich soil one may also find a niche for
clumps of such spring wildflowers as jack-in-the-pulpit.
Mostly green in flower, *Arisaema triphyllum* is incomparable
in form, always a happy conversation piece. White-flowered
bloodroot, *Sanguinaria canadensis,* another denizen of the forest floor, is named for its bright red sap. The plant has thick,
rounded, horizontal leaves paired with waxy white cups of
flowers, in form and bearing something like a water lily; 'Mul-
tiplex' is a popular double-flowered form. *Geranium maculatum* would also grow well in dappled shade. It has violet
blooms and, like other hardy geraniums, has handsome seedheads and foliage, often coloring brightly in autumn. Not quite
as cold-tolerant as jack-in-the-pulpit or bloodroot, the spotted
geranium will survive zone 4 winters.

Others worthy of cultivation here might include the crested
iris, *Iris cristata,* Solomon's-plumes, *Smilacina;* violets, *Viola;*
and bellworts, *Uvularia.* The low-growing *Maianthemum,*
false lily-of-the-valley, is similar to its cousin *Convallaria.* Likewise, it spreads to produce a bed of oval leaves, punctuated
in spring by lyres of small white flowers followed by red berries. In a rocky setting or for variety of texture, try *Sedum
ternatum.* Though chiefly considered a ground cover, it sends
up sprays of titanium-white flowers in early summer and makes
beds of fine succulent leaves.

The burnished bright yellow flowers of marsh marigold,
Caltha palustris, can be found in wet woodland clearings and
moist meadows in many parts of the country. Don't confuse it with the similarly named *Calla palustris,* or wild calla,
which has a much narrower northerly range and is not likely
to succeed where summers are hot. May apple, *Podophyllum
peltatum,* prefers a place that is moist at least in spring, though
it will tolerate drier ground. Its nodding white spring flowers,
strange fruit, and umbrella-like leaves earn it a place in any
moist woodland.

Native or Not

Most of these woodlanders are widely distributed in North America. Others are more regional. The exquisite bunchberry, *Cornus canadensis,* favors the North, *Galax* the South, and celandine poppy, *Stylophorum diphyllum,* a more westerly range. Whatever the species, it is probably wise to start with those that occur naturally in your area; local wildflower societies and gardening clubs may be an excellent source of information on obtaining plants and seeds.

Erythronium, dog-tooth violets and their tribe, includes an important group of garden plants for deciduous woodland, each enjoying its own native range in North America or elsewhere. Like so many of the earliest spring bulbs, they take advantage of the late winter sun before leaves of deciduous trees have come out. These perennials grow from fleshy bulbs which send up a pair of tongue-shaped, sometimes handsomely mottled leaves and a solitary lilylike flower in spring. Most grow 8 to 12 inches tall; the native North Americans have flowers of creamy white or yellow.

Popular *E. tuolumnense* is native to the West Coast and has large, 1¼ inch flowers and plain green but glossy leaves. The eastern species, *E. americanum,* the lovely yellow adder's-tongue or trout lily, has leaves which suggest the mottled sides of brook trout. Flowers are similar to the western species named above. These are hardy to zone 4 and suitable for naturalizing in light woods, in rock gardens, or under deep-rooted shrubs in moist, humusy soil. Plant 4 to 6 inches deep in early fall as soon as bulbs are purchased, or transplant immediately after flowering. Like lilies, they should never be allowed to dry out.

You may choose to take the purist approach, growing only those plants native to your area, but once you see them you'll certainly be tempted by garden forms as well as exotic relations. There are, for instance, selections of rue anemone, bloodroot, and *Trillium grandiflorum* with double flowers; these last longer than those with single blooms. Crested iris and wild geranium have white-flowered forms of great delicacy.

Deeper Shade

In denser shade, especially under trees, there's little light in summer and the soil is often very dry. Many plants have adapted to this by making growth while the soil is moist from winter rains and flowering in the spring sunshine before the trees leaf out. They may then go summer-dormant as Virginia bluebells and Dutchman's-breeches do. A few take advantage of winter light by making new growth in autumn, holding their leaves through winter, flowering in spring, and then going dormant. One of the toothworts, the widely distributed *Dentaria diphylla,* adapts to the climate of the region where it is growing. In the North it goes winter-dormant and retains its leaves well into summer. In the South it goes summer-dormant, makes new leaves in autumn, and remains handsome through winter before flowering in spring. This low, spring-blooming perennial has opposite leaves and small white flowers.

Among the finest of perennials for moderate to full shade, epimediums prefer a fairly deep, humus-rich soil, but will put up with a lot less and can be counted on to hold their leaves through summer in quite dry soil. They fall into two categories, clump-formers such as *Epimedium × youngianum* 'Niveum', and spreaders such as *E. × versicolor* 'Sulphureum'. One of the best is yellow-flowered 'Frohnleiten', which is evergreen where winters are not severe.

Where these do well, try also *Vancouveria hexandra,* which is slow to establish but then quite a rapid spreader. *Geranium macrorrhizum,* which comes in various shades of pink and an impure white, is very adaptable. The foliage of some forms is aromatic and it earns its place in the shade garden for its leaves alone, but it flowers quite well with only a few hours of morning or dappled sun.

The Christmas rose, *Helleborus niger,* prefers cool climates and even then is difficult to please. The Lenten rose, *H. orientalis,* is much less persnickety and often self-sows by the thousands in the warmer regions. Provided it gets good light and a little sun in winter or spring, it tolerates deep shade in summer — under a low-branched dogwood, for instance. Purchased seed is seldom fresh enough to germinate, so buy a plant or two to start you off. Once established, all it asks is a light top dressing of compost every few years, and the removal of old battered leaves in late winter so that they don't detract from the beauty of the flowers, which start in late winter and remain effective for months.

Ground Covers for Shade

MARY ANN MCGOURTY

Ground covers are considered the problem solvers of the garden because they are frequently used in adverse growing conditions or difficult terrain. For example, under the branches of many large trees, where there is little sunlight and the soil is dry and root-filled, ground covers adapted to dry shade compete successfully with the trees for available water and nutrients.

Appropriate ground covers can also decrease maintenance of steep or rocky areas. The gardener can stabilize such sites against soil erosion and eliminate mowing by planting carpetlike ground covers with long fibrous roots.

Although frequently used to solve landscape problems, ground covers have intrinsic beauty of their own. To use them to best advantage, consider the wide variety of colors, textures, and forms available, keeping in mind that the foliage is of primary interest. Foliage colors range from silvery blue to glossy dark green, gold, and maroon; and textures and forms vary from blocky and leathery to needle-fine and ferny.

Designing with Ground Covers

Ground covers can be used, like lawn grasses, to cover a large area or for a small accent. They can be grown alone to define or enclose space, or to unify disparate plantings of trees and shrubs. To maintain a feeling of openness, choose low-growing plants; to screen the base of a leggy shrub or fill the area under a large tree, taller plants are appropriate. Knee-high ground covers can help define the edges of pathways where people are invited to walk.

There is no definitive height limit for a ground cover; in fact, exact height is less important than the relative scale of plants in an overall garden design. For example, a prostrate ground cover would be lost in front of a large house; likewise, a stand of spreading evergreens 2 feet high would be out of place in a small rock garden. It is mostly a matter of choosing plants that are appropriate in size for the site.

It is also important to choose ground covers that are appropriate in vigor to the area in question. Some are so aggressive that they become weedy menaces, even on larger properties. Others are so slow to increase that they take years to create a dense cover in even a small area. Each kind of ground cover has its own growth rate, and a little background reading and a few visits to other gardens should give you some idea of which plants are vigorous enough or restrained enough for your garden. Best not to think you can cover a small area quickly with an aggressive plant, as there is no magic to make it stop growing when it has filled the space. In large areas it is possible to add interest by planting two or more kinds of ground covers adjacent to one another, or even to intermingle them. The limiting factor is that the plants should be of similar vigor, or one will crowd out the others. They should also be of similar height to create a unified appearance, but contrasting leaf textures or colors will enhance interest.

Deciduous or Evergreen

Whether you choose deciduous or evergreen plants depends on how you want the garden to look year-round. Where only deciduous ground covers are used, the whole effect may disappear with the early winter. If only evergreen ground covers are employed, the changing seasons produce little variation, and the garden may look static or monotonous. Usually a combination works best; the deciduous plants will lose their leaves, providing a change of scene, and the evergreen ones will give structure and interest for winter.

Evergreen ground covers are particularly valuable in sites

that are prominent year-round, such as near doors and walk-
ways or in locations most often viewed from house windows.
Ground covers for shade with long season interest include ivy
(*Hedera helix*), myrtle or periwinkle (*Vinca minor*), winter
creeper (*Euonymus fortunei* cultivars), European wild ginger
(*Asarum europaeum*), and pachysandra (*P. terminalis*). Pachysandra has been so overused as to become a cliché in many
areas, but a recent selection with very shiny leaves, 'Green
Sheen', adds new interest to an old standby. Where they are
hardy, British Columbia wild ginger (*Asarum caudatum*),
creeping lilyturf (*Liriope muscari*) and dwarf lilyturf (*Ophiopogon japonicus*), are possible choices for evergreen cover.
Some evergreen shrubs useful as ground covers are Siberian
carpet cypress (*Microbiota decussata*), low-growing yews
(*Taxus*), and, where they are hardy, *Sarcococca hookerana
humilis* and low-growing azaleas (*Rhododendron*) such as the
North Tisbury and Robin Hill hybrids. If year-round cover is
needed in sunny areas, it is best to use low-growing needle
evergreens.

One common mistake is planting broad-leaved evergreens
such as pachysandra or myrtle in a sunny location. They may
survive but will have yellowish foliage instead of the desired
lush, dark green appearance. Winter sun and wind can also
damage evergreen ground covers on exposed sites. Especially
in northern climates where the soil is frozen for much of the
winter, evergreen plants cannot replenish moisture lost to the
elements, and their leaves become scorched and dry. Even in
a shaded or sheltered location, some winter damage can occur,
but this can usually be overcome by shearing and fertilizing
the plants in early spring.

Flowers a Bonus

Many people select a ground cover based only on its flowering
potential, failing to consider its year-round appearance. Even
plants with long bloom periods rarely flower for more than 6
weeks, and the gardener is left with foliage for the rest of the
growing season, or if the plant is evergreen, for the whole year.
Thus the texture, form, and height of the foliage should be
the main considerations, with flowers only an added benefit.
There are, however, some ground covers with both good foliage and attractive flowers. Among deciduous sorts are epimediums, daylilies (*Hemerocallis*), *Lamium* 'White Nancy',
and *Astilbe chinensis* var. *pumila*. Southern native green-and-
gold (*Chrysogonum virginianum*) has a burst of golden starry
flowers in May with repeats well into summer. Semi-evergreen
choices (in the North) include *Geranium macrorrhizum* with

scented leaves, and *Waldsteinia ternata*. For evergreen ground cover with the showiest flowers, the nod goes to the Robin Hill and North Tisbury azaleas, although they are reliably hardy only to zone 6.

When considering a ground cover for a large area, choose one that will make a uniform carpet. The mounding effect of some ground covers may be acceptable in smaller areas, but the undulating lines of varying heights can appear busy or distracting in large areas. Conversely, the long unbroken horizontal expanse of a single kind of plant can be boring. Here a tapestry planting could be effective, using ground covers of similar height and vigor. Or an intermittent grouping of plants with strong vertical lines can provide a needed focal point. These accent plants should be of strong constitution to compete with the roots of lower-growing, established ground covers. A few likely candidates for this "jack-in-the-box" planting include ferns such as cinnamon (*Osmunda cinnamomea*), interrupted (*Osmunda claytoniana*), lady (*Athyrium filix-femina*), and Christmas (*Polystichum acrostichoides*). Hostas and tall Solomon's-seal (*Polygonatum*), or daylilies (*Hemerocallis*), are also worth a try.

Jack-in-the-box planting with ground covers is also a useful way to handle early spring-flowering bulbs. This works best under deciduous trees, as these areas are not shaded in spring when bulbs need sunlight to carry on photosynthesis and store energy for the following year. After the bulbs flower, their foliage becomes unsightly, but should not be removed until it has died off completely. If the bulbs are interplanted with an evergreen ground cover, the yellowing foliage can be hidden among the carpeting leaves. *Pachysandra terminalis* is not well suited for this treatment, as few bulbs can compete successfully over the longer term with the dense roots of pachysandra. Several deciduous ground covers are compatible with early spring bulbs, which have usually finished flowering before leaves of the ground cover appear. Choose plants which are late to emerge, such as hardy plumbago (*Ceratostigma plumbaginoides*), or those which have large leaves and a horizontal growth habit, such as hostas, daylilies, or *Brunnera macrophylla*. Their expanding leaves will hide the evidence of dying bulb foliage and fill the gap left when the bulbs are dormant. The best bulbs to use are the early-flowering ones, which will gain energy for the next season before the larger plants cover them.

Plants with small leaves or fine texture have a place in the ground cover scheme, too, as they can creep into narrow spaces — around stepping stones and between cracks in sidewalks. Something will eventually grow in these nooks and crannies, and it might as well be a plant of your choice, rather than weeds. Small-scale plants are also useful for softening the lines of stone terraces and steps. A few with prostrate habit, or nearly so, that will thrive in shade and tolerate a little foot traffic are pearlwort (*Sagina subulata*), *Ajuga reptans* cultivars, sweet woodruff (*Galium odoratum*), and moneywort (*Lysimachia nummularia*), although the last is aggressive if not restrained. Two small-leaved cultivars of *Euonymus fortunei*, 'Kewensis' and 'Minima', have the additional advantage of being evergreen.

Light Up the Shade

Plants with variegated leaves are at their best culturally in shade, or at least where they are protected from hot afternoon sun; otherwise, the lighter-colored part of the leaves will scorch. Coincidentally, they are at their best aesthetically in shade, where their white, cream, or yellow markings can reflect light and brighten up a dark area. There is an ever-increasing selection of variegated hostas, and the gardener has only to choose the pattern of variegation and leaf size that appeals.

Lamium maculatum is a vigorous, stoloniferous ground cover with a white splash down the middle of each small leaf. It is most useful in a large area or where it can be restrained, such as between a house and a driveway. Two popular selections, 'Beacon Silver' and 'White Nancy', have more variegation and, hence, are less aggressive. The latter has white flowers in spring, which increases its visibility and effectiveness at a distance. Occasional seedlings that echo the species will occur and should be removed to keep a planting homogenous. *Lamiastrum galeobdolon* 'Herman's Pride', a clump-former, is much less aggressive than the species from which it is derived and is suited to small- or medium-size areas. Its silvery leaves veined in green give a subtle lighting effect in shade, on 12-inch-high plants; in spring small yellow flowers appear in the leaf axils.

It is best to limit the number of different variegated plants in an area, or it becomes a horticultural zoo. The patterns begin to clash with one another, and the overall effect is one of disquiet. Likewise, even a single kind of variegated plant used to cover a very large area tends to appear too busy.

Light can also be injected into shaded areas through the use of blue-leaf hostas, which come in different leaf sizes and degrees of blueness. Large-leaved *Hosta sieboldiana* 'Elegans' is popular, but its use is limited under needle evergreens, as its cup-shaped leaves catch and hold falling debris. Under such circumstances it is better to choose those *Hosta* × *tardiana* sorts which don't have cup-shaped leaves. Blue-leaf hostas attain their best color in light or partial shade and revert to a greener color as light intensity diminishes.

The silvery green leaves of *Ajuga reptans* 'Silver Carpet' are effective light reflectors. It has the same uniform ground-hugging habit as the species and produces 6-inch spikes of light blue-violet flowers in spring. An occasional shoot may revert to green, and it should be removed. *Ajuga reptans* 'Gray Lady' and 'Kingwood' are similar, if not identical.

Dealing with Dryness

Frequently the limiting factor in establishing a ground cover planting in shade comes not from lack of light, but rather from the presence of roots in the soil. Shallow-rooted trees such as maples and beeches present a special challenge. In these cases, the more attention you pay to soil preparation, the more likely you are to be successful in creating a dense cover. Remove as many small roots as possible, then incorporate large amounts of organic matter (peat moss, compost, or aged manure) to increase moisture retention in the soil. Peat moss is the most satisfactory soil amendment because it is virtually weed-free. Compost and manure frequently contain weed seeds, which can cause special maintenance problems later in ground cover plantings. Even after plants are established, they will probably require extra supplements of fertilizer and water, as they are competing with the trees for available nutrients.

Dry shade is one of the most difficult gardening situations, but there are some ground covers which are reasonably well adapted for these conditions. At the top of the list are the epimediums. These semi-evergreen perennials spread by creeping roots to form a uniform cover 9 to 15 inches tall, depending on the cultivar. In early spring, sprays of starlike flowers of pink, white, yellow, or red dance over the plants on wiry stems. The new foliage of some cultivars, including *Epimedium* × *rubrum* and *E.* × *versicolor* 'Sulphureum', is light green with reddish margins. By midseason the leaves are dark green and leathery, then *E.* × *rubrum* takes on mahogany hues in autumn. Where foliage is persistent, it may be left over winter, but it should be cut to the ground in early spring before flowers appear.

Less familiar to most gardeners but well-adapted for dry shade is *Symphytum grandiflorum*. It is related to comfrey and has spreading rhizomatous roots. The large, oval, deciduous leaves are covered with bristly hairs, and in spring it has pale yellow nodding flowers on 10-inch stalks. It is not a particularly showy plant, but makes a dense ground cover under difficult conditions. Catalogs frequently list it as *Pulmonaria lutea.* There are two other garden workhorses that are worth a try in dry shade. Hostas, especially those that have thick, leathery leaves, are adapted for conservation of available water by minimizing transpiration. So are daylilies, whose tuberous roots are essentially for water storage.

Gardeners frequently try to establish plantings of familiar lily-of-the-valley (*Convallaria majalis*) or sweet woodruff (*Galium odoratum*) in dry shade under trees or shrubs. Neither is well suited for these conditions, and the plantings are rarely successful over the longer term.

Soggy Soil

At the other end of the scale is the damp garden, usually near the edge of a stream or seep, or in low-lying areas where drainage is poor. It is good to determine whether the area is evenly moist year-round, or whether it is wet during spring runoff with average moisture during the rest of the growing season. In either case, it should be possible to establish a planting of ground covers adapted for moist soil. On a site that is actually wet for a large portion of the year, choices are much more limited, as most plants will not thrive if they are wet while they are winter-dormant.

Any list of perennials for a shaded site with above-average moisture would certainly include astilbes. The best one for ground cover use is *A. chinensis* 'Pumila', as it is a mat-former rather than a clump-former like most of the others. Its ferny leaves make a dense, refined carpet which contrasts well with ground covers of coarser texture. The 12-inch spikes of mauve-pink flowers in August and September are particularly valuable, as there is frequently a scarcity of blooms in the shaded garden at that time.

Ajuga reptans and its cultivars thrive in shade with extra moisture; in fact, they can become invasive. Use them with caution in areas where they can escape into adjacent lawn. 'Burgundy Glow' is somewhat less robust than most cultivars and has attractive green, maroon, and white leaves. However, it requires more light for best leaf coloration. Also less aggressive is *Ajuga pyramidalis,* which is essentially a clump-former and has dark green leaves. In early summer it is topped by 10-inch spikes of clear blue flowers. If grown in dry soil, ajugas become spotty and do not make a dense cover.

Moneywort (*Lysimachia nummularia*) creeps by trailing prostrate stems that root easily at the joints. In shady, moist places where grass will not grow, this shallow-rooted plant carpets the ground quickly and is an effective lawn substitute, although it will not tolerate high-volume foot traffic. In early summer, bright yellow flowers appear in the axils of the round leaves. The golden-leaf form, 'Aurea', is somewhat less aggressive but is also a reliable ground cover.

The old standbys, hostas and daylilies, grow well with extra soil moisture; in fact, under these conditions daylilies may become too tall for ground cover use on some sites. Their graceful, arching leaves can form clumps 2 to 3 feet tall and as wide, with the bonus of colorful flowers in summer. Most hostas thrive in these conditions, and none better than old-time *H. lancifolia*. It has narrow, glossy green leaves and in late summer its deep lavender flowers add color to the shaded garden. Since *H. lancifolia* has been around for some time, it is less expensive than most of the newer cultivars, a consideration if a large number of plants are needed. If an injection of light is needed to brighten up a dark area, try *Hosta undulata* 'Albomarginata'. Its medium-size leaves have white margins, and each plant makes a handsome clump in short order.

Planting and Care

Most ground covers are rough-and-tumble plants, but it is unrealistic just to stick them into holes in the ground and expect them to create a dense cover that smothers weeds already present. Because ground covers live for many years in the same spot, it is worth the effort to prepare the soil well before planting. Incorporation of organic matter and fertilizer allows them to establish good root systems in an environment free of competing weeds. A more in-depth discussion of soil preparation begins on page 19.

If you are planting a new bed, lay the plants out on the ground according to your design and move them around until they are evenly spaced. A staggered row pattern gives a better visual impression and helps control erosion on slopes. If the bed is too wide to reach across without stepping into the prepared soil, place a board across the bed and use it as a bridge.

The number of plants it will take depends on several factors: the plants' growth rate, how quickly you want complete coverage, and your budget. The closer you space plants, the faster they will cover an area, and the less weeding and mulching will be needed. As a guide, most ground covers bought as flats of rooted cuttings will fill in adequately if planted on 6- to 9-inch centers — that is, planted 6 to 9 inches apart. When installing ground covers in 2- to 4-inch pots, space them 12 to 18 inches apart. Shrubs and other plants in larger containers can be planted on 2- to 3-foot centers. Mulch the area well to keep weed growth under control until plantings completely cover the area. Some ground covers will fill in faster if you cut back old leggy top growth in late winter to encourage dense new growth.

Traditionally, ground covers have been associated with care-free gardening, but they do require regular care, especially until they are established. Pay particular attention to weed control, so they won't spread seed and spread. Plants will require yearly feeding with a balanced fertilizer and supplementary watering during dry spells. This is especially true on sites where new plants are competing with established trees and shrubs.

The ultimate success of the garden depends on regular care, as well as selecting the correct types of plants for the growing conditions. Match the vigor of ground covers to the size of the growing area, and choose plants based on the beauty of their foliage.

Foliage Plants for Shade

JUDY GLATTSTEIN

As the year progresses from spring to summer, autumn to winter, the quality of light in a woodland garden changes. The greatest amount of sun is available to the low-growing herbaceous plants before the woody plants leaf out. In response, plant growth begins on the forest floor with the herbaceous plants, then deciduous and evergreen shrubs begin their yearly growth, followed by understory trees, and finally the lofty canopy of hardwood trees. Plants such as daffodils and some native wildflowers emerge in spring, flower, set seed, and go dormant by early summer. The influence of increasing shade concentrates flowering in the spring. To understand how plants of the deciduous forest respond to available light throughout the year is to understand why foliage is so important in the shade garden. If we look only at flowers the shady border has limited interest once spring has passed, as most perennials are in bloom for only two or three weeks. The selection of annuals for the shady garden is limited. Anyone with a shady garden must select for foliage as well as flowers if the garden is also to be interesting in summer, fall, and winter.

Garden plants with attractive foliage, such as ferns, hosta, and astilbe, are doubly useful; they disguise the resting place of dormant bulbs in summer and provide interesting foliage shape, texture, and color when flowers are scarce. Perennials with evergreen leaves, like Christmas fern (*Polystichum acrostichoides*), galax (*Galax urceolata*), bergenia, hellebores, and partridgeberry (*Mitchella repens*), are especially useful in winter. In summer, shade-loving annuals with attractive foliage such as coleus and caladium are effective.

What to Look For

What makes a good foliage plant? Most important, it must be suitable for the site in which it is to grow in terms of hardiness, soil type, available moisture, and extent of shade. Next, it should be resistant to pests and diseases; mildew-covered foliage, leaves chewed by deer, or slugs draw the wrong kind of attention. The leaves should be present in good condition for an extended part of the gardening season. Consider your options carefully, weighing evergreen foliage for winter interest against a deciduous plant with good fall color. The leaves on an individual plant should be attractive on their own and in combination with nearby plants.

Beyond these rather objective criteria, personal taste will dictate the requirements of a good foliage plant. Grasslike sedges add a graceful, supple line. Bold, architectural form is provided by large scale perennials such as rhubarb. The lacy texture of a 5-foot-tall cinnamon fern balances its stature. Leaves exist in an exciting range of shapes, sizes, and textures, and in a surprising variety of colors other than green.

Combinations

You can create a pleasing richness of design by making use of the form or outline of the leaf, playing shape against shape — simple to bold, plain to complex. A garden needs pattern and balance, and placing too many plants with similar leaf shapes together would be repetitious and boring. From a design standpoint, perhaps the simplest foliage plants to work with are those with linear, grasslike shape, such as sedges, liriopes, and daylilies. For contrast, use those plants that have rounded or heart-shaped leaves, such as hosta or Siberian bugloss (*Brunnera macrophylla*), and those with a lacy texture, such as ferns or astilbe.

A sense of proportion creates pleasant groupings. In general, use smaller, daintier plants in greater quantity, and fewer large, bold plants. For example, a dwarf hosta such as *H. venusta* has thumbnail-size leaves; you will need quite a few to make a good show. On the other hand, there are hostas such as 'Frances Williams' that have broad, 18-inch leaves, and just one specimen would be enough to set off a sweep of ferns.

When working with plants that are more nearly the same size, group several specimens together. Suppose in a shady corner there is room for a dozen plants. One of each of a dozen different plants will look cluttered and disorganized. If instead you plant six liriope, three medium-size hostas, and three maidenhair ferns (*Adiantum pedatum*), the resulting design will be stronger and more attractive.

Green and Other Colors

At one time in England there was a vogue for the green garden, which relied on green foliage alone to create a peaceful, serene atmosphere. Since plants and the color green are nearly synonymous, we often forget to think of green as a color at all. Yet there are many different greens, some with a shift toward blue; others, like chartreuse and pea green, toward yellow; deep somber greens such as olive and yew; and the clear hues of cucumber and moss.

And not all leaves are green. Gray or silver foliage, rare in shade-loving plants, produces cool, frosty results especially striking at dusk when combined with white flowers. *Lamium* 'Beacon Silver' and 'White Nancy', and Japanese painted fern (*Athyrium goeringianum* 'Pictum') provide these elusive tones. Just imagine the fern with white impatiens.

Golden foliage can also be attractive in shady areas, where it lightens and brightens the woodland in summer. Many hostas have this sunny hue; 'Wogan Gold' and 'Kabitan' are much smaller than 'August Moon' and 'Piedmont Gold'. Plants with dark green foliage and complimentary form, such as Christmas fern, bear's foot hellebore (*Helleborus foetidus*), or liriope show off these golden plants to advantage.

Darkest of all is the foliage of *Ophiopogon planiscapus* 'Arabicus' which has an almost black, linear leaf and keeps its color well in the shade. Most purple-leaved plants need good light to hold the deepest color. Many of the red-flowered astilbes such as 'Fanal', 'Feur', 'Glut', and 'Red Sentinel' have leaves which are coppery or bronze early in the season. Remember that dark colors tend to be less visible in shade. Brighten the combination with white or pale pink impatiens or begonias. Combine the ophiopogon with Japanese painted fern, perhaps in a container set at the edge of a path to create a jewel-box effect.

Variegated Leaves

If leaves are partly green, partly colored, they are said to be variegated. These markings may be blotches or spots, or simply differently colored veins. The leaves may be edged, striped, or zoned in a different color. White areas lack the pigment to carry out photosynthesis. Such variegated plants tend to be less vigorous than their green counterparts, or even yellow variegated kin which do contain other photosynthetic pigments.

Variegated ground covers are worth seeking out. *Pachysandra terminalis* 'Silver Edge' has a nice white edge to the leaf, and there are myrtles (*Vinca minor*) with either a white or a gold edge. A number of English ivies (*Hedera helix*) exist with leaves marked gold or silvery white. Variegated hostas are legion, with a multitude of combinations of white or yellow with green, chartreuse, or blue-green. Typically the center or edge of the leaf contrasts with the main portion. To avoid an agitated appearance, don't plant a lot of different variegated plants together. Use variegated plants as a focal point, or as a counterpoint to solid colors of green or glaucous blue.

Perhaps you have a hosta with a white-edged leaf. Rather than plant it with another hosta, plain or variegated, try lungwort (*Pulmonaria saccharata*), which has leaves spotted with silver. Both the hosta and the lungwort have a simple leaf shape. To vary the texture, add a lacy fern or an astilbe such as the white-flowered 'Bridal Veil'. To complete the composition, a green liriope would add a pleasing, dark green, linear pattern. Liriope offers other possibilities: the cultivar 'Silvery Sunproof' has green and white striped leaves, and there is one with golden yellow variegation.

Consider another variegated plant, the shrubby dogwood, *Cornus alba* 'Elegantissima' with its distinctive white-edged leaves. Rather than underplanting it with a similarly variegated hosta, try a ground cover with plain green leaves or something with white flowers. White impatiens would make a crisp foil for the dogwood, highlighting the variegation without being distracting. Like the dogwood, variegated *Kerria japonica* 'Picta' has charming, white-edged leaves which will maintain interest long after its single yellow flowers have gone.

Variegated Solomon's-seal (*Polygonatum odoratum* 'Variegatum') has oval, light green leaves edged in white. Small, greenish, bell-like flowers dangle in clusters on arching stems 18 inches tall. It is very handsome when combined with the heart-shaped green leaves of Siberian bugloss, a perennial which has flowers just like forget-me-nots.

Leaves splashed with silver provide a different pattern. Nothing is nicer for shade than the low-growing oval leaves of lungwort. They appear in early spring, dark green splashed and spotted silver. Its flowers are pink in the bud, turning blue as they open into small bells. The cultivars 'Mrs. Moon' and 'Margery Fish' have leaves exceptionally spotted silver, and 'Sissinghurst White' has white flowers. Pulmonarias combine well with primroses and ferns in spring, and the combination continues to look well after flowering.

Seasonal Effects

Coleus and caladium are among the shade-tolerant annuals with attractive foliage. The leaves of coleus are beautifully marked or colored with chartreuse, copper, red, bronze, or cream, often edged and/or splashed with green. Try using yellow-leaved coleus with glaucous blue hosta, and red-leaved coleus with the Japanese painted fern. The translucent, heart-shaped leaves of caladium may be white, pink, or red, and edged, veined, or splashed with green. Tropical in origin, they lend a certain flamboyance to the summer garden, either bedded out or in a container. White caladiums with white impatiens and the August lily hosta (*Hosta plantaginea*) make a sweetly scented, serene trio late in summer.

The adventuresome may want to explore beyond traditional offerings. Some plants that are usually considered houseplants make wonderful foliage accents in the shade. Set out from stem cuttings in late spring or early summer, they will look good until frost. Try the silver-and-purple-leaved varieties of inch plants (*Tradescantia* spp.) in combination with violet and lavender-flowered impatiens. With its white-striped leaves a different inch plant, one of the *Zebrina* species, looks good with white impatiens. Moses-in-the-cradle (*Rhoeo discolor*) is another foliage houseplant with potential.

Bold, Architectural Foliage

Bergenia (*Bergenia cordifolia*)
Hosta species and hybrids
Rodgersia species

Linear, Swordlike Foliage

Daylilies (*Hemerocallis* spp. and cultivars)
Grasses (*Hakonechloa macra* 'Aureola')
Lilyturf (*Liriope muscari*)

Mondo grass (*Ophiopogon japonicus*)
Rushes (*Luzula* spp.)
Sedges (*Carex* spp.)

Lacy, Fine-Textured Foliage

Doll's-eyes, baneberry (*Actaea pachypoda, A. rubra*)
Astilbe (*Astilbe* × *arendsii*)
Goatsbeard (*Aruncus dioicus*)
Meadow rue (*Thalictrum* spp.)
Sweet cicely (*Myrrhis odorata*)

Evergreen Foliage

Allegheny spurge (*Pachysandra procumbens*)
Alumroot (*Heuchera americana*)
Bergenia (*Bergenia cordifolia*)
Christmas fern (*Polystichum acrostichoides*)
Christmas rose (*Helleborus niger*)
European wild ginger (*Asarum europaeum*)
Galax (*Galax urceolata*)
Heartleaf ginger (*Asarum virginicum*)
Lenten rose (*Helleborus orientalis*)
Lilyturf (*Liriope muscari*)
Oconee bells (*Shortia galacifolia*)
Partridgeberry (*Mitchella repens*)
Stinking hellebore (*Helleborus foetidus*)
Wintergreen, checkerberry (*Gaultheria procumbens*)

Ferns

Broad beech fern (*Thelypteris hexagonoptera*)
Christmas fern (*Polystichum acrostichoides*)
Cinnamon fern (*Osmunda cinnamomea*)
Common polypody (*Polypodium virginianum*)
Goldie's fern (*Dryopteris goldiana*)
Interrupted fern (*Osmunda claytoniana*)
Maidenhair fern (*Adiantum pedatum*)
Marginal shield fern (*Dryopteris marginalis*)
Narrow beech fern, long beech fern (*Thelypteris phegopteris*)
Ostrich fern (*Matteuccia struthiopteris*)
Sensitive fern (*Onoclea sensibilis*)

Silver Foliage

Japanese painted fern (*Athyrium goeringianum* 'Pictum')
Lamium 'Beacon Silver', 'White Nancy'

Golden Foliage

Golden grass (*Milium effusum* 'Aureum')
Coleus 'Pineapple Wizard'
Hosta cultivars such as 'Kabitan', 'Piedmont Gold', etc.
Lamium maculatum 'Aureum'

Red or Purple Foliage

Caladium
Cimicifuga racemosa 'Atropurpurea'
Coleus 'Othello', 'Red Velvet'
Heuchera micrantha 'Palace Purple'
Oxalis regnellii

Variegated Foliage

Caladium
Hosta spp. and cultivars
Ivy (*Hedera helix* cultivars such as 'Cavendishii', 'Glacier') etc.,
Lamiastrum 'Herman's Pride'
Lilyturf (*Liriope muscari* 'Variegata')
Lungwort (*Pulmonaria saccharata*)
Wind-combed grass (*Hakonechloa macra* 'Aureola')

Ferns

MOBEE WEINSTEIN

Ferns are a tremendous asset to any planting, and indispensable to the shade gardener. In recent years, these primordial green plants have become increasingly popular and now more nurseries include ferns in their offerings. An enthusiast might create a garden using ferns alone, but most of us will want to incorporate them into mixed plantings. Astilbes, hostas, and azaleas combined with ferns make especially striking combinations.

Though a large and diverse group, these elegant foliage plants usually look their best in informal or natural settings. They make excellent backgrounds for herbaceous plants, and underplantings for shrubs. While most can be planted in masses, larger species can also be used as specimens. Ferns work beautifully when planted among rocks; they can soften the harsh edges of rough boulders, creep into cracks in walls, and fill in crevices of outcroppings.

Logs and tree stumps are natural partners for ferns in woodland settings. Ferns look well along a meandering path, at the base of a fence post, beside a bench, or even in large containers. In summer they provide a cooler and lusher feeling than any other group of plants. Although most garden ferns die back in the fall, some are excellent evergreens.

Selection and Use

Understanding their habit of growth will help you to determine which ferns are best suited for your needs. Fiddleheads, the coiled young fern leaves, burst into growth with the onset of spring. As the season progresses, they unfurl and mature. Most of the garden ferns range from 6 inches to 4 feet in height. As years pass, colonies spread out and large clumps expand, reaching their full potential as landscape plants.

The stem or rhizome of the fern creeps along just at or below ground level and can frequently go unnoticed. Fern roots are typically very slender and shallow. If they are short-creeping, such as the autumn fern, *Dryopteris erythrosora,* then the plant will form a central clump. If they are long-creeping, such as the hay-scented fern, *Dennstaedtia punctilobula,* then the plant will form more of a colony.

Hay-scented fern, soft and delicate, spreads very quickly. Its lacy, classic fronds reach up to 2½ feet. Deciduous, hardy, good on slopes in part to deep shade, the species admirably tolerates extended wet and dry spells. Plant it on the verges of a wild garden, among rocks, or in those odd corners where one might like grass but it won't thrive.

Leaves, or fronds, are the most conspicuous and abundant part of a fern. In most ferns, the young fronds uncoil from fiddleheads in spring. These are delightful alongside spring-blooming bulbs, wildflowers, and violets. Fronds are very diverse in their size, shape, texture, and color, and of course are the hallmark of a fern. Often, the fronds (and the rhizome as well) are covered with hairs or scales which further enhance the texture and color of the fern. Fronds may be once, twice, or thrice compound, with main branches splitting off into side branches.

Their form can be as simple as the strap-shaped hart's-tongue fern, *Phyllitis scolopendrium.* Its bright green, leathery fronds form clumps to 1½ feet tall. Such a distinctive species makes excellent specimens. Evergreen in milder climates, it prefers moist, well-drained soil with a limestone composition. Crushed oyster shells may improve soil texture and alkalinity.

Once-compound fronds like the common polypody, *Polypodium vulgare,* are of medium texture, growing more in the shape of a feather. Fully hardy, it grows to 1 foot tall and thrives on acidic, rocky soils. Plant it at the base of a rock, in wall crevices, or in stony humus in open, dappled shade. Finely dissected, more compound fronds tend to have a lacy, delicate appearance such as the northern maidenhair fern, *Adiantum pedatum.* A low grower, it forms 1-foot-tall mats and is hardy and evergreen.

Fronds can be thick and leathery, with a glossy finish such

as the tassel fern, *Polystichum polyblepharum*. Its lustrous, bristly fronds form gorgeous clumps to 2 feet high, and it is hardy and evergreen in milder climates. Others, like the lady fern, *Athyrium filix-femina*, are thin and soft.

There are a few ferns that have brightly colored variegated fronds, like the ever-popular Japanese painted fern, *A. goeringianum* 'Pictum'. Perhaps the best fern for landscaping is the Japanese shield fern, *Dryopteris erythrosora,* with bright red spore cases and a shape that suggests tiny shields. The leaves emerge a coppery red, then settle into green, then color again in the cool fall weather and remain evergreen. Marginal shield fern, *Dryopteris marginalis,* forms clumps up to 2 feet tall. Fully hardy, it likes constant moisture and dappled or high shade.

Above all, perhaps, ferns offer many shades of green. One can choose from the deep forest green of Christmas fern, *Polystichum acrostichoides*, the chartreuse of hay-scented fern, or even the bluish green of marginal shield fern. Its leathery fronds grow in clumps 2½ feet tall.

Ferns bear spores, often on showy fertile fronds, instead of flowers. Spores are usually found on the underside of fronds. The common polypody has large golden dots, while one will see narrow, hooked lines on the ladyfern. In between sterile leaflets of the interrupted fern grow soft, cinnamony tufts of spores. The fertile fronds of the sensitive fern, *Onoclea sensibilis,* are wiry branching structures strung with brown, beadlike spore cases which remain intact through winter.

Sensitive fern is one of the easiest to grow. With its wide-bladed, scalloped, light green leaflets, it brightens low, damp areas in part to medium shade, and forms large, somewhat invasive colonies. It is best in larger gardens and woodland settings. Deciduous sterile fronds grow 1 to 2 feet tall. Although the plant is very winter-hardy, its leaves turn brown with a touch of frost, which earns it the name sensitive fern.

How to Grow

Growing ferns is not too demanding, provided that certain conditions are met. Most species widely available to gardeners will thrive in loose, moist, humusy, well-drained soil in light shade. Special niches may be created in which to grow some of the rarer or more difficult ones.

For the most part, ferns require morning sun to light shade. The best settings are those with dappled shade provided by a high canopy of deciduous trees, those that receive a few hours of morning sun, and even those with a northern exposure, provided they are open. Afternoon sun is usually too strong.

Ferns need a soil that is well-drained, loose, and rich in organic matter. If your soil is swampy, you will have to improve the drainage first. You might be able to do this by working the soil and breaking through a hard pan or you may have to lay drainage tiles.

You will probably need to incorporate some organic matter, even if your soil is relatively good garden loam. Most ferns are denizens of open woodland and forest floor and luxuriate in a crumbly duff. Both sandy and clayey soils will benefit from this. Peat moss is most common and easily available, but I prefer a good leaf mold, garden compost, or composted manure, all of which are excellent additives.

Since ferns have shallow root systems made up of small roots, it is important that the soil remain loose and open. Ferns often appreciate crumbly rocks or pebbles mixed into a humusy soil. Avoid walking on the soil or anything else that causes compaction because their root systems cannot tolerate it.

Moisture

A properly prepared soil will be open and hold plenty of moisture without being soggy. There are, however, a few species that can tolerate wet feet, including sensitive fern, ostrich fern (*Matteuccia struthiopteris*), and cinnamon and royal ferns, *Osmunda cinnamomea* and *O. regalis*.

Ferns need fairly consistent moisture throughout the year. If growing conditions are ideal and weather cooperates, you may never need to water. But chances are you will have to provide moisture on occasion. A soil that dries out too quickly is going to require more frequent watering in summer. Water deeply and thoroughly when you do. Ferns also lose moisture to drying winds, and exposed sites should be modified or avoided.

Planting

As with any other planting, evaluate your setting before you select any ferns. As you become more and more familiar with your garden you will probably find that you have several microclimates. This allows for some flexibility and offers a place for experimentation.

Plant ferns in spring or fall. Start by digging a hole wider than the root ball of your fern. More organic matter may be added at this time. Bonemeal will help the plants get established, unless there are dogs, skunks, or other animals about; if so, use superphosphate fertilizer instead. Always keep in mind the ultimate size of what is being planted so that you can space plants appropriately.

Set the fern in the hole slightly higher than its original soil level to allow settling to restore it to the proper depth. The growing crown, the juncture between root and stem, should never be buried. Once in place, backfill the hole and firm the soil. Water thoroughly. New plantings will most likely require subsequent watering until well established.

Maintenance

After several years you may notice that some clump formers seem to be raised well above the soil level. This naturally occurs and indicates that it is time to lift them and replant. Dig up the plant, remove any old, dead, or decaying parts, and replant, once again positioning the crown just above the soil level. In some species multiple crowns are produced and after awhile they become very thick and crowded. Lift and separate these crowns and replant each one.

Ferns benefit from a soil mulch. It conserves moisture, maintains a more even soil temperature, keeps weeds down, and prevents packing of the soil surface and splashing of the plants which can come from a heavy rainfall. Organics such as shredded leaves or bark chips will help to improve the soil structure as they decompose. Replenish every spring.

Ferns in the garden require little fertilizing. If conditions are less than ideal, you could provide an annual application of a complete fertilizer at the beginning of the growing season. Organic or slow-release fertilizers are best. Quick-acting and concentrated formulas can burn plants or force growth that is soft and lush and too weak to withstand stress. If the soil has been well prepared and mulched, plants may never need any additional nutrients.

Maintaining neat and healthy ferns isn't a big task. Fern beds may need weeding, especially in the early years. As ferns have shallow root systems, it is best not to disturb the soil around them but to pull the weeds by hand. In spring, tidy up the plants before they put out their new flush of growth for the season. Remove the dead fronds by cutting them off near the crown. On some species, usually the deciduous kinds with thin leaves, you can safely pull off the old fronds by hand. With many, however, especially those that are evergreen or have leathery leaves, pulling damages the crown or dislodges the entire plant.

Fortunately, ferns cultivated outdoors are seldom affected by pests. Slugs and snails are the only real offenders. They are particularly fond of the maidenhair fern. Look for bitten foliage and shiny trails. To control them, pick them off by hand or put out beer traps. Otherwise, you can expect ferns to be trouble-free, rewarding plants for the shade garden.

Lawns

WARREN SCHULTZ

When it comes to that place in the sun, nothing shines like turf. Lawn grass is the ultimate ground cover for sunny areas. It feels good underfoot. It needs little maintenance, aside from mowing. It's long-lived — a single sowing can establish a lawn that lasts for decades. Grass spreads rapidly and forms a tough, wear-tolerant mat to keep weeds down. Grass survives, even thrives, from the far North to the deep South, staying green in all but the most severe conditions. And when the going gets too tough for grass it doesn't roll over and die, it goes dormant to spring back again when the time is right.

There are turf varieties that have disease and insect resistance. Some have drought and heat tolerance. Many resist wear and tear. It's plain that there are plenty of reasons why there are 33 million acres of lawn in America.

In fact, grass is so good that homeowners often try to grow it where it doesn't belong, or at least where it will be challenged. And perhaps the greatest challenge to grass is shade. Lawn grass, for the most part, is a sun-lover. It evolved over centuries in pastures and sunny savannahs, and it's still happiest where the sun shines. But here in America, shade is growing as fast as the national debt.

All of those trees planted in the suburbs 30 or 40 years ago have matured. They're blocking the sun, creating waves of shade that wash over our neighborhoods. In fact, it's estimated that as much as 20 percent of American turf is growing, or trying to grow, in the shade.

The Importance of Sunshine

Grass, like all plants, depends on the sun to live. The grass plant uses solar energy, through photosynthesis, to combine carbon, oxygen, and hydrogen into sugars, carbohydrates, and fibers. Carbohydrates serve as the main source of energy for growing grass plants. And after they're produced in the shoots, they're stored in the roots to fuel further growth. However, the less light available, the less photosynthesis the plant can manage, the less carbohydrate fuel the plant can accumulate and use. That, in a nutshell, is why grass grows poorly in the shade. And why it needs some special care.

Even at its best, lawn grass manages to use only 1 or 2 percent of solar energy for photosynthesis. When the amount of sunlight available is reduced through shading, the grass struggles to survive. Carbohydrate production is reduced. Turf grows less vigorously. It falls behind in the competition with weeds and is more susceptible to diseases. And there are often side effects to shade that cause problems for lawn grass. However, there are several ways to help grass live and even thrive with reduced solar energy. You have to be willing to invest some time and treat that shady patch a bit differently than the rest of your lawn, altering your mowing, fertilizing, watering, and disease prevention techniques.

But first, you should take some time to examine the conditions. All shade is not the same. It varies in intensity, duration, and cause. And those variables will play a role in how you handle it.

First, you have to decide whether the shade is just too deep to bother with. Seventy percent is the cutoff number. If the shade lasts all day with more than 70 percent of sunlight blocked, or if it lasts more than 70 percent of the day, you should probably give up on lawn grass and try one of the more shade-tolerant ground covers. Or, if the deep shade exists in a limited area around a tree trunk, for example, consider replacing the grass with a bark mulch.

While you're at it, take a look at what's causing the shade. It could be buildings, fences, garden structures, shrubs, or trees. Shade under a tree is the hardest to deal with. Grass grown under trees has two strikes against it. First, there's the dearth of sunlight, but just as troublesome is the competition from tree roots. Regardless of the size and age of the tree, most of its feeder roots grow within the top few inches of soil.

If you're willing to take the time to start over with that tree-shaded spot, and are preparing the soil for seeding, you can prune the roots of established trees, thinning the top layer without damaging the tree. And if you're planning to sow one of the more shade-tolerant grasses, it might be a good idea. However, there are less dramatic steps you can take to compensate for that competition.

Food and Water

Even when rainfall seems adequate, shady turf may be suffering from drought. It may look brown, thin, or be infested with weeds. They are all symptoms of lack of water — a common side effect of shady conditions. Tree canopies often block rainfall and irrigation from reaching the soil and the grass roots. Much of the water that does reach the soil is absorbed by tree roots. For best results, shade-grown grass needs to receive more water than the rest of your lawn.

The standard recommendation for sunny turf is 1 inch of water per week. For shady areas, increase that amount by half. As with the rest of the lawn, water deeply and thoroughly. Light, frequent watering does little good. Instead, water should be applied slowly and perhaps once a week as necessary so that it penetrates to a depth of at least 6 inches.

When should you water? It's often recommended that turf should not be watered late in the day, on the theory that water left standing on the blades overnight will encourage disease. However, there is a new, somewhat radical school of thought that suggests that the evening is the *best* time to water, at least in humid areas of the country. The thinking is that the grass will be wet from dew during the evening anyway. By watering late in the day, you give the turf a chance to dry out in the morning.

Just as shady turf needs more water, it needs more fertilizer, too. Again, tree roots are competing for the fertilizer you apply, and because shady turf is unable to manufacture as much food, an extra boost is essential. Turf grown in the shade is often starving, even if it is regularly fertilized with the rest of your lawn. And hungry grass spreads slowly, leaving bare patches and an opportunity for more rugged weeds to move in.

Because the blades are not receiving their full ration of solar radiation for photosynthesis, we need to step in and step up their fertilizer regime. As a general rule, you should increase fertilizer rates by half. For fescue that amounts to 2 to 3 pounds of nitrogen per 1,000 square feet per year. Bluegrass, ryegrass, bentgrass, zoysia, and Bermuda grass will require 3 to 4 pounds per year. In the North, spring and fall are the best times to fertilize. In the South, apply from June to August.

Mowing

Aside from increasing the dose of fertilizer, there's a simple way to increase the plants' ability to make food. Because light is at a premium in the shade, the photosynthetic rate is reduced and there's a shortage of food produced. Perhaps you can't significantly increase the amount of light reaching any given blade, but you can increase the amount of blade surface available for photosynthesis. You do that simply by allowing the grass to grow higher than normal. Let it grow an extra ½ to 1 inch as compared to sun-grown grass. For example, the best mowing heights for some grass species grown in the shade are: 4 inches for tall fescue, 3 inches for Kentucky bluegrass, 2½ inches for fine fescue and ryegrass, and 1 inch for Bermuda grass and zoysia.

That doesn't mean letting the grass get shaggy. It doesn't mean less frequent mowing. In fact you should take more care with your mowing schedule on shady grass. Mowing may be the most stress your lawn has to face. It's certainly the most regular one. The less area you cut, the less you stress, the longer the roots get, the better equipped they are to handle the competition from tree roots.

Disease Prevention

The lack of sunlight, shortage of water and fertilizer, the less-than-ideal growing conditions all make shade-grown grass an easier target for diseases.

With only one exception — St. Augustine decline virus — all turf diseases are caused by fungi. And in most cases, fungi prefer the environmental conditions of moistness and shade. So when trying to grow a lawn in the shade, it's especially important to keep a close eye out for localized disease breakouts.

There are two diseases that are particularly attracted to shaded turf: powdery mildew and pythium. Powdery mildew is of the same family as the disease that strikes your phlox, zinnias, and zucchini. It's normally not a serious problem for turf, except Kentucky bluegrass which is quite susceptible. And if that Kentucky bluegrass is growing, or trying to grow in shade, and if that shady area has poor air circulation, then it can be a problem.

You can recognize powdery mildew from small patches of white or gray fungus on the blades. As it progresses, the tissue beneath the discolored patches becomes yellow. Eventually, the turf takes on the appearance of having been dusted with powder. That powder can be wiped off the leaves.

Powdery mildew is a constant threat, especially if conditions are humid. The best cure is prevention. Reduce the shade as much as possible by pruning the trees as much as possible. Increase air circulation by pruning or removing nearby shrubs. Unfortunately, part of the shade prescription actually encourages powdery mildew: the disease is favored by heavy nitrogen fertilizer, so it's important to adjust your fertilization routine if powdery mildew appears. On the other hand, high mowing can help slow the spread, especially if you remove the clippings. Finally, if you're reseeding a shaded area, stay away from Kentucky bluegrass (especially the 'Merion' variety.) Rather, choose a resistant variety of fine fescue such as 'Dawson', 'Fortress', 'Gracia', 'Reliant', 'Reptans', or 'Ruby'.

Pythium can be a destructive disease under the right conditions, and those conditions include shade. It's a disease of cool-season grasses, especially bentgrass, though it may occur on ryegrass overseeded in the South. Fortunately, it requires very specific conditions to occur: daytime temperatures above 86 degrees, nighttime temperatures about 68 degrees, and humidity over 90 percent for two days. And of course, shaded areas are often more humid than surrounding areas.

Pythium shows up first as circular patches of brown measuring one to several inches in diameter. As the disease progresses they form large, irregular clusters of dark, water-soaked grass. The blades may feel slimy and show cottony mycelium in the morning.

Again, prevention is the best cure. Reduce shade, increase air flow as above, and, because grass is more susceptible when suffering from a calcium deficiency, add dolomitic limestone annually to increase the calcium level.

Choosing Varieties

All the extra care will help your turf cope with shade, but you'll still be fighting a losing battle if you're trying to grow the wrong species or variety of grass in the shade.

Fortunately, some grass species and varieties have been bred and selected to better handle that low light than others. Grass is a sun-loving plant, but some species and varieties are more efficient than others at utilizing solar energy.

Breeders have been setting their sights on shade-loving grasses. Over the past decade or so, several new developments have made growing grass in limited sun an easier task. Breeders now select for shade tolerance and rate new varieties for their ability to survive without full sun. There are several new varieties that will grow well in up to 70 percent shade.

Though to most homeowners one variety or even species of grass is indistinguishable from the next, it's not true that grass is grass. The good news is that some species in general are much more shade-tolerant than others. The bad news is that one of the species of northern grasses that can tolerate shade the least is that all-time favorite, Kentucky bluegrass.

If you're having problems growing grass in the shade, that might be your problem. With a few varietal exceptions, Kentucky bluegrass ranks near the bottom of the heap when it comes to shade tolerance. And what's at the top? One class of grasses that is becoming more and more popular, the fescues. Fescues are coming on strong. They seem like perfect grasses for these times. They are the most shade tolerant of all grasses. They stand up to wear and tear. Most are resistant to diseases, some varieties even resist insect damage. And they don't require heavy fertilization to look good.

Rutgers University recently concluded a four-year trial of lawn grass varieties to determine how they would perform in the heavy shade. Eight of the top ten varieties were fescues. They were 'Rebel' tall fescue, 'Reliant' hard fescue, 'Scaldis' hard fescue, 'Jamestown' chewings fescue, 'Biljart' hard fescue, 'Banner' chewings fescue, and 'Fortress' red fescue. The two non-fescue varieties that scored well were 'A-34' Kentucky bluegrass and 'Pennfine' perennial ryegrass.

There is one other species that consistently grows well in the shade, provided it receives plenty of moisture: rough bluegrass (*poa trivialis*). It resembles a Kentucky bluegrass, but the blades are coarser and of a lighter green color. Because it spreads by stolons, it can form a dense turf.

In the deep South, Bahia grass is made for the shade. Best varieties are 'Argentine', 'Paraguay', and 'Wilmington'. Because Bahia grass is killed by temperatures below 20 degrees, southern lawn owners in cooler areas should use centipedegrass (including 'Oaklawn' and 'Tennessee Hardy') in shady areas.

In the South, the most popular grass, Bermuda grass, is the one that's least suitable for the shade. Better species for shady areas are St. Augustine and zoysia. However, when northern grasses, such as Kentucky bluegrass, tall fescue, and perennial rye are grown in the South, they can handle more shade than when grown in the North.

As with all other aspects of shady turf culture, sowing requires a little extra care. Grass grown in the shade has enough problems: lack of light, competition from roots, lack of water. Don't let soil be one of them. Take extra care to insure that the soil is friable and fertile. You may find under certain mature trees that the "soil" is actually a dense mat of fibrous feeder roots. You won't harm the tree by thinning that layer lightly with a rotary tiller, verticutter, or by hand with a garden rake. It also pays to top-dress with a half-inch layer of topsoil or shredded compost before sowing.

Because of the less than ideal conditions, grass seed will not germinate as reliably in shady areas. To insure good coverage, sow at twice the recommended rate. Make sure that it's made good contact with the soil throughout by raking or rolling lightly. Follow standard procedure as far as watering is concerned. Make sure to keep the soil surface evenly moist at all times until the grass germinates. Mulch very lightly with sawdust or weed-free straw, or cover with a floating row cover. But take it easy on the water once the grass has come up. Mowing newly germinated grass calls for a light touch, too. Give the new grass a chance to put on some growth before you trot out the mower. Let it grow to its maximum recommended height, then cut off less than a third of the blade. For example, let fine fescue grow to about 3 inches before cutting it back to 2½.

If you have a struggling but serviceable lawn, you can replace it gradually without digging it up or doing a lot of work, by overseeding with an improved, shade- tolerant variety (one that is sod forming). Rake the area roughly, and sow the new variety at 1½ times the recommended rate. Keep well watered, as for any newly sown grass.

Once your new shade-tolerant grass is up and established, it will still require extra care. Make sure to keep a close eye on that shady patch, monitoring it for disease problems or signs of moisture or fertilizer stress. Mow frequently and lightly. Pull weeds when they appear. With a little bit of pampering, you'll find that it is possible to have a good-looking lawn, even where sunshine is sparse.

City Shade

LINDA YANG

The search for city sunlight can be a challenge. Just because the real estate agent says your back yard, patio, terrace, rooftop, or balcony faces south, don't expect to be blinded by sunbeams all day — or even part of the day. If any bit of structure comes between your space and the sky for any significant length of time there will be areas where dark hours outnumber light. It's hard to miss a day-long shadow from a 20-story building, but structure doesn't mean only a huge skyscraper. You might have part-time shade courtesy of a tall fence, a dense canopy of trees, a corner of a neighbor's house, or even the top floors of your own.

The only way to manage city shade is to determine the light you actually have. Which means getting outside and looking — not just once but several times. And unless your memory is better than mine, be sure to take along a pencil and something sturdy on which to note the spots where the direct rays touch. Jot down their approximate length of stay, if they're from the gentle morning sun or that of the leaf-wilting afternoon, and don't forget to add the season you're out there.

What if you have a space that seems to have its sunlight "by appointment only"? I promise you a plant for every condition — but only you can appraise the condition you find.

Now, before marching off to the nearest nursery to match

your light with appropriate plants, take a minute to ponder your course of design. A successful city garden reflects not only its owner's personal taste, but a pragmatic response to the peculiar constraints of space. At one extreme is the formal composition. It is distinguished by symmetrical, even sparse plantings (a paired set of neatly clipped crabapples or topiary yews) and crisp mathematical order in the placing of walks and furnishings. Axes and geometrical lines predominate, and architectural features or ornaments are chosen for neat patterns and classical form.

In marked contrast is the naturalistic approach with seemingly random, asymmetrical paths and furnishings. It is distinguished by irregular groupings of plants (like blowsy clusters of Solomon's-seal and snakeroot) and curved or undulating pathways predominate. While scale and proportion remain important, neither plants nor furnishings are symmetrically balanced nor positioned as mirrored images.

While city views may include "borrowed scenes" of breathtaking skyscapes or rooftop spires, the crucial vistas are seasonal perspectives seen from indoors all year. Fortunately, nature and the horticultural breeder have created deciduous and evergreen shrubs and trees in a broad palette of shapes, sizes, tones, and textures. So whatever design route you take, some woody plant is sure to help you achieve your design while adding four seasons of interest.

You might, for example, bend the flexible limbs of a Japanese holly (*Ilex crenata*) to create a bower or highlight a view. Or position a row of neatly clipped azaleas to edge a parapet wall or outline a boundary, coax flowering golden-chain trees into a mini-*allée*, or use small-leaved cotoneasters (*C. microphyllus*) to soften the edge of a planter or carpet a slope.

Where space is minimal, even a single specimen adds year-round perspective. Among the slow-growing, shade-tolerant species that are amenable to the pruning needed for tight control are Japanese maple (*Acer palmatum*), birch (*Betula* species), maidenhair tree (*Ginkgo biloba*), and honey locust (*Gleditsia triacanthos*).

Trees and shrubs can also add flowers on high. Where there's need for a brightener for spring try star magnolia (*Magnolia stellata*), crabapple (*Malus* species), callery pear (*Pyrus calleryana*), Carolina silverbell (*Halesia carolina*), kousa dogwood (*Cornus kousa*), shadbush (*Amelanchier canadensis*), chokeberry (*Aronia arbutifolia*), or Cornelian cherry (*Cornus mas*). Outstanding summer bloomers include the sourwood tree (*Oxydendrum arboreum*) and summer-sweet (*Clethra alnifolia*), while the Chinese witch hazels (*Hamamelis mollis*) can be counted on for long-lasting fragrant golden blossoms in early winter.

Unfortunately, the city is filled with ugly intrusions you may have to disguise, and where multi-seasonal cover-ups are needed, evergreens are the plants to use. Take advantage of the countless small-leaved rhododendrons and azaleas to obscure a chain-link fence, a neighbor's rotting shed, a forest of roof pipes, a water tower, or an oppressive brick wall. Other superb baffles or textured winter screens are *Skimmia japonica, Pieris japonica, Leucothoe fontanesiana,* and Oregon grape holly (*Mahonia aquifolium*).

While shrubs and trees are crucial elements through the four seasonal acts, it takes a broad supporting cast to make the city drama complete. From spring through autumn, other horticultural characters add a kaleidoscope of tones, textures, scents, and shapes. Summer's colorful stars for the shady city place include such reliable perennials as turtlehead (*Chelone lyonii*), astilbe (*Astilbe* spp.), and *Corydalis lutea;* fail-safe annuals like the wishbone flower (*Torenia fournieri*), coleus (*Coleus blumei*), and red salvia (*Salvia splendens*); and even scrumptious herbs like bay (*Laurus nobilis*), Chinese garlic chives (*Allium tuberosum*), and basil (*Ocimum basilicum*).

You won't find tomatoes ripening in city shade, but you can count on dazzling your guests with freshly harvested lettuce and spinach that can be truly gourmet.

And if yours is a rooftop or balcony, or you've simply run out of space in the ground? Try a container. Windowboxes and terra cotta pots make welcoming homes for summer flowers, while large tubs harbor hardy plants the rest of the year. I have found that any shrub or perennial that survives winter in the vicinity, in the ground, will also survive winter on top of the ground in a large container. This is because soil is a natural insulator. There's no need for winter wrapping or moving to protected areas when there's enough soil in the tub. This means that where perennials or trees are concerned, the bigger the container, the better.

But with space at a premium, how little a tub is big enough for winter plant survival? In New York City, where I garden (on the cusp of zones 6 and 7), a practical minimum tub size for hardy species — trees, shrubs, perennials, and vines — is 14 inches — wide, high, and long. In colder areas this minimum must be increased; in warmer climes it can be reduced.

Now someone out there is sure to complain that my 14 inches is a rather conservative figure. And I can agree, having seen 3-foot-high yews perfectly happy in an 8-inch windowbox. The problem instead is one of maintenance — and it is inversely proportional to container size. Grow hardy plants in tiny tubs and your watering and fertilizing chores will multiply monumentally.

The choice of container is endless. Anything you find that's appropriate for your design is appropriate for your plants providing it is also weather-resistant, made of a nontoxic material, and has several holes on the bottom for drainage. My favorites are old wooden barrels, both the clean and shiny ones and those that have not yet been "finished." Cast cement and sculpted stone are also handsome, but often too heavy for upstairs gardens. On balconies and rooftops, or wherever weight is a worry, plastic or fiberglass is best. Once disdained as the ugly ducklings of the container world, these products have had marvelous face-lifts and now come in truly attractive shapes, patterns, and shades.

One advantage to gardening above ground is that container soil can be customized. You can give your rhododendrons plenty of peat, and let the clematis have their lime. But there's also something to be said for keeping life simple, and for my large containers I have an all-purpose blend: one part topsoil, one part perlite, and one part peat moss or compost. Add a dollop of dehydrated cow manure and 5–10–5 fertilizer — a heaping handful for each 6 inches of container height.

The time of year also affects the light in town. The vernal equinox, which falls within the third week of March, marks the official beginning of spring. The sun is poised above the equator and day length equals night length. From this point until the end of June, daylight hours noticeably lengthen as the sun continues its climb above most city obstructions. This is the time when even the deepest canyon shines. This is also the time when north-side gardeners have longer, brighter days.

Unfortunately, summer's dazzling light is not guaranteed for all. If yours is one of a series of tiered balconies stacked each above the other like open dresser drawers, you will look up and find a ceiling, not open sky. A balcony ceiling means that as spring changes to summer and the sun climbs high, the back of your space will be covered by your upstairs neighbor's shadow.

Still, there's no need for despair. Ceilings were made for the hanging basket. Even the gloomiest corner can be draped with suspended pots of tropical foliage like grape ivy (*Cissus rhombifolia*), spider plant (*Chlorophytum comosum*), croton (*Codiaeum* species), or Swedish ivy (*Plectranthus coleoides*). Some color can be added here and there by tucking in such fail-safe flowers as begonia, impatiens, or browallia. You can then insure continual bloom by feeding them regularly with a high-phosphorus fertilizer (the middle number of the 3 on the label), and rotating them weekly to the balcony's bright front side.

Then too, there's no need to let that ceiling stop you from having at least one container of hardy perennials, so long as you also supply the year-round rain. Containers are just fine for perennials like hostas or ferns and shrubs like winged euonymus (*Euonymus alata* 'Compacta') or bush honeysuckle (*Diervilla lonicera*). And why not a small weeping tree? Weeping trees, after all, grow down, not up, so they naturally fit under a ceiling. Appropriately scaled weepers for containers in shady spots include the weeping flowering crabapple, weeping Siberian pea tree (*Caragana arborescens* 'Pendula') and weeping Sargent hemlock (*Tsuga canadensis* 'Pendula').

In any case, no city gardener can be choosy about light. Making the most of limited sun also means finding and amplifying reflections. In the summer for example, several hours after the midday sun has dropped behind the buildings that surround me, my plants shimmer in a brilliant, occasionally eerie glow. It is indeed the afternoon sun — but reflected into my shady space by helpful neighboring structures. Reflections from myriad shiny windows and bright or glazed brick walls hardly equal the open sky, but they do mean extra moments of useful light. Add to this glow with a strategically sited mirror or by painting the adjacent wall or ceiling white.

What about those pockets of truly impenetrable shade? There really is a plant for every place, and this includes the group dismissed as invasive. Rapid spreaders and sprawlers are just the answer for spots so troublesome nothing else grows, and when all else fails, some invaders to turn to are Boston ivy (*Parthenocissus tricuspidata*), dead nettle (*Lamium maculatum*), English ivy (*Hedera helix*), goutweed (*Aegopodium podagraria*), *Houttuynia cordata,* and pachysandra (*Pachysandra terminalis*).

After your plants are in place, it's time to start cleaning. A biweekly hosing should suffice for back yard plants, while streetside species, especially near heavy traffic, should be doused each season with a mild dishwasher detergent. The city is, after all, a sooty place, and if you notice your sills are grimy, you'll notice your plants' leaves are, too. The problem of leaf soot is more than mere aesthetics. Dirt and dust reduce the light that reaches the leaves, and compound the challenge of shade. Since dirty leaves have a harder time "breathing" — that's trading carbon dioxide and pollutants for oxygen — their need, and yours, is clear. Help your city's air and keep your shady plants clean.

Shade Gardening in the South

PETER LOEWER

I'm a latecomer to both shade gardening and the South. My first garden was in the North — about 125 miles northwest of New York City — and my second garden is within the city limits of Asheville, North Carolina.

Upstate New York has vicious winters, especially in the area around the Catskill Mountains. While many parts of the state were covered with snow, our area endured sleet and freezing rain. When temperatures plummeted — and they often did — to 30 degrees below zero, there was rarely any snow cover. When snow did fall, it came around Thanksgiving, giving way to rain and sleet for Christmas. The January thaw would melt some of the icicles on the gutter's edge, then temperatures would fall again and spring would appear sometime in late April. In a typical winter the ground would freeze to 7 feet.

In the mountains of western North Carolina, winter usually comes around the end of December. There will be two or three nights where the temperature will reach zero, then, by the end of February, the winter jasmine is in full flower and the Lenten roses are in the midst of bloom — the snowdrops have already passed. There is little or no snow, and unless you are high in the mountains the ground rarely freezes deeper than 1½ inches.

Up North I had enough work to do in the infrequent sunshine and, except for a few wildflowers, did very little shade gardening. Here in the South the situation is completely reversed.

Any comparison of the two climates starts with the sun. During the summer, western North Carolina temperatures rarely reach 90 degrees and it's hotter on the south shore of Long Island than here in the mountains. But the intensity of the sun is something else again.

You first become acquainted with the southern sun when on a sunny January day you are sitting in a car, somewhere in the Carolinas, in the parking lot of any mall or shopping center. Outside the car the air might be 25 degrees, but inside the car temperatures soon rise and you're forced to open the window. In July, the same situation would result in your opening every window and then, in desperation, running to the nearest air-conditioned room as fast as you could.

Once you leave the mountains and travel east to the Atlantic coast, not only are cool mountain temperatures left behind but you enter a world of often unbearable humidity. In areas slightly above sea level, afternoon temperatures often reach the upper 90s and the humidity is in the same league. In fact, unless your garden is high in the mountains, it is often more important for a plant to be tolerant of heat than of cold.

USDA zone 6, the Upper South, includes a small slice of Maryland, West Virginia, half of Kentucky, and a bit of upper Arkansas. Since winter temperatures here match those of Philadelphia, there are few of the difficulties found in true southern gardening.

Most of the major gardening problems begin in zone 7, the Middle South. This area includes most of Maryland, most of Virginia, the western half of North Carolina, Tennessee, the middle third of Arkansas, and the mountainous regions of Mississippi, Alabama, Georgia, and South Carolina.

Zone 8 is the Lower South. It includes the southern part of those states in zone 7 plus half of Louisiana and some of Texas.

By the time you live in zone 9, the coastal zone, winter temperatures rarely go below 20 degrees and for all practical purposes you are on your way to the tropics.

So where does shade gardening come in? In zones 7 and 8 the climate is one of extremes: too much rain or too much drought; too much heat or too much cold; and always, especially in the summer, too much heat and too much humidity. So shade gardening becomes very attractive for a number of reasons — especially if you are partial to the English style of gardening.

Shade Definitions in the South

The first mistake the average gardener from the North or the Midwest makes after moving to the South is to underestimate the power of the southern sun. They wonder why their peonies burn around the edges and why pachysandra turns yellow when out in the open and why daylilies get such a bedraggled look.

If you love the look of an English garden, with its layers of color and the mixed textures of the leaves, sooner or later you have to come around to gardening in the shade. The sun is much too hot for the majority of perennials that excel around London to keep their attractiveness in zones 7, 8, and 9.

Deciduous shade

Deciduous trees are especially valuable in the southern shade garden because sunlight falls through their high branches before leaves begin to unfold. Plants that are at their best in early spring love the open sun of early spring — and that includes most of the popular spring bulbs. There are quite a number of tulip, daffodil, and hyacinth cultivars that will perform beautifully in the South, including some that even bloom in zone 9.

A great many wildflowers delight in the sunlight of late winter, and these same plants will lose their leaves by June. So even if you garden in an area that is beset with summer heat and lack of rain, there is no reason not to carpet your woodland garden — or naturalize your lawn — with spring bulbs and other flowers.

Various members of the genus *Cyclamen* do especially well in the South. These are not the blowsy flowers of the holidays but wild species that are at their best in deciduous shade or at the roots of evergreens, shaded by tree branches situated high above the corms.

And don't overlook the beauty of the Spanish bluebells or wood hyacinths (*Endymion hispanicus*). They come in blue, pink, or white, and are best under a deciduous tree where they can blossom in mid-spring, die back by June, and be replaced by a bed of ferns, especially Japanese painted fern (*Athyrium goeringianum* 'Pictum') or one of my all-time favorites, the hay-scented fern (*Dennstaedtia punctilobula*). If the bluebells seed about, the little plants are easily removed, and the same is true of hay-scented ferns.

Dappled shade

Dappled shade is our most valuable asset in the southern garden. And the best shade provider is a tree. Our garden is surveyed at one acre but because it is on the side of a hill, the available land is more like 1½ acres.

I went out and counted the trees on our land. There are eight oaks of various species all over 60 feet high, seven American dogwoods, one thirty-year-old metasequoia (*Metasequoia glyptostroboides*), one mature umbrella-tree (*Magnolia tripetala*), one very old 70-foot tulip tree (*Liriodendron tulipifera*), one 50-foot white pine (*Pinus strobus*), one large Canada hemlock (*Tsuga canadensis*), one small sorrel tree (*Oxydendrum arboreum*), one 20-foot red Japanese maple of an undetermined cultivar, an ancient laurel (*Kalmia latifolia*), a golden-chain tree (*Laburnum* × *watereri*), a small redbud (*Cercis canadensis*), a chain of five black locusts (*Robinia pseudoacacia*), countless native and cultivar rhododendrons, and a snowball tree (*Viburnum* × *carlcephalum*), a documented purchase from 1955.

Except for the front lawns, only two sections of our garden are located in full sun. One is the vegetable garden. Here from 10:00 A.M. to 4:00 P.M. tomatoes do beautifully in full sun and cucumbers twine around a number of mahonias that edge that part of the garden. But all the lettuces are shaded from shortly after noon and on into the afternoon. Without that protection, lettuces would bolt long before the end of June.

On the west wall of the house is a collection of herbs bordered by a gunnera (*Gunnera chilensis*) at one end and a 'Queen Elizabeth' rose at the other. (Even though I planted the gunnera with a large plastic dishpan underneath its root system for water, it still wilts every afternoon by 2:00.)

Without our ceiling of shade provided by the many trees, it would be impossible to grow a number of my favorite perennials to perfection. All the large-leaved hostas, my Himalayan rhubarb (*Rheum palmatum*), ground covers including all the ivies and the myrtles, hydrangeas (both the French and the oak-leaved), the dwarf rhododendrons, the mahonias, and my prized Japanese aucuba (*Aucuba japonica* 'Variegata') — are better for living in light shade. All day the sunlight is filtered by that high canopy of leaves. Even on a windless day the sunbeams never shine in one place for more than a few moments, and though soon replaced by another shaft of light, the leaves are never burned.

Up North, except for the wild daylily (*Hemerocallis fulva*) and the lemon lily (*H. lilioasphodelus*), most of the hybrids require almost a full day of sun. Here in the South, they bloom well in dappled shade and a few hardy souls will bloom in partial shade but the number of blooms is decidedly less.

Bamboos, too, are especially fine under the tall-tree umbrellas. There are two that are especially fine bamboos for Southern gardens. Both are runners but can be kept under control, especially if they have to fight with ivy or are planted with a walkway or strong edge to halt their progress.

The first is the Kuma bamboo (*Sasa veitchii*), one of the finest plants for shade gardening whether partial or full. This plant first entered American gardens about one hundred years ago. During the late spring, summer, and before the first frosts of autumn, this bamboo looks like any other of the landscape types. But after the first frost, the edges of the leaves are burned, making the plant look like it's variegated — but it isn't. From late autumn through the winter and on into spring, the Kuma bamboo is one of the finest landscape elements I've ever seen.

The second is the running bamboo (*Arundinaria viridistriata*). This bamboo is colorful in the full sun, but when given dappled shade the rich chartreuse and golden hue of the leaves is especially prominent. Everyone who sees this plant immediately wants a piece of the action.

Partial shade

Partial shade — especially when it comes from noon to 3:00 P.M. — is best for a number of plants, including Lenten roses (*Helleborus orientalis*) — used as a ground cover in our garden), a few ornamental grasses like wild oats (*Chasmanthium latifolium*) and the variegated miscanthus (*Miscanthus sinensis* 'Variegatus'), a number of different lilies (Orientals and Asiatic), and a particularly attractive form of the English ivy called 'Buttercup', this last a cultivar with leaves of golden yellow when given a half-day of sun, but lime green when kept in the shade.

Down South, most climbing and shrub roses will bloom if they only get half a day of sun, as long as they do get plenty of sun in the early spring before the leaves emerge. These same roses will also do well in light shade. Even hybrid teas will bloom with gusto in partial shade.

Surprisingly, many of the black-eyed Susans (*Rudbeckia* spp.) are candidates for some shade, especially in the afternoon. I would never have known, since most garden books specify full sun, but they do seed about, and this year fledgling plants sprouted in the bed that is home to *Lilium auratum*, a species of *Ligularia* (these are planted with plastic buckets beneath their roots for extra water), and a line of liriope (*Liriope muscari* 'Variegata'). Not only are the Susans flowering, but their bright orange blossoms are especially effective against the shady background of the rhododendron and fern thicket behind their bed.

In fact, it's a safe bet that most perennials — except for those wedded to the sun like the daisies, the sun roses (*Helianthemum* spp.), blazing-stars (*Liatris* spp.), oriental poppies (*Papaver orientale*), and the yuccas (*Yucca* spp.), will bloom well in southern gardens when given partial shade.

Full shade
In the South, full shade is home to a surprising number of plants, including a few excellent ground covers, a host of ferns, and a number of wildflowers.

Among the ground covers that do well in these positions are bishop's weed (*Aegopodium podagraria* 'Variegatum'). Sold as a foolproof plant and generally considered a weed, it is both of these, but when shaded the leaves never burn and the white areas really gleam.

Carpet bugleweed (*Ajuga reptans*) is another tough ground cover for Southern shade. Varieties with purple leaves hold their color in partial shade and usually turn a fresh green in full shade.

Doll's-eyes (*Actaea pachypoda*) are overlooked in the shade garden until the fall when their branches appear, full of white berries each with a black spot at the bottom (like a doll's eye) and each on a red stem. The berries are poisonous. They are native to the rich woods of the mountains and the Piedmont of North Carolina.

Wild ginger (*Asarum* spp.) always works in the shade garden. *A. shuttleworthii* loves full shade as long as you provide a rich, moist soil loaded with humus. They do flower, but you must look close to the ground for their strange, brown, juglike blossoms that are pollinated by beetles instead of bees.

White wood asters, *Aster divaricatus* (*corymbosus*), dislike the hot sun their field-loving relatives enjoy, and instead revel in the shade of the woods. They're especially appealing in shady city gardens as they're tolerant of poor and thin soil. The long black stems will flop around but end in clusters of white flowerheads up to 1 inch across. Gertrude Jekyll would plant it in small spaces where it would "serve to draw attention to those generally neglected shrub edges."

In the North, bergenias (*Bergenia* spp.) will succeed in full sun if given a moist soil. In the South the leaves burn. In our garden the bergenias are shaded by hydrangeas, mock orange, and an oak tree, yet they do well and flower every spring.

Galax (*Galax urceolata*) is a lovely woodlander that forms rosettes of a foliage so choice it is often stolen from the woods by unscrupulous flower arrangers and florists. It would be superb ground cover even if it didn't flower, but the tall scapes with their tiny white flowers are a definite plus. It doesn't take to coastal gardens.

Although it could be listed as a vine, the common English ivy (*Hedera helix*) also does full duty as a ground cover. The species and its many cultivars are something special for full shade in a southern garden. And that perfect ground cover also excels at climbing trees, especially since there is no damage to their holdfasts. But English ivy is at its best when it matures into its arborescent form and is known as tree ivy. Instead of continuing life as a climber, it now stays put and becomes a bushy shrub. The adult leaves change shape, losing their pointed lobes and rounding out their profile. Then clusters of greenish yellow flowers are produced in late summer, flowers that are especially attractive to bees. After pollination the flowers change into small, round, green fruits that ripen to blue-black, bearing a grapelike bloom. In fact, what struggles in the North can easily become a pest in the South — but as a ground cover, growing ivy beats cutting a lawn.

And the South is blessed with a number of ferns that call it home, preferring plenty of shade and a deep, woodsy, moist soil. Not only will most of the northern species do well in the middle South, there are many species that resent cold that will also grace a woodland garden.

Deep or heavy shade

That part of garden that never sees the rays of the sun is in deep shade; even at midday, it's full of shadow. Whether it is an area beneath old evergreens or behind a high wall, it's often too dark for even mosses to grow. Even the southern sun has difficulty here. While deep shade is welcomed on many sunny summer afternoons, no plant will last for any length of time in such surroundings. Probably the best you can do is set aside such an area for a rotating display of tropical houseplants. We have such an area shaded by first an oak, second an old dogwood, and third a star magnolia. Under that triple threat nothing would grow with any sense of dignity. So today, the greenhouse ferns summer there with a number of shade-loving orchids hanging in pots from the branches.

Some Shrubs for Shade

The following shrubs grow well in open, partial, or full shade.

The American boxwood (*Buxus sempervirens*) has wonderful and lustrous evergreen foliage and does well in the cooler sections of the Piedmont. It responds to an occasional light pruning but I must confess, we leave our hedge to grow as it will. Partial shade is best but these shrubs will grow in full shade.

Shame on the southern gardener who does not have at least one camellia (*Camellia japonica*) in his or her garden, and preferably three or four. These shrubs do well throughout zones 7, 8, and 9. And they must have at least partial shade to provide that rich evergreen foliage. They do need protection from stiff winter winds and on those few nights in the winter when temperatures fall to zero, I simply cover the bush with a blanket and it always blooms from late January to early March. If you must use a full-sun location, plant these shrubs on the north side of your house.

The winged spindle tree (*Euonymus alata*) is a deciduous shrub that can become weedy in the South. But its glorious autumn color that can rival the bracts of a poinsettia is certainly worth removing unwanted seedlings. And the wings on the corky twigs are always of interest during the winter. Partial shade is best.

The strawberry bush (*Euonymus americana*) grows well in good soil and is a great shrub for naturalizing. The flowers of May are often missed but the orange fruits of fall with their scarlet seeds are beautiful to behold. They do well in full shade.

Our dog-hobble bush (*Leucothoe fontanesiana*) is planted in front of an old wall and shaded by first a dogwood and then a huge white oak above all. It's easy to grow, does well in city gardens, and will adapt to partial or full shade. It makes a great underplanting in a woodland garden.

Heavenly bamboo or nandina (*Nandina domestica*) is really a member of the barberry family and does exceptionally well in partial shade. The evergreen leaves are always attractive and the red berries are especially decorative. They even do well in northern Florida. Old plants can be rejuvenated by cutting back the canes, but, like rhododendrons, only do one-third of the plant per year.

The yew *Taxus × media* does well in our garden, where it's shaded by a tall red oak and numerous rhododendrons. While it can reach 14 feet, we trim ours to vaguely reflect the look of an Italian garden. The shade it provides in turn makes a marvelous habitat for a number of ferns and a clump of *Iris cristata*.

Vines for the Shade

I recommend two vines for shade. The first is the climbing hydrangea (*Hydrangea anomala petiolaris*). Give it good soil and partial shade — a stone wall is excellent — and it will climb without support, producing hydrangea-like flowers in May. You can also plant it so it climbs a tree. This vine does not do well in zone 9.

Virginia creeper (*Parthenocissus quinquefolia*) is a native American vine with glossy green five-fingered leaves that turn a brilliant red in the fall. Not only will they vine, they also make an excellent ground cover if you prevent them from climbing trees. They do well throughout the South, especially in partial shade.

Throughout the South the evergreen wintercreeper (*Euonymus fortunei*) will perform as a ground cover in full shade when tree supports are lacking, or it will climb using aerial roots on trees or walls, and just ramble over rocks.

Providing Shade and the Value of Trees

If you are starting a Southern garden and there are few, if any, trees on the property, the first thing you should do is make a plan of the garden area and immediately plant some trees. It's not necessary to wait for a lifetime in order to have shade in the garden. There are many fast-growing trees that will cut down the power of the Southern sun. Choosing trees like dogwoods — especially the Chinese (*Cornus kousa*), shad-bush (*Amelanchier arborea*), sourwood (*Oxydendrum arboreum*), the chaste tree (*Vitex agnus-castus*), and a number of the smaller Japanese maples (*Acer* spp.) — will soon provide garden shade.

Don't overlook small, fast-growing trees like the staghorn sumac (*Rhus typhina*). If cut down to the ground every fall, this small tree will perform as a tropical-looking bush every spring. Or if the original tree is allowed to form suckers, you will soon have a shady grove of sumac plus the magnificent fall color of the leaves.

And if you are building your own home on a wooded tract of land, before you begin, learn the names and habits of the shrubs and trees that are on your land. Native rhododendrons, wild dogwoods, a host of ferns, and other native plants will only add to the worth of your shade garden. With selective trimming and clearing up underbrush, the possibilities for your shade garden are expanded. Chopping down full-grown trees is a vast undertaking costing hundreds of dollars, so before you even begin to cut, try pruning the lower branches to let in more light to provide that marvelous dappled shade. It always makes more sense to tailor the garden to the land rather than the land to the garden. Remember that in the South a garden in shade is a marvelous place to sit and worry about cultivation chores and weeding.

Some Other Trees for Shade

In addition to the trees mentioned previously, the following will quickly provide shade.

The silk tree (*Albizia julibrissin*) is a fast-growing, umbrella-form tree that in many Southern gardens can become a weed, but the ferny leaves bring a tropical look to the garden. Height is between 20 and 30 feet with a 30-foot spread. The pink powder puff flowers are a definite plus.

The various witch hazels, especially the Chinese (*Hamamelis mollis*), not only produce additional shade, their autumn colors and winter blossoms should be welcome everywhere. Chinese witch hazels top at 20 feet. Don't grow them in zones 8 or 9 as it's too hot.

Russian olive (*Elaeagnus angustifolia*) quickly grows to provide additional shade. This small tree will reach a height of 20 feet. Extremely sweet-smelling flowers appear in the spring. Russian olives are almost ancient at 14 years of age. They do well in coastal areas of the South.

Finally, the Japanese stewartia (*Stewartia pseudocamellia*) needs afternoon shade in order to prevent the scorching of the leaves. Showy white flowers appear in the spring and resemble camellias, hence the species name.

Soil Conditioning

The condition of soil for the shade garden is very important. In full Southern sun, most plants must struggle if they are in dense, poorly drained, clay-packed soil (soil in the South is a euphemism for red clay). In the shade, that type of soil could be deadly — especially when overhanging trees prevent a lot of rainwater from falling on the soil.

What do you do about the soil? First, you remember that clay is full of minerals and is far superior for plant growth than many other types of soil. After all, the mountains and plains of the South support a wide variety of plants on that stubborn soil.

Start to collect falling leaves from your own trees and your neighbors'. Buy or rent a leaf shredder and begin composting those leaves immediately and also start a kitchen compost heap. Always haunt nursery centers in the fall and buy up bags of topsoil or composted cow or sheep manure when it's on sale — it's all grist for the same mill. And, unless it's small, don't bite off the whole garden at once. Start improving one small spot and keep at it. By mixing all this organic matter with the clay, over a few short seasons the soil will improve.

Watering in the Shade

A few words on watering. Whether you water in the morning or afternoon, try to get it out of the way before the night falls. This helps to prevent the double threat of mold and mildew, a situation that is especially prevalent in the shade garden.

I've used both ground irrigation and sprinklers, and today I'm more inclined to recommend above-ground watering of plants. If you are gardening in the shade and have a number of trees, think about running thin piping up the tree trunks to a height of 8 feet and letting your water fall like rain. If you do use this system, remember to water enough to completely saturate the soil, giving mature plants a good drink. This also helps to prevent the development of shallow root systems.

And be sure you mulch your plants not only to cut back on weeds, but to help to conserve the water that is already in the soil.

The Color Plates

The color plates and the plant encyclopedia feature a variety of plants that will grow well (or moderately well) in shade gardens. The color plates are grouped according to plant types: trees, shrubs, perennials, annuals, bulbs, ground covers, vines, grasses, and ferns. Within each group, the plants are arranged alphabetically by genus and species.

Each plate is accompanied by a short description that gives the plant's botanical and common names, its height, its bloom season (if appropriate), a description of the amount of shade it will take, its hardiness zone limit, and the page on which you will find the encyclopedia entry.

A Word about Color

Color, more than many visual attributes, is in the eye of the beholder. What one person describes as blue, another may call lavender or even purple. And it is not just the names that vary. Sun and shade, time of day, and neighboring colors can all affect what we actually see. A leaf that looks rich red in midday may be a deep lavender in late-afternoon shade.

As you look at the photos on the following pages, remember that the camera, no less than the eye, captures colors as they appear at a certain moment. Add to that the natural variation among plants and the difficulty of reproducing colors precisely, and you will understand why you should not count on your plant having exactly the color you see in the photograph.

Trees

Acer japonicum   *Full-moon Maple*   *Part to light shade*
'Aconitifolium'   *Height: 8–10 ft.*   *p. 277*
                            Purple flowers
                            in spring
                            Gorgeous fall
                            color
                            Zone 6

Amelanchier ×   *Apple Serviceberry*   *Part to moderate*
grandiflora   *Height: to 25 ft.*   *shade*
                            White or pinkish   *p. 288*
                            flowers
                            Zones 4–8,
                            semi-hardy 3

Amelanchier laevis

Allegheny Serviceberry
Height: to 35 ft.
Fall color
Zones 4–8,
semi-hardy 3

Part to moderate shade
p. 289

Cercis canadensis

Eastern Redbud
Height: to 35 ft,
usually less
Flowers in early spring
Zone 4

Part to light shade
p. 318

Cornus florida   Flowering   Part to light shade
                            Dogwood   p. 333
                            Height: to 30 ft.
                            Fall color
                            Bright red fruit
                            Zone 5

Cornus florida   Red Flowering   Part to light shade
var. rubra   Dogwood   p. 333
                            Height: to 30 ft.
                            Bright fruit
                            Fall color
                            Zone 5

Cornus kousa *Kousa Dogwood* *Part to light shade*
Height: to 20 ft. *p. 333*
Flowers later than
native dogwood
Zones 5–8

Cornus kousa *Kousa Dogwood* *Part to light shade*
Height: to 20 ft. *p. 333*
More trouble-free
than native
dogwood
Zones 5–8

Cornus mas

Cornelian Cherry
Height: to 20 ft.
Flowers in early
spring
Edible fruit
Zones 5–7

Part to light shade
p. 333

Halesia carolina

Silverbell Tree
Height: to 40 ft.
Stunning against
tall evergreens
Zones 5–8

Part to light shade
p. 362

**Magnolia ×
soulangiana**

*Saucer Magnolia
Height: to 30 ft.
Fine specimen for
moist acid soil
Zone 5*

*Part to light shade
p. 399*

Magnolia stellata

*Star Magnolia
Height: to 15 ft.
Fragrant flowers
Zone 4*

*Part to light shade
p. 399*

Malus floribunda
Crabapple
Height: to 25 ft.
Red and yellow
fruit
Dependable tree
Zones 4–8
Part shade
p. 402

**Malus 'Indian
Magic'**
Crabapple
Height: to 20 ft.
Fruits remain
through winter
Zones 4–8
Part shade
p. 402

Paulownia tomentosa	*Empress Tree* *Height: to 50 ft.* *Fragrant flowers in long clusters* *Fast growing* *Zone 6*	*Part shade* *p. 424*

Tsuga canadensis	*Canada Hemlock* *Height: to 90 ft.,* *usually shorter* *Zones 4–7; semi-* *hardy 3 and 8*	*Part to full shade* *p. 464*

Shrubs

***Abeliophyllum
distichum***

*Korean Abelialeaf
Height: 3–5 ft.
Blooms in early
spring
Fragrant
Zone 5*

*Light shade
p. 276*

***Acer palmatum
'Dissectum'***

*Cutleaf Japanese
Maple
Height: to 12 ft.
Brilliant fall color
Specimen plant
Zone 5*

*Part to light shade
p. 277*

Aesculus parviflora

Bottlebrush Buckeye
Height: 8–12 ft.
Blooms in summer
Zone 4

Part to light shade
p. 283

Aesculus pavia

Red Buckeye
Height: 12 ft.
Flowers in late spring
Zone 5

Part to light shade
p. 283

Aronia | Red Chokeberry | Part to light shade
arbutifolia | Height: to 8 ft. | p. 294
| Fruit persists into |
| winter |
| Zone 4 or 5 |

Aucuba japonica | Aucuba | Part to full shade
| Height: to 10 ft. | p. 301
| Evergreen |
| Scarlet berries on |
| female plants |
| Zone 7 |

Berberis julianae   *Barberry*   *Part to light shade*
                         Height: 6–8 ft.   *p. 305*
                         Evergreen
                         Blue-black berries
                         in fall
                         Zone 6–8

Berberis   *Barberry*   *Part to light shade*
thunbergii   *Height: 4–6 ft.*   *p. 305*
'Atropurpurea'   *Fall color*
                         Many cultivars
                         available
                         Zones 4–8

Buddleia
alternifolia
'Argentea'

Butterfly Bush
Height: to 20 ft.
Fragrant flowers
in summer
Attracts butterflies
Zone 6

Part shade
p. 309

Callicarpa
americana

French Mulberry
Height: 5–8 ft.
Pink flowers
followed by
showy berries
Zone 7

Part to light shade
p. 311

Calycanthus floridus

*Carolina Allspice
Height: 4–8 ft.
Fragrant flowers
Aromatic bark
Zone 5*

*Part to light shade
p. 313*

Camellia japonica 'Rev. John G. Drayton'

*Camellia
Height: 20–25 ft.
Evergreen
Blooms fall to
spring
Zone 8*

*Part to light shade
p. 314*

***Camellia
sasanqua*
'Showa no Sakae'**

*Sasanqua Camellia
Height: 6–10 ft.
Evergreen
Blooms fall to
winter
Zone 8*

*Part to light shade
p. 314*

***Chaenomeles
speciosa*
'Toyo Nishiki'**

*Flowering Quince
Height: 6–10 ft.
Blooms in early
spring
Good hedge shrub
Zones 5–8*

*Part shade
p. 319*

Clerodendrum **trichotomum**   Harlequin Glorybower
Height: 10–15 ft.
Fragrant flowers in summer
Blueberries in fall
Zone 7

Part to light shade
p. 326

Clethra alnifolia **'Pink Spires'**   Sweet Pepperbush
Height: 3–8 ft.
Fragrant flowers in summer
Zone 4

Part to full shade
p. 327

Comptonia
peregrina

Sweet Fern
Height: to 5 ft.,
often much less
Leaves aromatic
Zone 3

Part shade
p. 329

Cornus racemosa

Gray Dogwood
Height: 8–15 ft.
Most effective in
summer
Zone 4

Part to full shade
p. 334

| **Cotoneaster divaricatus** | *Spreading Cotoneaster Height: 3–7 ft. Blooms in spring Handsome and easy to grow Zone 5* | *Part shade p. 335* |

| **Daphne mezereum** | *February Daphne Height: to 5 ft. Blooms in early spring Fragrant Zone 6* | *Part to light shade p. 340* |

Daphne odora   *Fragrant Daphne*   *Part to light shade*
                    Height: to 4 ft.   *p. 340*
                    Evergreen
                    Fragrant flowers
                    in spring
                    Zone 7

Dirca palustris   *Leatherwood*   *Part to light shade*
                       Height: 3–5 ft.   *p. 345*
                       Flowers in early
                       spring
                       Likes moist soil
                       Zone 5

Eleagnus pungens
'Variegata'

Thorny Eleagnus
Height: to 15 ft.
Evergreen
For difficult
conditions
Zone 7

Part to moderate
shade
p. 347

Enkianthus
campanulatus

Enkianthus
Height: 8–12 ft.
or more
Blooms in spring
Zone 5

Part to light shade
p. 347

**Euonymus
japonica
'Matanzaki'**

Japanese
Euonymus
Height: to 15 ft.
Half-evergreen
Zone 7

Part to full shade
p. 350

**× Fatshedera ×
lizei**

Fatshedera
Height: to 6 ft.
Evergreen
Blooms in fall
Zone 8

Part to full shade
p. 352

Fatsia japonica

Japanese Aralia
Height: 10–12 ft.
Evergreen
Blooms in fall
Zone 8

Full shade
p. 353

Fothergilla gardenii

Dwarf Fothergilla
Height: to 3 ft.
Fragrant flowers
in spring
Fall color
Zone 5

Part to light shade
p. 355

Fothergilla major   Large Fothergilla   Part to light shade
                        Height: 4–10 ft.   p. 356
                        Fragrant flowers in
                        spring
                        Fall color
                        Zone 5

Gardenia   Gardenia   Part to light shade
jasminoides   Height: 4–6 ft.   p. 358
                        Evergreen
                        Very fragrant
                        Blooms fall to
                        spring
                        Zone 8

Hamamelis ×
intermedia
'Arnold Promise'

Hybrid Witch
Hazel
Height: to 20 ft.
Fragrant
Blooms winter to
spring
Zone 5

Part to full shade
p. 363

Hamamelis
virginiana

Common Witch
Hazel
Height: to 20 ft.
Blooms in fall
Fragrant
Zone 4

Part to full shade
p. 363

Hibiscus syriacus
'Althea'

Rose-of-Sharon
Height: 5–15 ft.
Blooms summer
to fall
Zone 5

Part shade
p. 370

Hydrangea
quercifolia

Oakleaf
Hydrangea
Height: to 6 ft.
Blooms in summer
Fall color
Zone 5

Part to light shade
p. 374

Ilex × attenuata
'Fosteri'

Foster's Holly
Height: 10–15 ft.
Evergreen
Prune to keep
as shrub
Zone 6

Part to light shade
p. 375

Ilex cornuta
'Rotunda'

Chinese Holly
Height: to 6 ft.
Evergreen
Tolerates dry soil
Zone 7

Part to light shade
p. 375

Ilex crenata   *Japanese Holly*   *Part to light shade*
'Helleri'   *Height: 5–10 ft.*   *p. 375*
     Evergreen
     Zone 6

Ilex × meserveae   *Meserve Holly*   *Part to light shade*
     Height: 8–12 ft.   *p. 375*
     Evergreen
     The best holly for
     Northern regions
     Zone 5

Ilex verticillata Winterberry Part to light shade
Height: 5–15 ft. p. 376
Red berries persist
into winter
Tolerates wet soil
Zone 4

Itea virginica Virginia Sweet Part to full shade
Spire p. 380
Height: 5–10 ft.
Fragrant flowers in
summer
Fall color
Zone 5

Jasminum
nudiflorum

Winter Jasminum
Height: 4–5 ft.
Blooms winter to
spring
Zone 7; zone 6
with protection

Part to light shade
p. 380

Kalmia latifolia

Mountain Laurel
Height: 7–15 ft.
Evergreen
Needs acid soil
Zone 5

Part to full shade
p. 381

Kerria japonica
'Pleniflora'

Japanese Rose
Height: 4–6 ft.
Blooms in spring
Zone 5

Part to full shade
p. 382

Leucothoe
axillaris

Coast Leucothoe
Height: to 4 ft.
Evergreen
Blooms in spring
Zone 6

Part to full shade
p. 385

Leucothoe
fontanesiana

Drooping
Leucothoe
Height: to 6 ft.
Evergreen
Blooms in spring
Zone 5

Part to full shade
p. 385

Ligustrum
japonicum

Japanese Privet
Height: 7–10 ft.
Evergreen
Blooms in spring
Good topiary
plant
Zone 7

Part to light shade
p. 386

Loropetalum
chinense

Loropetalum
Height: 6–12 ft.
Fragrant flowers in
spring
Needs acid soil
Zone 7

Part to full shade
p. 393

Mahonia
aquifolium

Oregon Grape
Holly
Height: 3–6 ft.
Evergreen
Fragrant flowers in
spring
Zone 5

Part to full shade
p. 400

Mahonia bealei   *Mahonia*   *Part to full shade*
                      Height: to 12 ft.   *p. 400*
                      Evergreen
                      Fragrant flowers
                      in spring
                      Zone 7

Malus sargentii   *Crabapple*   *Part shade*
                       Height: to 14 ft.   *p. 402*
                       Blooms in spring
                       Fruits late summer
                       Zones 4–8

**Nandina
domestica
'Alba'**

*Heavenly Bamboo
Height: 6–8 ft.
Evergreen
Showy red berries
Zone 7*

*Part to moderate
shade
p. 414*

**Osmanthus
heterophyllus
'Myrtifolius'**

*Holly Osmanthus
Height: 15–20 ft.
Evergreen
Fragrant flowers
in fall
Zone 7*

*Part shade
p. 419*

**Philadelphus
coronarius**

*Mock Orange
Height: to 10 ft.
Very fragrant
flowers in spring
Zone 5*

*Part to light shade
p. 428*

**Pieris japonica
'Wada'**

*Pieris
Height: 3–10 ft.
Evergreen
Choice specimen
plant
Zone 5*

*Light to full shade
p. 431*

**Pittosporum
tobira**

*Pittosporum
Height: 6–18 ft.
Evergreen
Blooms in spring
Useful hedge plant
Zone 9*

*Part to full shade
p. 431*

**Prunus
laurocerasus**

*Cherry Laurel
Height: to 20 ft.
Evergreen
Blooms in spring
Zone 7*

*Part to full shade
p. 437*

Rhododendron   *Florida Flame*   *Light shade*
austrinum   *Azalea*   *p. 440*
                     Height: 6–12 ft.
                     Fragrant flowers in
                     spring
                     Zone 7

Rhododendron   *Piedmont Azalea*   *Part to light shade*
canescens   *Height: 6–10 ft.*   *p. 440*
                     Fragrant flowers
                     in spring
                     Zone 7

| **Rhododendron catawbiense** | Catawba Rhododendron Height: 6–10 ft. Evergreen Blooms in spring Zone 5 | Part to light shade p. 441 |

| **Rhododendron mucronulatum 'Cornell Pink'** | Korean Rhododendron Height: to 8 ft. Profuse, very early flowers Zone 5 | Part to light shade p. 441 |

Rhododendron
PJM hybrid

PJM
Rhododendron
Height: 3–6 ft.
Evergreen
Very hardy
Zone 4

Part to light shade
p. 441

Rhododendron
'Snow'

Kurume Azalea
Height: 4–6 ft.
Evergreen
Many colors
available
Zone 7

Part to light shade
p. 442

**Rhododendron
'Toucan'**

*Exbury Azalea
Height: to 4 ft.
Flowers in many
colors
Zone 5*

*Part to light shade
p. 442*

**Rhodotypos
scandens**

*Jetbead
Height: 4–6 ft.
Blooms in spring
Tolerates pollution
Zone 5*

*Part to full shade
p. 443*

Ribes alpinum *Alpine Currant* *Part to light shade*
Height: 5–8 ft. *p. 443*
Blooms in spring
Good for hedges
Zone 3

Skimmia *Skimmia* *Part to full shade*
japonica *Height: 3–5 ft.* *p. 451*
Evergreen
Male and female
plants needed for
berries
Zone 8; 7 with
protection

**Stewartia
pseudocamellia**

*Stewartia
Height: 25–30 ft.
Flowers in early
summer
Zone 6*

*Light shade
p. 454*

**Symphoricarpos
albus**

*Snowberry
Height: to 4 ft.
Blooms in spring
Zone 3*

*Part to light shade
p. 455*

Ternstroemia gymnanthera

Ternstroemia
Height: 4–10 ft.
Evergreen
Blooms in summer
Zone 7

Part to full shade
p. 458

Vaccinium corymbosum

Highbush
Blueberry
Height: 8–12 ft.
Brilliant fall color
Wet, acid soil
Zone 4

Part to light shade
p. 466

**Viburnum ×
carlcephalum**

Viburnum
Height: 6–10 ft.
Very fragrant
Zone 5

Part to light shade
p. 467

**Viburnum
dilatatum**

Viburnum
Height: 6–10 feet
Blooms in spring
Showy fruit in fall
Zone 5

Part to light shade
p. 467

Perennials

Aconitum carmichaelii

Azure Monkshood
Height: 3–4 ft.
Blooms in late
summer
Poisonous
Zone 3 or 4

Light shade
p. 279

Aconitum napellus

Common
Monkshood
Height: to 4 ft.
Blooms in late
summer
Poisonous
Zone 5

Part shade
p. 279

**Adenophora
confusa**

*Ladybells
Height: to 3 ft.
Blooms mid to
late summer
Zone 4*

*Part shade
p. 280*

**Amsonia
tabernaemontana**

*Blue Star
Height: to 2 ft.
Blooms in late
spring
Zone 4*

*Part to light shade
p. 289*

**Anemone ×
hybrida**

*Japanese Anemone
Height: 1–5 ft.
Blooms late
summer
to early fall
Zone 6*

*Part to light shade
p. 291*

**Anemone
pulsatilla**

*Pasqueflower
Height: to 12 in.
Blooms in spring
Needs neutral or
alkaline soil
Zone 5 to 8*

*Part to moderate
shade
p. 291*

Anemone sylvestris 'Snowdrop'

Wood Anemone
Height: to 18 in.
Blooms in late
spring
Zone 4

Part to light shade
p. 291

Aquilegia caerulea

Rocky Mountain
Columbine
Height: 2–3 ft.
Blooms in late
spring
Zone 4

Part to light shade
p. 292

Aquilegia
canadensis

Common
Columbine
Height: to 18 in.
Blooms in late
spring
Zone 4

Part to light shade
p. 292

Aquilegia
'Dragon Fly'

Garden Columbine
Height: 1–3 ft.
Blooms in late
spring
Zone 5

Part to light shade
p. 292

Arisaema triphyllum

Jack-in-the-pulpit
Height: 1½–2½ ft.
Woodland plant
for rich, moist soil
Zone 4

Light to full shade
p. 293

Aruncus dioicus

Goatsbeard
Height: 4–6 ft.
Blooms in early
summer
Prefers moist soil
Zone 4

Part to light shade
p. 296

Asphodeline lutea   *Asphodel*   *Part shade*
                        Height: 2–3 ft.   *p. 299*
                        Blooms in early
                        summer
                        Fragrant
                        Zone 6

Astilbe ×   *Astilbe*   *Part to full shade*
arendsii   *Height: 2–4 ft.*   *p. 299*
'Deutschland'   *Blooms in spring*
                        Needs moist soil
                        Zone 5

***Astilbe chinensis*
'Pumila'**

Chinese Astilbe
Height: 8–12 in.
*Blooms in late
summer
Best astilbe for
dry soil
Zone 5*

Part to full shade
p. 299

***Astilbe tacquetii*
'Superba'**

Astilbe
Height: 3–4 ft.
*Blooms in
midsummer
Does well in South
Zone 5*

Part shade
p. 300

Bergenia
'Margery Fish'

Bergenia
Height: 9–18 in.
Blooms in spring
Many hybrids
available
Zone 3

Light to full shade
p. 307

Brunnera
macrophylla

Siberian Bugloss
Height: 12–18 in.
Blooms in spring
Zone 4

Part to light shade
p. 309

Calceolaria 'John Innes'

Calceolaria
Height: to 6 in.
Blooms in early
summer
Zone 7

Part to light shade
p. 311

Caltha palustris

Cowslip, Marsh
Marigold
Height: 1–2 ft.
Blooms in spring
Moist to wet soil
Zone 4

Part shade
p. 312

Campanula latifolia

Great Bellflower
Height: 2–4 ft.
Blooms in summer
Zone 4

Part to light shade
p. 315

Campanula persicifolia var. alba

Peach-leaved
Bellflower
Height: 2–3 ft.
Blooms in early
summer
Zone 4

Part to light shade
p. 315

Chelone lyonii   *Pink Turtlehead*   *Part shade*
                      Height: to 3 ft.   *p. 321*
                      Blooms in late
                      summer
                      Needs constant
                      moisture
                      Zone 4

Cimicifuga   *Black Snakeroot*   *Part to moderate*
racemosa   *Height: to 6 ft.*   *shade*
                      Blooms in   *p. 323*
                      midsummer
                      Best for wild
                      garden
                      Zones 4–7

**Coreopsis
verticillata
'Golden Shower'**

*Threadleaf
Coreopsis
Height: 2–3 ft.
Blooms in
midsummer
Drought tolerant
Zone 4*

*Part shade
p. 331*

**Dicentra
cucullaria**

*Dutchman's-
Breeches
Height: 5–8 in.
Blooms in spring
Good for wild
gardens
Zone 4*

*Light to full shade
p. 343*

Dicentra 'Luxuriant'

Bleeding Heart
Height: 12–18 in.
Blooms spring to
fall
More heat tolerant
than others
Zone 4

Part to full shade
p. 343

Dicentra spectabilis

Common Bleeding
Heart
Height: 1–2 ft.
Blooms in spring
Zone 3 or 4

Part to full shade
p. 343

Digitalis grandiflora

Yellow Foxglove
Height: to 3 ft.
Blooms in early
summer
Zone 4

Part to light shade
p. 344

Disporum flavum

Fairy-Bells
Height: 2–3 ft.
Good for dry
shade
Zone 4

Part to full shade
p. 346

Disporum sessile Japanese Fairy- Part to full shade
'Variegatum'   Bells   p. 346
                   Height: 1½–2 ft.
                   Good for dry
                   shade
                   Zone 5

Dodecatheon   Shooting-star   Part to light shade
meadia   Height: 1–2 ft.   p. 346
                  Blooms in spring
                  Requires well-
                  drained soil
                  Zone 5

Eupatorium coelestinum

Mist Flower
Height: to 2 ft.
Blooms late
summer
to early fall
Zone 5

Part to light shade
p. 350

Filipendula palmata

Meadowsweet
Height: 2–4 ft.
Blooms in summer
Needs very moist
soil
Zone 4

Part to light shade
p. 355

Filipendula rubra   Queen-of-the-
Prairie
Height: 4–7 ft.
Blooms in summer
Needs very moist
soil
Zone 3

Part to light shade
p. 355

Geranium   Cranesbill
'Johnson's Blue'   *Height: to 2 ft.*
Blooms in late
spring
to early summer
Zone 4

Part to light shade
p. 360

**Geranium
maculatum**

*Wild Geranium
Height: 12–20 in.
Blooms spring to
early summer
Zone 5*

*Part to light shade
p. 360*

**Helleborus
lividus**

*Hellebore
Height: to 2 ft.
Blooms in winter
or early spring
Zone 8*

*Part to full shade
p. 367*

Helleborus niger   *Christmas Rose*   *Part to full shade*
                       Height: to 12 in.   *p. 367*
                       Blooms winter to
                       early spring
                       Zone 4

Helleborus   *Lenten Rose*   *Part to full shade*
orientalis   *Height: to 18 in.*   *p. 367*
                 Blooms early to
                 midspring
                 Easiest hellebore
                 to grow
                 Zone 5

**Heuchera
sanguinea**

*Coral-Bells
Height: 1–2 ft.
Blooms in summer
Attractive foliage
Zone 4*

*Part shade
p. 370*

Iris cristata

*Crested Iris
Height: 4–6 in.
Blooms in mid-
spring
Zone 4*

*Part shade
p. 379*

Kirengeshoma palmata

Kirengeshoma Height: 4 ft. Blooms late summer to fall Zone 5

Part to full shade p. 383

Ligularia × przewalskii 'The Rocket'

Rocket Ligularia Height: 4–6 ft. Blooms in summer Zone 4

Part to light shade p. 385

Lobelia cardinalis

Cardinal Flower
Height: 3–6 ft.
Blooms in summer
Prefers moist soil
Zone 3

Part to light shade
p. 391

Lobelia siphilitica

Blue Lobelia
Height: 2–4 ft.
Blooms in late summer
Needs moist soil
Zone 5

Part to light shade
p. 391

Lupinus
'Russell Hybrid'

Lupine
Height: 2–3 ft.
Blooms in early
summer
Not for hot, dry
areas
Zone 5

Part shade
p. 395

Lysimachia
punctata

Yellow Loosestrife
Height: 2–3 ft.
Blooms late spring
to early summer
Moist to wet soil
Zone 5

Part to light shade
p. 397

Malva alcea

Hollyhock Mallow
Height: 2–4 ft.
Blooms in summer
Prefers dry soil
Zone 4

Part to light shade
p. 403

**Meconopsis
cambrica**

Welsh Poppy
Height: to 2 ft.
Showy but difficult
Zone 6

Part to light shade
p. 406

Mertensia virginica   *Virginia Bluebells*   *Part to full shade*
                          Height: to 2 ft.   *p. 408*
                          Blooms in early
                          spring
                          Zone 4

Monarda didyma   *Bee Balm*   *Part shade*
                     Height: 2–3 ft.   *p. 412*
                     Blooms in summer
                     Attracts butterflies
                     and hummingbirds
                     Zone 4

Monarda
fistulosa

Wild Bergamot
Height: 3–4 ft.
Blooms in summer
Drought tolerant
Zone 4

Part shade
p. 412

Omphalodes
cappadocica

Navelwort
Height: 6–10 in.
Blooms in spring
Tolerates dry
shade
Zone 6

Part to full shade
p. 418

Omphalodes verna

Blue-eyed Mary
Height: to 8 in.
Blooms in spring
Needs moist, well-drained soil
Zone 5

Full shade
p. 418

Phlox divaricata 'Mrs. Crockett'

Wild Sweet William
Height: to 18 in.
Blooms in spring
A choice woodland flower
Zone 4

Part to full shade
p. 429

Phlox paniculata   *Garden Phlox*   *Part shade*
'Mt. Fujiyama'   *Height: 3–4 ft.*   *p. 429*
                          Blooms in summer
                          Zone 4

Physostegia   *Obedient Plant*   *Part shade*
virginiana   *Height: 3–4 ft.*   *p. 430*
                          Blooms in summer
                          Zone 4

Polygonatum Solomon's-Seal   Part to full shade
odoratum   Height: to 3½ ft.   p. 433
var. *thunbergii* Blooms in spring
                 Tolerates dry soil
                 in full shade
                 Zone 5

Primula helodoxa Amber Primrose   Light shade
                      Height: ½–3 ft.   p. 435
                      Blooms in early
                      summer
                      Moist to wet soil
                      Zone 6

Primula japonica   Japanese Primrose   Light shade
                       Height: 8–16 in.   p. 435
                       Blooms in late
                       spring
                       Needs ample
                       moisture
                       Zone 6

Primula sieboldii Japanese Star   Light shade
                       Primrose   p. 436
                       Height: to 12 in.
                       Blooms in spring
                       More drought
                       tolerant than other
                       primulas
                       Zone 5

Primula vulgaris
English Primrose
Height: to 6 in.
Blooms in late
spring
Mulch in hot
summers
Zone 5

Light shade
p. 436

Shortia galicifolia
Oconee Bells
Height: to 8 in.
Blooms in early
summer
Good for rock
gardens
Zone 5

Part to full shade
p. 450

Smilacina racemosa

False Solomon's-Seal
*Height: to 3 ft.
Blooms in spring
Zone 4*

Part to full shade
p. 451

Stylophorum diphyllum

Celandine Poppy
*Height: to 18 in.
Blooms in late spring
Good for wild garden
Zone 5*

Part to full shade
p. 454

Tanacetum
vulgare
var. *crispum*

Tansy
Height 2–3 ft.
Blooms in summer
Leaves strongly
aromatic
Zone 3 or 4

Part shade
p. 456

Thalictrum
rochebrunianum

Meadow Rue
Height: 3–5 ft.
Blooms in summer
Needs staking
Zone 5

Part shade
p. 459

Tradescantia ×
andersoniana
'Pauline'

Spiderwort
Height: 2–2½ ft.
Blooms late spring
to summer
Zone 5

Part to light shade
p. 462

Tricyrtis hirta

Toad Lily
Height: to 3 ft.
Blooms in early
fall
Needs acid soil
Zone 6

Part to full shade
p. 463

Trillium grandiflorum

Snow Trillium
Height: 12–18 in.
Blooms mid- to
late spring
Needs constantly
moist soil
Zone 5

Part to full shade
p. 463

Uvularia grandiflora

Big Merrybells
Height: to 2½ ft.
Blooms in late
spring
Good for wild
gardens
Zone 5

Light to full shade
p. 465

***Veronica latifolium* 'Crater Lake Blue'**

Veronica
Height: 12–18 in.
Blooms late spring
and summer
Zone 4

Part to light shade
p. 466

Viola cornuta

Horned Violet
Height: 5–8 in.
Blooms in late
spring
Best in cool, moist
summers
Zone 5

Part to moderate
shade
p. 469

Viola odorata
'Royal Robe'

Sweet Violet
Height: 6–8 in.
Blooms in late
spring
Many cultivars
Zone 6

Part to moderate
shade
p. 469

Viola striata

Striped Violet
Height: 4–16 in.
Fragrant flowers
in summer
Zone 5

Part to moderate
shade
p. 469

Annuals

Abutilon hybridum   Flowering Maple
Height: 1 to 3 ft.
Good container
plant
Must have
afternoon shade

Light shade
p. 277

Ageratum houstonianum 'North Sea'   Ageratum
Height: to 14 in.
Blooms until late
fall
Pink or white
forms also
available

Part to light shade
p. 285

Asperula orientalis

Woodruff
Height: to 12 in.
Fragrant
Prefers warm
weather
and moist soil

Part to light shade
p. 298

Begonia × semperflorens-cultorum

Wax Begonia
Height: 8 to 12 in.
Blooms
continuously
Good bedding
plant

Part to moderate
shade
p. 304

Begonia ×
semperflorens-
cultorum 'Gin'

Wax Begonia
Height: 8 to 12 in.
Blooms
continuously
Good bedding
plant

Part to moderate
shade
p. 304

Browallia
speciosa
'Blue Bells'

Browallia
Height: 8 to 12 in.
Best in warm
weather
and moist soil

Part shade
p. 308

Campanula medium Canterbury Bells
Height: 2 to 4 ft.
Prefers cool
weather
Part to light shade
p. 315

Cheiranthus cheiri Wallflower
Height: to 2½ ft.
Good cut flower
Prefers cool
weather
Part shade
p. 320

Chrysanthemum
parthenium
'White Stars'

Feverfew
Height: to 3 ft.
Perennial often
grown as annual
Reseeds freely
Zone 5

Part shade
p. 322

Cirsium
japonicum

Plumed Thistle
Height: to 2½ ft.
Adds interesting
texture
Prefers cool
weather

Part shade
p. 323

**Cleome
hasslerana**

*Spider Flower
Height: 4 to 5 ft.
Drought tolerant
Excellent accent
plant
Prefers warm
weather*

*Part to light shade
p. 325*

**Coleus ×
hybridus**

*Garden Coleus
Height: to 3 ft.
Hundreds of
cultivars available
Prefers warm
weather*

*Part to full shade
p. 328*

**Collinsia
grandiflora**

*Bluelips
Height: 8 to 15 in.
Prefers dry soil
Not heat resistant*

*Part shade
p. 328*

**Consolida
ambigua**

*Rocket Larkspur
Height: 1–2 ft.
Prefers cool
weather
Good cut flower*

*Part shade
p. 330*

**Consolida
orientalis**

*Larkspur
Height: 1–2 ft.
Prefers cool
weather*

*Part shade
p. 330*

**Cosmos
bipinnatus**

*Cosmos
Height: 3–4 ft.
Drought tolerant
Good cut flower*

*Part to light shade
p. 334*

Dianthus barbatus

Sweet William
Height: 1–2 ft.
Fragrant flowers
in spring

Part to light shade
p. 342

Digitalis purpurea 'Foxy'

Annual Foxglove
Height: to 4 ft.
Best in cool, moist
coastal climates

Part shade
p. 344

Eustoma
grandiflora

Prairie Gentian
Height: 2–3 ft.
Prefers warm
weather,
moist soil

Part shade
p. 351

Exacum affine

Persian Violet
Height: 1–2 ft.
Excellent pot plant
Prefers warm
weather

Part to full shade
p. 352

Helianthus annuus

Common Sunflower
Height: to 12 ft.
Flower heads:
12 in. across
Drought tolerant

Part shade
p. 365

Helianthus annuus × hybrida

Hybrid Sunflower
Height: to 12 ft.
Flower heads:
12 in. across
Drought tolerant

Part shade
p. 365

**Helianthus
annuus
'Italian White'**

*Hybrid Sunflower
Height: to 12 ft.
Flower heads:
12 in. across
Drought tolerant*

*Part shade
p. 365*

**Impatiens
balsamina**

*Garden Balsam
Height: 2–2½ ft.
Many colors
available
Prefers warm
weather*

*Light to full shade
p. 377*

Impatiens 'New Guinea'

Impatiens
Height: 1–2 ft.
Some varieties
require full sun

Part shade
p. 377

Impatiens wallerana

Impatiens
Height: 1–2 ft.
Many colors
available
Prefers warm
weather

Light to full shade
p. 378

**Lobularia
maritima**

*Sweet Alyssum
Height: to 12 in.
Good edging plant
Prefers cool
conditions*

*Part shade
p. 392*

**Lobularia
maritima
'Rosie O'Day'**

*Sweet Alyssum
Height: to 12 in.
Good edging plant
Fragrant
Prefers cool
conditions*

*Part shade
p. 392*

Lunaria annua

Honesty
Height: 1½–3 ft.
Prefers cool
weather
Pods used in dried
bouquets

Part to light shade
p. 394

**Lupinus
subcarnosus**

Bluebonnet
Height: 8–10 in.
Not heat-resistant
Needs moist soil,
good drainage

Part shade
p. 395

Machaeranthera
tanacetifolia

Tahoka Daisy
Height: 1–2 ft.
Drought tolerant
Long flowering
season

Part shade
p. 398

Malcolmia
maritima

Virginia Stock
Height: 6–12 in.
Fragrant
Prefers cool
weather

Part to light shade
p. 401

**Matthiola
longipetala**

Evening Stock
Height: to 18 in.
Very fragrant
Cannot tolerate
heat

Part shade
p. 405

Mimulus guttatus

Monkey Flower
Height: 12–14 in.
For California
Prefers cool
weather

Part to light shade
p. 409

Myosotis sylvatica

*Forget-Me-Not
Height: 6–18 in.
Prefers cool
weather*

*Part to full shade
p. 413*

Nemophila maculata

*Five-Spot
Height: to 12 in.
Cool weather plant
Good for high
altitudes*

*Part shade
p. 414*

**Nemophila
menziesii**

*Baby-Blue-Eyes
Height: to 12 in.
Cool weather plant
Good for high
altitudes*

*Part shade
p. 414*

Nicotiana alata

*Flowering Tobacco
Height: to 5 ft.
Fragrant
Prefers warm
weather*

*Part to light shade
p. 415*

Nierembergia hippomanica var. violacea 'Purple Robe'

*Cupflower
Height: 6–15 in.
Needs moist soil
Prefers warm
weather*

*Part to light shade
p. 416*

Oenothera erythrosepala

*Evening Primrose
Height: 2–8 ft.
Night-blooming
Good for sandy or
poor soil*

*Part shade
p. 417*

Omphalodes
linifolia

Navelwort
Height: to 12 in.
Prefers cool
weather, neutral
to alkaline soil

Part to light shade
p. 418

Pelargonium ×
domesticum

Martha
Washington
Geranium
Height: to 18 in.
Needs cool nights

Part to light shade
p. 426

**Pelargonium ×
hortorum**

*Common
Geranium
Height: 1–3 ft.
Good pot plant*

*Part to light shade
p. 426*

**Penstemon
'Scarlet and
White'**

*Gloxinia
Penstemon
Height: 2–3 ft.
Popular West
Coast plant
Prefers cool
weather*

*Part shade
p. 427*

**Primula
malacoides**

Fairy Primrose
Height: 4–18 in.
Prefers moist soil,
cool weather

Part to light shade
p. 435

Primula obconica

German Primrose
Height: to 12 in.
Prefers moist soil,
cool weather

Part to light shade
p. 435

**Primula ×
polyantha**

*Polyanthus
Primrose
Height: to 12 in.
Prefers moist soil,
cool weather
The easiest
primrose*

*Part to light shade
p. 435*

Reseda alba

*White Mignonette
Height: to 3 ft.
Prefers rich soil
and cool weather*

*Part shade
p. 439*

Rudbeckia hirta
'Gloriosa Daisy'

Black-eyed Susan
Height: 2–3 ft.
Tolerates heat
and drought

Part to light shade
p. 444

Sabatia angularis

Rose Gentian
Height: to 3 ft.
Needs damp soil
and cool weather

Part shade
p. 445

Schizanthus ×
wisetonensis

Butterfly Flower
Height: 1–2 ft.
For California
gardens

Part to light shade
p. 448

Senecio ×
hybridus

Cineraria
Height: 1–3 ft.
Good pot plant
For coastal
California

Part shade
p. 449

Torenia fournieri *Wishbone Flower* *Part to light shade*
Height: 10–12 in. *p. 461*
Good for hanging
baskets
Prefers warm
weather

Trachelium *Throatwort* *Part to light shade*
caeruleum *Height: 1–4 ft.* *p. 461*
Prefers warm
weather

Viola tricolor

*Johnny-Jump-Up
Height: to 12 in.
Good to plant
over spring bulbs
Prefers cool
weather*

*Part to light shade
p. 470*

**Viola ×
wittrockiana**

*Pansy
Height: to 9 in.
Many colors
available
Prefers cool
weather*

*Part to light shade
p. 470*

Summer
Bulbs

Agapanthus
africanus

African Lily
Height: 1½–3½ ft.
North of zone 8,
store over winter

Part to light shade
p. 284

Begonia grandis

Hardy Begonia
Height: 1–2 ft.
The hardiest
begonia
Zone 6

Part to full shade
p. 304

**Begonia ×
tuberhybrida**

*Tuberous Begonia
Height: to 18 in.
Very showy
Many forms
available
Tender above
zone 10*

*Part to full shade
p. 304*

**Caladium 'June
Bride'**

*Caladium
Height: 18 in.
Stunning foliage
plant
Tender above
zone 10*

*Light to full shade
p. 310*

Caladium 'White
Queen'

*Caladium
Height: 18 in.
Beautiful accent
plant
Tender above
zone 10*

*Light to full shade
p. 310*

**Cardiocrinum
giganteum**

*Cardiocrinum
Height: to 12 ft.
An immense,
striking plant
Needs cool, moist
soil
Zone 7*

*Part to light shade
p. 316*

**Crinum
americanum**

*Swamp Lily
Height: 1½–2 ft.
Showy accent
plant
Zone 9*

*Part to light shade
p. 336*

**Crinum
bulbispermum**

*Common Crinum
Height: to 3 ft.
The most popular
crinum
Zone 7, with
protection*

*Part to light shade
p. 336*

**Crinum ×
powellii**

*Hybrid Crinum
Height: to 2 ft.
Showy accent
plant
Zone 8*

*Part to light shade
p. 336*

**Crocus
longiflorus**

*Autumn Crocus
Height: to 5 in.
Flowers and leaves
appear together
Zone 5*

*Light shade
p. 337*

Crocus medius *Autumn Crocus* *Light shade*
Height: to 10 in. p. 337
Flowers appear
before leaves
Zones 6 or 7

Cyclamen *Sowbread* *Part to full shade*
hederifolium *Height: 3–6 in.* p. 338
Good for rock
gardens
Zone 7

**Hemerocallis
aurantiaca**

Daylily
Height: to 3 ft.
*Easy plant in
any location*
Zone 7

Part to light shade
p. 368

**Hemerocallis
fulva**

Tawny Daylily
Height: to 5 ft.
*Common roadside
escape*
Zone 3

Part to light shade
p. 368

Hemerocallis
hybrids

Hybrid Daylilies
Height: 1–5 ft.
Thousands of
named varieties,
many colors
Zone 4

Part to light shade
p. 368

Hemerocallis
'Hyperion'

Hybrid Daylily
Height: 1–5 ft.
Easy plant in
any location
Zone 4

Part to light shade
p. 369

| ***Lilium*** **'Bellingham'** | *American Hybrid Lily* *Height: 4–8 ft.* *Many colors available* *Zone 4* | *Part to light shade* *p. 388* |

| ***Lilium* 'Black Dragon'** | *Aurelian Hybrid Lily* *Height: 5–8 ft.* *Fragrant* *Zone 4* | *Part shade* *p. 388* |

Lilium 'Cascade'   *Madonna Lily*   *Part shade*
                         Height: 3–4 ft.   *p. 388*
                         One of the oldest
                         garden plants
                         Zone 5

Lilium   *Red Asiatic Hybrid*   *Part shade*
'Enchantment'   *Height: 2–3 ft.*   *p. 338*
                         Vigorous, easy to
                         grow
                         Zone 4

Lilium
'Golden Showers'

Yellow Aurelian
Hybrid
Height: 4–6 ft.
Fragrant
Zone 5

Part shade
p. 388

Lilium
'Imperial Silver'

White Oriental
Hybrid Lily
Height: 5–6 ft.
Fragrant
Zone 5

Part shade
p. 389

Lilium 'Jamboree'   *Red Oriental*   *Part shade*
                           Hybrid   *p. 389*
                           Height: 4–6 ft.
                           Fragrant
                           Zone 5

Lilium martagon   *Turk's-Cap Lily*   *Part to light shade*
var. album   *Height: 4–6 ft.*   *p. 389*
                           Tolerates more
                           shade than
                           other lilies
                           Zone 4

Lilium parryi   *Lemon Lily*   Part shade
                     Height: 4–6 ft.   p. 389
                     Fragrant
                     California native
                     Zone 7

Lilium   *Wood Lily*   Part shade
philadelphicum   *Height: 2–3 ft.*   p. 389
                     Native to Eastern
                     U.S.
                     Zone 5

Lilium superbum   Turk's-Cap Lily   Part shade
                       Height: 5–8 ft.   p. 389
                       Native to Eastern
                       U.S.
                       Zone 5

Lilium   Washington Lily   Part shade
washingtonianum   Height: 4–6 ft.   p. 390
                       Fragrant
                       California native
                       Zone 7

*Ground
Covers*

Aegopodium podagraria 'Variegatum'

Variegated
Goutweed
Height: to 12 in.
Good for difficult
places
Can be invasive
Zone 4

Part to full shade
p. 282

Ajuga reptans 'Burgundy Glow'

Ajuga
Height: to 4 in.
Blue or white
flowers in
spring
Zone 3

Part to full shade
p. 285

Alchemilla mollis   Lady's-Mantle   Light to full shade
                        Height: to 15 in.   p. 287
                        Flowers in early
                        summer
                        Zone 4

Andromeda   Bog Rosemary   Part to light shade
polifolia   Height: to 12 in.   p. 290
                        Evergreen
                        For damp soil
                        Zone 3

Anemone
canadensis

Canada Anemone
Height: to 2 ft.
Flowers in early
summer
Zone 4

Part to light shade
p. 291

Asarum
canadense

Wild Ginger
Height: 6–8 in.
Needs moisture
Zone 4

Light to full shade
p. 297

Asarum europaeum

European Wild Ginger
Height: to 5 in.
Evergreen
Moist soil
Zone 5

Light to full shade
p. 298

Aubretia deltoidea

False Rockcress
Height: to 6 in.
Blooms in early spring
Zone 5

Part shade
p. 301

**Bergenia
cordifolia
'Profusion'**

*Heartleaf Bergenia
Height: 12–18 in.
Most widely
grown species
in East
Zone 3*

*Light to full shade
p. 306*

**Bergenia
crassifolia**

*Siberian Tea
Height: to 18 in.
Good for West
Coast
Zone 3*

*Light to full shade
p. 306*

Ceratostigma plumbaginoides

Leadwort
Height: to 12 in.
Flowers in fall
Zone 5, with
protection

Part to light shade
p. 317

Chrysogonum virginianum

Green-and-Gold
Height: 4–10 in.
Blooms in late
spring
Zone 5

Part to light shade
p. 322

Convallaria majalis

Lily-of-the-Valley
Height: 6–12 in.
Very fragrant
Zone 4

Part to full shade
p. 330

Cornus canadensis

Bunchberry
Height: to 6 in.
Difficult; needs
cool weather
Zone 2

Part to full shade
p. 332

**Epimedium ×
rubrum**

*Red Epimedium
Height: to 12 in.
Blooms in spring
Zone 5*

*Part to full shade
p. 348*

**Epimedium ×
versicolor
'Sulphureum'**

*Persian Epimedium
Height: to 12 in.
Blooms in spring
Zone 5*

*Part to full shade
p. 348*

Epimedium ×
warleyense

Warley Epimedium
Height: 9–12 in.
Blooms in spring
Zone 5

Part to full shade
p. 348

Epimedium ×
youngianum
'Niveum'

Snowy Epimedium
Height: 8–10 in.
Blooms in spring
Zone 5

Part to full shade
p. 348

Euonymus
fortunei
'Silver Queen'

Winter Creeper
Height: to 2 ft.
Evergreen
Many cultivars
available
Zone 4

Part to full shade
p. 349

Galax urceolata

Galax
Height: to 2½ ft.
Evergreen
Blooms in summer
Zone 5

Part to full shade
p. 356

Galium odoratum

Sweet Woodruff
Height: to 12 in.
Blooms in spring
Fragrant
Zone 5

Part to full shade
p. 357

Gaultheria procumbens

Wintergreen
Evergreen
Height: to 4 in.
Bright red berries
Zone 5

Part to full shade
p. 358

Geranium macrorrhizum   Bigroot Cranesbill
Height: 12–18 in.
Blooms in early
summer
Zone 5

Part to light shade
p. 360

Hosta fortunei 'Aureo-marginata'   Fortune's Hosta
Height: to 2 ft.
Light purple
flowers
Blooms in summer
Zone 4

Light to full shade
p. 372

Hosta 'Ginko Craig'

*Ginko Craig Hosta
Height: to 10 in.
Useful for edgings
or rock gardens
Zone 4*

*Part to full shade
p. 372*

Hosta 'Krossa Regal'

*Krossa Regal
Hosta
Height: to 3 ft.
Lavender flowers
Blooms late
summer
Zone 4*

*Light to full shade
p. 373*

Hosta lancifolia   *Narowleaf Hosta*   *Light to full shade*
Height: to 2 ft.   p. 373
Blooms in late
summer
Best ground cover
hosta
Zone 4

Hosta sieboldiana   *Siebold Plantain*   *Light to full shade*
Lily   p. 373
Height: to 30 in.
Lilac flowers
Blooms in
midsummer
Zone 4

Lamiastrum galeobdolon 'Herman's Pride'

*Yellow Archangel
Height: to 12 in.
Yellow flowers
Zone 4*

*Part to moderate
shade
p. 383*

Lamium maculatum 'White Nancy'

*Spotted Dead
Nettle
Height: to 9 in.
Blooms in summer
Zone 4*

*Part to full shade
p. 384*

Liriope muscari
'John Birch'

Lilyturf
Height: to 18 in.
Evergreen
Zone 6

Part to full shade
p. 390

Lysimachia
nummularia

Moneywort
Height: to 2 in.
Needs moist soil
Zone 4

Part to light shade
p. 397

Mazus reptans   *Mazus*   *Part shade*
                        Height: to 2 in.   *p. 405*
                        Blooms in summer
                        Use between
                        stepping stones
                        Zone 6

Mitchella repens   *Partridgeberry*   *Part to full shade*
                        Height: to 2 in.   *p. 411*
                        Evergreen
                        A woodland plant
                        Zone 4

Myosotis
scorpioides
var. *semperflorens*

Forget-Me-Not
Height: 12–18 in.
Blooms spring
to fall
Needs moist soil
Zone 5

Part to light shade
p. 413

Ophiopogon
japonicus

Mondo Grass
Height: to 12 in.
Evergreen
Good under trees
Zone 7

Part to full shade
p. 419

Pachysandra procumbens

Pachysandra
Height: 8–10 in.
Evergreen in South
Zone 5

Part to dense shade
p. 421

Pachysandra terminalis

Pachysandra
Height: to 12 in.
Evergreen
Zone 5

Part to full shade
p. 421

***Paxistima
myrsinites***

Oregon Boxwood
*Height: to 2 ft.
Evergreen
Zone 5*

*Part to full shade
p. 425*

***Phlox stolonifera*
'Blue Ridge'**

*Creeping Phlox
Height: to 12 in.
Blooms in late
spring
Prefers moist soil
Zone 4*

*Part shade
p. 429*

**Polemonium
reptans**

*Creeping
Polemonium
Height: 8–12 in.
Blooms in spring
Needs moist,
well-drained soil
Zone 4*

*Part to moderate
shade
p. 432*

**Polygonum
bistorta
'Superbum'**

*European Bistort
Height: 2–3 ft.
Blooms in early
summer
Zone 4*

*Part to light shade
p. 433*

Pulmonaria
angustifolia

Blue Lungwort
Height: 6–12 in.
Blooms in spring
Zone 4

Part to full shade
p. 438

Pulmonaria
saccharata
'Mrs. Moon'

Bethlehem Sage
Height: 8–14 in.
Blooms in spring
Zone 4

Part to full shade
p. 438

Rhododendron indicum

Indicum Dwarf
Azalea
Height: 6–18 in.
Width: to 30 in.
Evergreen
Zone 6

Part to light shade
p. 441

Rhododendron North Tisbury

North Tisbury
Azalea
Height: to 15 in.
Width: to 4 ft.
Evergreen
Zone 6

Part to light shade
p. 441

| *Rhododendron* **Robin Hill** | *Robin Hill Azalea* *Height: 12–15 in.* *Width: 18–30 in.* *Evergreen* *Zone 6* | *Part to light shade* p. 442 |

| *Sarcococca* *hookerana* var. *humilis* | *Sweet Box* *Height: 6–24 in.* *Evergreen* *For West Coast and South* *Zone 6* | *Part to full shade* p. 445 |

Saxifraga ×
urbium

London Pride
Height: to 12 in.
Blooms in spring
Best in Pacific
Northwest
Zone 5

Part to full shade
p. 447

Sedum spurium
'Dragon's Blood'

Two-row
Stonecrop
Height: to 6 in.
Blooms in late
summer
Tolerates dry soil
Zone 3

Part to light shade
p. 448

**Skimmia
reevesiana**

Skimmia
Height: to 2 ft.
Evergreen
Zone 7

Part to full shade
p. 451

**Symphytum
grandiflorum**

Ground-cover
Comfrey
Height: 8–12 in.
Excellent for dry
soil
Zone 5

Part to moderate
shade
p. 456

Taxus baccata
'Repandens'

Spreading English
Yew
Height: to 2 ft.
Evergreen
Tolerates dry soil
Zones 6–8

Part to full shade
p. 457

Taxus cuspidata
'Densa'

Cushion Japanese
Yew
Height: to 18 in.
Evergreen
Tolerates dry soil
Zone 5

Part to full shade
p. 458

Tiarella cordifolia

*Foamflower
Height: to 6 in.
Likes moist,
well-drained soil
Zone 5*

*Light shade
p. 460*

Vinca minor

*Myrtle
Height: to 10 in.
Evergreen
Flowers in spring
Zone 5*

*Part to light shade
p. 468*

Vines

Adlumia fungosa   *Climbing Fumitory*   *Part shade*
                        Height: to 25 ft.   *p. 282*
                        Blooms in summer
                        Zone 5

Akebia quinata   *Fiveleaf Akebia*   *Part shade*
                        Height: to 30 ft.   *p. 286*
                        Can be aggressive
                        Zone 5

Aristolochia durior

Dutchman's-Pipe
Height: to 30 ft.
Creates dense
cover
Zone 5

Part to light shade
p. 294

Bignonia capreolata

Cross Vine
Height: to 50 ft.
Good for trellises
and fences
Zone 7

Part shade
p. 307

Clematis paniculata

Sweet Autumn Clematis
Height: to 30 ft.
Fragrant flowers in late summer
Zone 5

Part to light shade
p. 324

Clytostoma callistegioides

Violet Trumpet Vine
Height: to 8 ft.
Evergreen
Blooms in spring
Zone 8

Part to light shade
p. 327

Decumaria barbara

Climbing
Hydrangea
Height: *to 30 ft.*
Suitable as wall
cover
Zone 7

Part to light shade
p. 341

Euonymus fortunei radicans 'Variegata'

Winter Creeper
Height: *to 12 ft.*
Best evergreen
vine for North
Zone 5

Part to full shade
p. 350

Ficus pumila

Creeping Fig
Height: to 40 ft.
Evergreen
Zone 9

Part to full shade
p. 354

**Gelsemium
sempervirens**

Carolina Jasmine
Height: 10–20 ft.
Evergreen
Fragrant
Zone 7

Part to light shade
p. 359

Hedera helix
'Baltica'

English Ivy
Height: to 50 ft.
Evergreen
Many cultivars
available
Zone 6

Part to full shade
p. 364

Hydrangea
anomala
petiolaris

Climbing
Hydrangea
Height: 50–60 ft.
Clings well to
walls
Good fall color
Zone 4

Part to light shade
p. 374

Menispermum
canadense

Moonseed
Height: to 12 ft.
Quick cover on
chain-link fences
Zone 5

Part shade
p. 407

Parthenocissus
quinquefolia

Virginia Creeper
Height: to 50 ft.
Fall color
Tolerates difficult
conditions
Zone 3

Light shade
p. 422

Parthenocissus tricuspidata

Boston Ivy
Height: to 60 ft.
Outstanding wall
cover
Zone 5

Light shade
p. 423

Vitis coignetiae

Crimson Glory
Vine
Height: to 50 ft.
Brilliant fall
color
Zone 5

Part to light shade
p. 471

Grasses

Acorus gramineus
'Variegatus'

Japanese Sweet
Flag
Height: to 12 in.
Evergreen
Tolerates wet soil
Zone 6

Part to light shade
p. 279

Alopecurus
pratensis
'Aureo-variegatus'

Meadow Foxtail
Height: to 4 ft.
Good for meadow
gardens
Zone 5

Part to light shade
p. 287

Arrhenatherum   Bulbous Oat Grass   Part to light shade
elatius bulbosum   Height: 12 in.   p. 295
'Variegatum'   Drought tolerant
                   Zones 5–8

Arundinaria   Pygmy Bamboo   Part to light shade
pygmaea   Height: to 12 in.   p. 296
                   Good for erosion
                   control
                   Zone 7

**Arundinaria
viridistriata**

Running Bamboo
Height: to 6 ft.
Good tub plant
Zone 7

Part to light shade
p. 297

**Bambusa
glaucescens**

Hedge Bamboo
Height: to 20 ft.
Useful for accents,
hedges
Zone 8

Part to light shade
p. 302

Carex conica 'Variegata'

Miniature Sedge
Height: to 6 in.
Tolerates wet soil
Zone 5

Part to light shade
p. 316

Carex grayi

Gray's Sedge
Height: to 2 ft.
Tolerates wet soil
Zone 3

Part to light shade
p. 316

Carex pendula   Drooping Sedge   Part to light shade
                          Height: to 2 ft.   p. 317
                          Evergreen
                          Tolerates wet soil
                          Zone 5

Chasmanthium   Northern Sea Oats   Part to light shade
latifolium   Height: to 5 ft.   p. 320
                          Ornamental spikes
                          may be dried
                          Zone 5

**Cyperus
alternifolius**

Umbrella Plant
Height: 2–4 ft.
Evergreen
Tolerates wet soil
Zone 9

Part to light shade
p. 338

Cyperus papyrus

Paper Plant
Height: 6–8 ft.
Evergreen
Tolerates wet soil
Zone 10

Part to light shade
p. 339

Deschampsia
caespitosa

Tufted Hair Grass
Height: to 2 ft.
Evergreen
Zone 5

Part to moderate
shade
p. 341

Hakonechloa
macra 'Aureola'

Golden Variegated
Hakonechloa
Height: to 8 in.
Good specimen
plant
Zone 5

Part to light shade
p. 361

**Helictotrichon
sempervirens**

*Blue Oat Grass
Height: to 2 ft.
Evergreen
Drought tolerant
Zone 4*

*Light shade
p. 366*

**Holcus mollis
'Albo-variegatus'**

*Variegated Velvet
Grass
Height: to 12 in.
Needs moist soil
Zone 5*

*Part to light shade
p. 371*

**Imperata
cylindrica
rubra**

Japanese Blood
Grass
Height: to 12 in.
Color intense all
season
Zone 6

Part to light shade
p. 378

Luzula nivea

Snowy Wood Rush
Height: to 2 ft.
Semi-evergreen
Flowers in spring
Zone 4

Part to full shade
p. 396

Luzula sylvatica   *Greater Wood   Part to full shade*
Rush   p. 396
Height: to 12 in.
Makes a dense
ground cover
Zone 5

Milium effusum   *Golden Grass   Part to full shade*
'Aureum'   *Height: 18 in.   p. 409*
Yellow flowers in
early summer
Zone 5

Miscanthus
floridulus

Giant Miscanthus
Height: to 10 ft.
White flower
plumes in fall
Zone 5

Part to light shade
p. 410

Miscanthus
sacchariflorus

Eulalia Grass
Height: to 6 ft.
Silvery flowers in
late summer
Zone 5

Part to light shade
p. 410

**Miscanthus
sinensis
'Gracillimus'**

*Maiden Grass
Height: to 5 ft.
Suitable for
waterside
plantings
Zone 5*

*Part to light shade
p. 410*

**Phalaris
arundinacea
picta**

*Ribbon Grass
Height: to 3 ft.
Valuable for
difficult areas
Zone 4*

*Part to full shade
p. 427*

Sasa palmata   Palm-Leaf Bamboo   Light shade
                         Height: to 7 ft.   p. 446
                         Best in wild
                         garden
                         Zone 6

Sasa veitchii   Kuma Bamboo   Light shade
                         Height: to 7 ft.   p. 446
                         Best in wild
                         garden
                         Zone 6 or 7

Spartina
pectinata
'Aureo-marginata'

Prairie Cord Grass
Height: to 6 ft.
Good for
waterside
planting
Zone 5

Light shade
p. 452

Spodiopogon
sibericus

Silver Spike Grass
Height: to 3 ft.
Best in moist or
wet soil
Zone 5

Part to light shade
p. 453

Ferns

**Adiantum
pedatum**

Northern
Maidenhair Fern
Height: 12–24 in.
Needs moist soil
Zone 3

Light to moderate
shade
p. 281

**Athyrium filix-
femina**

Lady Fern
Height: to 2 ft.
Not drought
tolerant
Zone 3

Light to full shade
p. 300

Athyrium goeringianum 'Pictum'

Japanese Painted Fern
Height: 10–15 in.
Needs moist soil
Zone 6 or 7

Moderate to full shade
p. 300

Cyrtomium falcatum

Holly Fern
Height: 24–30 in.
Evergreen
Zone 10

Light shade
p. 339

Matteuccia
struthiopteris

Ostrich Fern
Height: to 4 ft.
Needs wet soil
Zone 3

Light shade
p. 404

Osmunda
cinnamomea

Cinnamon Fern
Height: to 3 ft.
Needs wet, acid
soil
Edible fiddleheads
Zone 3

Light shade
p. 420

Osmunda regalis   *Royal Fern*   *Light shade*
                      Height: to 4 ft.   *p. 420*
                      Wet, acid soil
                      Fall color
                      Zone 2

Polystichum   *Christmas Fern*   *Light to moderate*
acrostichoides   *Height: 18–24 in.*   *shade*
                     Evergreen   *p. 434*
                     Zone 3

Encyclopedia
of Plants

Abeliophyllum
A-bee-li-o-fill'um
Oleaceae. Olive family

Description
A single, deciduous, shrubby species, native to Korea. Grown for its fragrant white forsythia-like flowers in early spring.

How to Grow
Plant in part to light shade, depending on climate. Adaptable to most soils. Flowers appear on wood of the previous year, so prune immediately after flowering. To encourage new growth, remove old stems to the ground every several years. Hard winters may kill flowerbuds, but not the plants themselves, in the northern extent of its range. Increased by softwood cuttings in summer, hardwood cuttings in fall, or by fresh seed.

Uses
Early spring color in informal shrub border or foundation planting. Flowers can be forced during winter for arrangements.

distichum p. 90
Korean abelialeaf. Stems arching and spreading, 3–5 ft. long. Leaves ovalish, smooth-edged, 1–3 in. long. Flowers white to pinkish, ⅝ in. wide, bell-shaped, in compact clusters. Its dark green leaves appear after the bloom and turn purple before falling in autumn. Zone 5.

Abutilon
A-bu'ti-lon. Flowering maple
Malvaceae. Mallow family

Description
About 150 species of tropical shrubs, rarely herbaceous, a few of which are grown as bedding plants.

How to Grow
Needs afternoon shade or continuous light shade. Start seeds indoors in midwinter at 70–75 degrees F and set in the garden after last frost. Abutilon makes a good show of color in warm weather. Propagate by taking tip cuttings before fall frost or in late spring.

Uses
Abutilon makes a good show of color in warm weather in containers and beds.

hybridum *p. 168*
Flowering maple, Chinese lantern. 1–3 ft. high. Alternate leaves resemble those of true maples; some varieties are variegated. Flowers 1½ in. wide, nodding, red, pinkish, purple, yellow, or white; bell- or trumpet-shaped. Many showy named forms. Tender perennial usually treated as annual or bedding plant.

Acer
A'ser. Maple
Aceraceae. Maple family

Description
About 150 species of north temperate zone, mostly deciduous trees and large shrubs. Many have attractive foliage that colors brilliantly in fall. Clusters of small, often showy flowers in spring, followed by winged seeds.

How to Grow
The plants described below enjoy part to light shade. Maples will grow in any good soil, with adequate moisture and drainage. Prune lightly to shape or to remove damaged wood. Irrigate during extended dry spells. Propagated from seed or softwood cuttings.

Uses
Specimens for lawn or mixed border.

japonicum 'Aconitifolium' *p. 80*
Full-moon maple. This cultivar has a round habit and deeply

divided leaves, growing 8–10 ft. tall. Leaves light green, turning an exceptional crimson in fall, and purple flowers; about ½ in. long and wide, in drooping, showy hanks in spring. Fruit with wings spreading almost horizontally, also attractive. The species is taller, at 12–25 ft high. Japan. Zone 6.

palmatum 'Dissectum' *p. 90   Pictured on p. 277*
Cutleaf Japanese maple. Slow-growing, to 12 ft. high, with spectacular autumn color. Branches weep; tree develops into a broad mound at maturity. This cultivar has especially finely divided leaves. 'Bloodgood', 'Oshi Beni', 'Crimson Queen', and 'Tamukeyama' are other outstanding cultivars with excellent fall foliage. Korea and Japan. Zone 5 or 6, depending on cultivar.

Aconitum
A-ko-ny′tum. Monkshood or wolfsbane
Ranunculaceae. Buttercup family

Description
A genus of more than 100 species of herbaceous perennials native to the north temperate zone, a few of which are of garden interest. All are dangerously poisonous if eaten, but not to the touch. Plants usually have thickened or tuberous roots, and leaves that are cleft or divided like a palm. Late-summer-blooming blue or purple flowers, rarely white or yellow, grow in heavy clusters at the end of spikes or side stalks. Each pealike bloom has one large, hoodlike petal and four smaller attendants.

How to Grow
Monkshoods prefer cool climates, part to light shade, and a rich, moist, well-drained soil, preferably with a pH of 5–6.

A. carmichaelii likes more shade than *A. napellus*; adequate moisture is critical in either case. May need staking, as they are somewhat weak-stemmed. Garden varieties should be treated as short-lived perennials. They bloom the second or third year from seed, and increase slowly. They can be divided, but in general dislike disturbance.

Uses
Showy plants for the late summer and early autumn, but owing to their poisonous sap they have no place in children's play areas.

carmichaelii p. 128
Azure monkshood. One of the most handsome garden plants in the genus. Normally 3–4 ft., sometimes taller. Leaves 3-lobed, often notched. Flowers blue, sometimes white, with spurlike hoods, each 1½ in. long and borne in loose 2–8-in. racemes. Also listed as *A. fischeri*. East Asia. Zone 3 or 4.

napellus p. 128   *Pictured on p. 278*
Common monkshood. Source of the drug aconite and cultivated for ornament. 3–4 ft. tall, leaves twice- or thrice-divided into narrow segments. Flowers blue, beaklike hood, 1–2 in. long and borne in a loose 2–8 in. long raceme. Extremely poisonous. Europe. Zone 5.

Acorus
Ak'or-us. Sweet flag
Araceae. Arum family

Description
Marsh herbs, hardy all over the U.S. The species described

below is usually sold and used as semiaquatic ornamental grass.

How to Grow
Plant in part to light shade. Easy to grow in moist or wet soil. Propagate by dividing the rootstock.

Uses
Suitable for bogs, watersides, or marshes.

gramineus 'Variegatus' *p. 254   Pictured on p. 279*
Japanese sweet flag. Fine-textured foliage grows in tufts to 12 in. high from a stout rootstock. Leaves have a creamy stripe; this variety is more widely grown than the plain green species. Flowers greenish, minute, on a stalkless spadix. Fruit berrylike. Japan. Zone 6.

Adenophora
A-den-off'o-ra. Ladybell
Campanulaceae. Bellflower family

Description
About 40 species of perennial herbs, mostly from eastern Asia. Closely related to campanulas and grown for their handsome blue to purple flowers.

How to Grow
Easy to grow in part shade and moist, well-drained soil.

Uses
Reliable color in the summer border; informal edgings and naturalizing.

confusa p. 129
Ladybells. 3 ft. high. Flowers bell-shaped, ¾ in. long, purple, loosely clustered on gently leaning stalks in mid- to late summer. Zone 4.

Adiantum
Ay-dee-an'tum. Maidenhair fern
Polypodiaceae. Polypody family

Description
A group of several hundred ferns, most native to temperate North America and Asia. Fronds are generally thin, delicate

in texture, suggesting in whole or in part the shape of a fan, and held atop dark, wiry stalks.

How to Grow
Prefer light to moderate shade and moist, well-drained soil containing plenty of organic matter. These ferns are not tolerant of drought, direct sun, or intense heat. Divide in spring or fall. The species listed below is somewhat slow to establish and may be pestered by slugs.

Uses
Woodland gardens, rockeries, against northern foundation walls and porches. Among the choicest and prettiest of hardy ferns, maidenhair invariably improves any spot it likes.

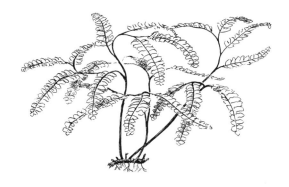

pedatum *p. 270   Pictured above*
Northern maidenhair fern. A deciduous, slow-spreading fern growing 12–24 in. tall. Lacy fronds with medium green leaflets fan out in arching whorls on polished black stalks. Zone 3. (Closely related *A. capillus-veneris,* the southern maidenhair fern, shorter, less hardy, and better suited to warmer regions.)

Adlumia
Ad-loom′i-a
Fumariaceae. Fumitory family

Description
A delicate, short-lived climbing vine, native to rich woods in eastern North America.

How to Grow
Easy in part shade and moist, rich but not overly acid, humusy soil. Protect from wind. Propagated by seed; self-sows once established.

Uses
Woodland. Cool and damp rock and retaining walls.

fungosa p. 244
Climbing fumitory, Allegheny vine, mountain fringe. Often climbing to 25 ft. high by slender tendrils. Leaves are alternate, fernlike. Flowers ¾ in. long, white or purple, resembling bleeding heart, *Dicentra* spp., growing in loose, drooping clusters in summer. Biennial. Zone 5.

Aegopodium
Ee-go-po'-di-um. Goutweed
Umbelliferae. Carrot family

Description
A small group of Eurasian perennials; a variegated form of one species is widely planted as a deciduous ground cover or edging.

How to Grow
Shade-loving, the species listed below will grow in part to full shade. Goutweed thrives in any soil condition, wet or dry, and can become weedy if not controlled. Deadhead flowers to prevent self-seeding. In heat and humidity it may get leaf blight. To increase, divide rootstocks in spring or fall.

Uses
Ground cover in dry shade. White leaves brighten dark areas.

podagraria 'Variegatum' p. 214
Variegated goutweed. Stout, coarse herb, 12 in. high. A useful foliage plant, 'Variegatum' has compound soft green foliage; leaflets have white margins. Flowers small, white, packed in flat umbels, not of great ornamental interest. Zone 4.

Aesculus
Es-kew-lus. Buckeyes and horse chestnuts
Hippocastanaceae. Horse chestnut family

Description
Thirteen species of deciduous North American and Eurasian shrubs and trees. Large, long-stalked leaves have 5–9 leaflets arranged like fingers on a hand. Trees bear large trusses of showy flowers in spring and leathery, sometimes spiny capsules

of one or two polished brown nuts in fall. Called "buckeyes" or "horse chestnuts," they are mealy and inedible, although pretty in arrangements and wreathes.

How to Grow
Plant buckeyes or horse chestnuts in part to light, dappled shade in any ordinary garden soil. The red buckeye is the more shade-loving.

Uses
Floriferous, distinctive large shrubs and specimen trees. Bottlebrush buckeye makes an appealing rustic thicket. Both species best in larger settings, and away from busy walks and drives where blossom and nut litter may pose problems.

parviflora p. 91
Bottlebrush buckeye. Mound-forming shrub, 8–12 ft. high and 3–15 ft. wide. Leaves have 5–7 leaflets, each 3½–8 in. long; turn yellow in fall. Outstanding in early summer when covered with foot-long candelabras of white flowers. Native to the southeastern U.S. and well-suited to that region, northward to zone 4.

pavia p. 91
Red buckeye. A round-headed shrub or small tree, 10–20 ft. high and equally wide. Leaves with 5–7 leaflets, slightly smaller than parviflora, often drop early in the fall. Grown chiefly for the 8-in.-long clusters of red or red and yellow flowers in late spring. Native to Virginia, south to Florida and Texas. Zone 5.

Agapanthus
Ag-a-pan'thus
Amaryllidaceae. Amaryllis family

Description
Lilylike plants with fleshy roots, often classed as summer-flowering bulbs. Tall flowerstalks rise from a rosette of long, strap-shaped leaves, crowned by a sphere of blue or white flowers in summer.

How to Grow
Enjoys part to light shade in the North, where it is often grown in pots. After its summer bloom is finished, it should be rested over the winter in a frost-free place. These vigorous growers need a large container. If kept in the same one from one season

to the next, they should be fed liberally with liquid manure. In the South they need more shade and may be cultivated in the open garden. Adaptable to a variety of soils. Mature plants can tolerate some drought.

Uses
Large, formal plant for containers, or seasonal bloom in warm climates. Pots of large specimens are excellent accents in pairs.

africanus *p. 198   Pictured above*
African lily, lily of the Nile. Plant 1½ to 3½ ft. tall. Leaves 20 in. long, rather thick. Flower stalk longer than leaves, the cluster consisting of about 12–30 striking blue flowers, 1½ in. long. There are many horticultural varieties, varying in size and flower color, which may range from white or pale blue to violet, and others with variegated leaves. South Africa. A tender bulb, it may be grown outdoors in zones 8 and 9; northward, strictly a pot specimen.

Ageratum
A-jur-a′tum
Compositae. Daisy family

Description
A group of nearly 30 species of chiefly tropical American annuals, one of which is perhaps the most popular of all edging plants, with soft flowers in blue, pink, or white, in compact long-blooming clusters.

How to Grow
Will thrive in light or dappled shade. Raise from seed indoors at 70–75 degrees F and set out after all danger of frost is past. Prefers warm weather.

Uses
Well suited to providing blue color and glossy foliage in summer bedding, edgings, containers.

houstonianum 'North Sea' *p. 168*
Common ageratum, flossflower. Usually 14 in. high. Leaves opposite, more or less oval with scalloped edges. Flowerheads just over ¼ in. wide with the texture of drapery tassels, the outside somewhat sticky. This cultivar is deep blue and blooms until late fall. 'Album' has white flowers; pink-flowered and dwarf varieties also available. Also sold as *A. mexicanum*. Central and South America. Tender annual.

Ajuga
Aj-oo'-ga. Bugleweed
Labiatae. Mint family

Description
European annual or perennial herbs, sometimes weedy. The species listed below is an excellent perennial ground cover.

How to Grow
Bugle is shade-loving and enjoys light to moderately full shade. It is easy to grow in ordinary, well-drained garden soil. Carpet-forming to the point of invasiveness under good conditions; where light, moisture, and soil are less to its liking, creeping stems tend to wander, seeking better areas to colonize. To rejuvenate tired plantings, dig up after bloom, improve soil, divide, replant.

Uses
Under spring bulbs, on banks and other areas which are difficult to cultivate, as a filler in borders and rock gardens.

reptans 'Burgundy Glow' *p. 214*
Ajuga or bugleweed. This cultivar has green, white, and dark pink to purple foliage. Leaves are opposite, oval, about 2 in. long, in crisp clusters 3 to 6 in. high. Plants bear a profusion of blue or purplish flowers on spikes 6–12 in. high in spring or early summer. 'Bronze Beauty' has dark foliage and blue flowers. These foliage selections hold color best in shade, but may need contrast of lighter rocks or leaves to show up. All are evergreen in mild winters, but subject to blight and other diseases in the South. The species has dark green leaves. Cold-hardy to zone 3.

Akebia
A-kee'bi-a
Lardizabalaceae. Akebia family

Description
Four species of Asiatic woody vines with distinctive, semi-evergreen foliage and loose clusters of small dark flowers in spring.

How to Grow
Best in part shade and well-drained soil. Propagate by division, cuttings, or seeds.

Uses
Vigorous coverage on walls, arbors, fences. Color, shape, and texture of leaves excellent on white or light surface. Nice complement to bamboo structures.

quinata p. 244
Fiveleaf akebia. A stout, twining climber, to 30 ft. high. Leaves have 5 leaflets, oblong and waxy. Flowers are fragrant, interesting, but small and dark: need to seen close-up. Can be aggressive, especially in warmer climates; control by cutting down to the ground in late winter. Zone 5.

Alchemilla
Al-ke-mill'a. Lady's-mantle
Rosaceae. Rose family

Description
200 species of European perennials, a few of which are of

interest to gardeners. Lobed or compound leaves with a silvery cast have serrated margins that catch and hold drops of rain and dew — to the general delight of onlookers.

How to Grow
Shade-loving; enjoys light to full shade, depending on moisture, climate, and exposure. Easy to grow in any ordinary garden soil and may be increased by division. In hot or dry climates, plant them in moist, humus-enriched soil.

Uses
Remarkable and mounding foliage for borders, edges, and ground covers.

mollis *p. 215   Pictured on p. 286*
Lady's-mantle. Plant grows to 15 in. high, producing a clump of erect, long-stalked leaves with shallow rounded lobes suggestive of a ruffed cloak. Flower clusters 2–3 in. wide. Bears chartreuse or yellowish flowers in late spring. Also sold as *A. vulgaris.* Zone 4.

Alopecurus
A-low-pee-cure′us
Gramineae. Grass family

Description
40 species of meadow grasses, mostly from the cooler parts of the north temperate zone. Medium-size grasses of upright, open habit with slowly creeping rhizomes. Spikelike, dense panicles of bloom.

How to Grow
Enjoys part to light shade. Prefers fertile, moist soil. Increase by division.

Uses
Meadow gardens or ground cover.

pratensis **'Aureo-variegatus'** *p. 254*
Meadow foxtail. Perennial, stems 2 ft. high. Leaves to 6 in. long, slightly rough; this cultivar has leaves with broad gold margins. Similar 'Aureus' has leaves of gold with green ribs. Flower spike buff-colored, dense, 1–3 in. long in spring. Zone 5.

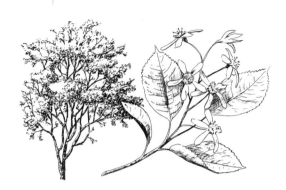

Amelanchier
Am-e-lang'ki-er. Serviceberry, shadblow, juneberry
Rosaceae. Rose family

Description
About 25 species of deciduous shrubs or trees which bloom profusely in spring and color reliably in fall. These two are native to the eastern U.S. They have alternate leaves with toothed edges. Flowers are small, white or pinkish, and abundant.

How to Grow
Serviceberries enjoy part to light shade; the plants will grow well in moderate shade, but flowering and fall color will be reduced. Easy to grow in ordinary to light, even sandy soil, provided moisture is adequate; mulch and irrigate in times of drought. Pruning is usually unnecessary, except to remove damaged branches. Specimens with multiple trunks attain an open vaselike habit with age.

Uses
Offers four seasons of interest in shrub borders, hedgerows. Edible fruits ripen in early summer, excellent for attracting songbirds like cedar waxwings. Cooks make berries into brilliant pink preserves with a fragrant apple flavor.

× *grandiflora* p. 80
Apple serviceberry or shadblow. Graceful in habit, reaching 25 ft. A naturally-occurring hybrid of *A. canadensis* and *A. laevis*, it differs little from its parents but has rather larger, sometimes pinkish flowers, 1¼ in. wide, in 3-in. racemes, produced in billowy clouds before the leaves unfold. Dark pink fruit the size of blueberries. Leaves turn chalk-yellow and soft orange in fall. Best in zones 4 through 8; semihardy zone 3.

laevis *p. 81*   *Pictured on p. 288*
Allegheny serviceberry or shadblow. A tree, to 35 ft., rarely
shrubby. Leaves purplish green when young, 3½ in. long,
rounded or slightly heart-shaped at the base, ultimately bright
green. Flowers, ½ in. wide, in slender nodding racemes, 3 in.
long, appearing with or after the leaves, and making a striking
contrast with the early foliage. Purplish fruits. Fall color ranges
from yellow-orange to cherry-red. Best in zones 4–8; semi-
hardy in zone 3.

Amsonia
Am-sown′i-a
Apocynaceae. Dogbane family

Description
Twenty species of herbaceous perennials with clusters of starlike blue flowers.

How to Grow
Easy to grow in part to light shade and ordinary soil. Cut
back after flowering to produce fresh new foliage for summer
and fall. Divide in spring or fall.

Uses
Borders.

tabernaemontana *p. 129*
Blue star, willow amsonia. A bushy perennial, to 2 ft. high,
with alternate leaves. Dense clusters of pale blue flowers in
late spring. Fall foliage yellow. Massachusetts to Texas.
Zone 4.

Andromeda
An-drom'i-da
Ericaceae. Heath family

Description
Two species of low-growing evergreen shrubs native to North America, Europe, and Asia.

How to Grow
Andromedas are suited for part to light shade, and need acid, humus-rich soil with plenty of moisture. Can be increased by rooting the creeping runners or top cuttings. Seed may be sown in moist peat moss.

Uses
Good plant for the damp garden and to face down larger ericaceous plantings. Not always an easy subject.

polifolia p. 215
Bog rosemary. Evergreen shrub to 12 in. high, with creeping rootstock. Leaves 1–1½ in. long, narrow, simple; leathery on top, glaucous beneath. Bell-shaped flowers pink or white, in nodding terminal umbels in spring. 'Nana' is a more compact form. Zone 3.

Anemone
A-nem'o-nee. Windflower
Ranunculaceae. Buttercup family

Description
About 120 species of herbaceous plants native to North America, Europe, and Asia. Most have compound leaves and showy flowers. Species range from 6 in. to 4 ft. tall and bloom from spring to fall. Many make excellent garden subjects.

How to Grow
Most anemones enjoy part to light shade. They grow best in rich, moist, but well-drained soil. Propagate from seed or division in spring. Established plants need little care. *A. pulsatilla* needs more shade in hot climates, neutral to alkaline soil, and excellent drainage, especially in winter.

Uses
A varied group with subjects for ground cover, border, edge, and rock garden.

canadensis *p. 216*
Canada anemone. To 2 ft. high. Maplelike 5-to-7-part leaves grow in rosettes. Flowers 2 in. long, white, on stalks held above the foliage in early summer. Invasive; better suited as ground cover, and in larger plantings, such as a naturalized colony on a moist bank. Northeastern North America. Zone 4.

× *hybrida* *p. 130*
Japanese anemone. Herbaceous perennial, 1–5 ft. high, depending on the cultivar. Flowers 2–3 in. wide, solitary, pink or white, in late summer and autumn. Can be aggressive, so give it plenty of space. Nice in larger borders; it forms an attractive low mound of foliage in spring and summer. Hybrid of Asian origin. Zone 6.

pulsatilla *p. 130*
Pasqueflower. Plants grow 9–12 in. high and have silky, fernlike leaves, 4–6 in. long. The bell-shaped 2-in. flowers are blue or reddish purple and may appear before the leaves in early spring. Feathery, smoke-gray seed clusters extend the season. There are varieties with lilac and red flowers and with variegated leaves. Works well as a border, edging, or rock garden plant; adds variety of form and texture to spring bulbs. Eurasia. Suitable for zones 5–8.

sylvestris 'Snowdrops' *p. 131*
Wood anemone. 18 in. high. 1 or 2 white, 2-in.-wide, fragrant, sometimes nodding flowers in late spring. Good in borders and shady wild gardens. Selected from the Eurasian species. Zone 4.

Aquilegia
A-kwee-lee'je-a
Ranunculaceae. Buttercup family

Description
About 70 species of herbaceous perennials, all from the north temperate zone. Leaves are twice- or thrice-compound, soft ruffled green like a maidenhair fern. Flowers of red, yellow, blue, purple, white, or bicolors in spring. Blooms are showy, usually with long hollow spurs on the petals.

How to Grow
Columbines enjoy part to light shade and well-drained soil. Short-lived perennials, they often die after 3–4 years, but are easily propagated by seed or division in spring, and often self-

sow. Foliage may look ragged after the plants bloom; combine with hostas or other camouflage. Leaf miners may disfigure the leaves but do not hurt the flowers.

Uses
Rock gardens, borders, woodland gardens.

caerulea *p. 131*
Rocky Mountain columbine. 2–3 ft. high. Flowers up to 2 in. wide with bluish purple sepals and white petals. Will not tolerate dry soils; afternoon shade will prolong flowering. Rocky Mountains. Zone 4.

canadensis *p. 132   Pictured above*
Common columbine. Herbaceous perennial, 1–2 ft. high. Flowers 1½ in. wide, with yellow petals and red sepals and spurs, in March to June. Native to dry, rocky woods from Canada to Florida and Texas. Zone 4.

'Dragon Fly' *p. 132*
Garden columbine. Herbaceous perennial, 1–3 ft. high. Large, 2-in. flowers in various colors open in late spring. Hybrid origins. Zone 5.

Arisaema
A-ri-see′ma
Araceae. Arum family

Description
A genus of over 100 species of perennial herbs with tuberous, acrid roots, divided or compound leaves, and a showy flower comprised of a spike in a spathe, metaphorically referred to in common speech as jack-in-the-pulpit.

How to Grow

The only commonly cultivated species are plants of rich, moist woods. Shade-lovers, they tolerate morning sun, but in general prefer light, dappled to full shade. With proper light, good humusy soil, and a moist site, they are of easy culture. Protect from heat, drought, and afternoon sun. Propagate by root division.

Uses

Woodland plantings and wildflower nooks. Plant has strong lines; soft, divided foliage of ferns, bleeding hearts, or columbines complement texture nicely.

triphyllum *p. 133   Pictured above*
Jack-in-the-pulpit. Root acrid, but heated and eaten by indigenous peoples. The purplish, striped, leafy, 3-in.-long spathe gracefully arches over the erect greenish yellow to white spadix. Large long-lasting leaves. Eastern U.S. Zone 4.

Aristolochia
A-ris-toe-loe′ki-a
Aristolochiaceae. Birthwort family

Description

A genus of 180 species of mostly tropical, woody vines and a few temperate species of vines and perennial herbs. Widely grown for their fine, rich foliage, and ability to cover unsightly objects quickly.

How to Grow

Enjoys part to light shade, fertile soil and adequate moisture, but tolerates less favorable conditions. Easy to grow from seed. Can also be increased by cuttings of ripened wood.

Uses
Ideal for providing quick summer shade and cover.

durior p. 245
Dutchman's-pipe, pipevine. Long-lived deciduous climber, to 30 ft. high. Leaves roundish or kidney-shaped, 6–14 in. wide, stalked. The coarse heart-shaped leaves overlap like shingles, creating a dense cover, ideal for shading porches. Yellowish brown, 1½-in.-long flowers, borne in early summer, are irregular to the point of being peculiar; suggestive of a tobacco pipe. Central U.S. Zone 5.

Aronia
A-rone′i-a. Chokeberry
Rosaceae. Rose family

Description
A small genus of North American deciduous shrubs grown for their showy white flowers which bloom in clusters in midspring, and their persistent berries with bitter taste.

How to Grow
Chokeberries enjoy part to light shade. They prefer acid, well-drained soil, but adapt to a variety of soils and wet or dry conditions. They are easy to propagate from seeds, from cuttings, or by layering. Thin out branches in winter or early spring.

Uses
Informal borders and the edges of woodland and wildlife gardens.

arbutifolia p. 92   Pictured above
Red chokeberry. Plants can reach heights of 8 ft. but rarely grow more than 4 ft. tall. They spread by underground suckers. The 2-in. leaves are toothed and oblong, shiny green and gray

underneath. In fall, they turn bright red. The 1½ in. clusters of white flowers with contrasting black stamens are followed in fall by brilliant red berries that last all winter. Zone 4 or 5.

Arrhenatherum
Ar-re-nath′er-rum. Oat grass
Gramineae. Grass family

Description
A genus of tall, coarse, oatlike European perennial grasses.

How to Grow
Plant bulbous oat grass in part to light shade. Quite drought tolerant once established, but likes fertile, well-drained soil. It does best in a cool climate; in warm areas, the plants perform best in spring and fall. Cut foliage back in summer if it becomes unattractive. Increase plants by division.

Uses
Mixed borders, raised beds, ground cover.

elatius bulbosum 'Variegatum' *p. 255*
Bulbous oat grass. This garden curiosity has small bulbils at the base of the stems; the plants form erect and spreading clumps. The rough, narrow leaves are 12 in. long. A narrow spike of purplish green flower forms on 3½ ft. stems in late spring or fall, followed by seedhead. This cultivar has attractive, white-striped leaves which show up well in shade and is not as invasive as the species. Best in zones 5–8.

Aruncus
A-run′kus
Rosaceae. Rose family

Description
A genus of herbs differing from the closely related *Spiraea* in having compound leaves. Flowers small, white, crowded into showy panicles, the male and female on different plants.

How to Grow
Enjoys light to partial shade and moist soil. Propagated by division.

Uses
Borders.

dioicus *p. 133   Pictured above*
Goatsbeard. A strong-growing perennial, 4–6 ft. high. Flowers
creamy white, ⅛ in. wide, nearly stalkless on the branches of
a wide-spreading, open cluster 6–10 in. high. North America
and Asia. Not well suited to the South. Zone 4.

Arundinaria
A-run-di-nay′ri-a. Bamboo
Gramineae. Grass family

Description
About 30 species of rhizomatous woody grasses (commonly
called bamboos), mainly from eastern and southern Asia, with
round, smooth, erect canes. Leaves flat, short-stalked; upper
leaves longer.

How to Grow
Enjoys part to light shade. Most require well-drained but
moist, fertile soil. Tall species benefit from wind protection.
Propagate by dividing off a section of rhizome in early spring
just as new growth begins. These aggressive spreaders may be
restrained by stout barriers below ground. Mow pygmy bamboo in late winter to encourage density. Cut *A. viridistriata*
to the ground in late autumn to maintain vivid color.

Uses
Although extremely invasive, useful in pots or for ground cover
and erosion control in difficult areas.

pygmaea *p. 255*
Pygmy bamboo. Canes to 12 in. high, bright green, round,
becoming purplish toward the flattened tip. Nodes prominent,
purple. Leaves narrow, to 5 in. long, sharp-pointed, bright

green and hairy above, silvery green beneath. Frequently offered as *Sasa pygmaea*. Zone 7.

viridistriata p. 256
Running bamboo. To 6 ft. high, usually less. Canes ¾ in. wide, new shoots creamy gold. Leaves narrow, to 8 in. long, tapering to a pointed tip, bright green with broad yellow-gold stripes. Gold coloration somewhat muted without adequate light. Distinctive tub or patio plant. Zone 7.

Asarum
Ass'-a-rum. Wild ginger
Aristilochiaceae. Birthwort family

Description
Low-growing herbaceous perennials with heart- or kidney-shaped leaves. Plants spread by creeping rhizomes to form large patches. Both leaves and rhizomes have a spicy, gingery aroma. Curious dark flowers small and hidden.

How to Grow
The wild gingers are shade-loving plants, needing protection from direct sun and heat and preferring light to full shade. They need humusy soil and plenty of moisture. Given these, they spread readily and are easily increased by division.

Uses
Ground cover for shady woodlands, northern exposures, and wild gardens.

canadense p. 216
Wild ginger. 6–8 in. high. Leaves 3–6 in. wide and heart-shaped. Flowers 1 in. wide, bell-shaped, purplish green on the outside and deep maroon inside. Eastern North America. Zone 4.

europaeum p. 217   Pictured on p. 297
European wild ginger. 5 in. high with evergreen, glossy, kidney-shaped leaves. Flowers 1 in. wide, bell-shaped, purplish green outside, deep maroon inside; darker colors predominating. Europe. This evergreen plant may need winter snow cover. Zone 5.

Asperula
As-per'u-la
Rubiaceae. Madder family

Description
A large genus of Old World herbs, some cultivated for ornament.

How to Grow
Sow seeds of this annual species in part to light shade, in a moist site, such as a stream bank. Prefers warm weather.

Uses
Ground cover.

orientalis p. 169
Woodruff. To 1 ft. high, with small leaves growing in whorled tufts. Numerous but tiny flowers, lavender-blue, fragrant, ⅜ in. long, borne in terminal clusters beneath which are found leafy bracts. Eurasia. Hardy annual.

Asphodeline
As-fo-de-line'e
Liliaceae. Lily family.

Description
A genus of perhaps 20 species of herbs found in the Mediterranean region and of interest chiefly because, in legend, lilylike asphodel covers the Elysian Fields.

How to Grow
Asphodel enjoys afternoon shade and is easy to grow in any well-drained garden soil. May need winter mulch in northern regions. Propagated by spring or fall root division.

Uses
Borders.

lutea *p. 134*
Asphodel, king's-spear. A thick-rooted herb, 2–3 ft. high. Narrow leaves are blue-gray and grasslike. Flowers numerous, yellow, star-shaped, fragrant, 1 in. across, clustered at the end of a 2–4 ft. tall spike. Southern Europe and Arabian Peninsula. Zone 6.

Astilbe
As-til'be
Saxifragaceae. Saxifrage family

Description
An increasingly popular genus of perennials grown for their profuse, plumelike clusters of tiny white, pink, or red flowers and attractive foliage.

How to Grow
Shade-loving, astilbes need afternoon or light to moderately full shade, and moist soil. Dry conditions cause leaves to turn brown and wither; *A. chinensis* and *A. tacquetii* tolerate better than × *arendsii*.

Uses
Excellent in mixed borders or massed in island beds.

× arendsii 'Deutschland' *p. 134*
Astilbe. Perennial, 2–4 ft. high with dark green or bronze leaves. This cultivar has white flowers. Others may be red or pink. Flowers in late spring. Hybrid in origin. Zone 5.

chinensis 'Pumila' *p. 135 Pictured above*
Chinese astilbe. 8–12 in. high perennial. Flowers mauve-pink in summer, minute but numerous in dense, erect plumes. Vigorous. Excellent for rock gardens and border fronts. China and Japan. Zone 5.

tacquetii 'Superba' *p. 135*
3–4 ft. high perennial. Foliage bronze-green. Very small magenta or reddish purple flowers borne in loose, feathery panicles from late summer to fall. Also does well in the South. China. Zone 5.

Athyrium
A-theer-ee-um
Polypodiaceae. Polypody family

Description
A small group of deciduous ferns widely distributed in temperate and tropical regions.

How to Grow
Shade-loving plants which tolerate a few hours of morning sun to moderately full shade, and rich, moist, well-drained soil containing plenty of organic matter. Divide in spring or summer.

Uses
Versatile, lacy ferns for borders, ground cover, woodland, wildflower and rock gardens. The painted fern makes a striking foliage accent; it likes more shade than the lady fern.

fielix-femina *p. 270*
Lady fern. Lacy, light green, finely cut fronds about 2 ft. tall. Spreads slowly. Eastern U.S. Zone 3.

goeringianum 'Pictum' *p. 271*
Japanese painted fern. Green fronds 1–1½ ft. tall, frosted silver with purple veins and stems. Look for 'Pictum Red', a brighter cultivar. Japan. Zone 6 or 7.

Aubrieta
Au-bree'sha
Cruciferae. Mustard family

Description
A small genus of Old World perennials. They have small, simple leaves and relatively large 4-petaled flowers in short clusters.

How to Grow
Plant false rockcress in part shade and light, well-drained soil.

Uses
The species listed here is popular as a mat-forming ground cover or edging, or in rock gardens.

deltoidea p. 217
False rockcress. 6 in. high. Leaves hairy. Flowers ¾ in. wide, typically lilac or purple. Many varieties available, some with pink flowers. Mediterranean. Zone 5.

Aucuba
Aw-kew'ba
Cornaceae. Dogwood family

Description
A small genus of Asiatic evergreen landscaping shrubs.

How to Grow
Aucubas may be suitable for part, light to moderate, and nearly full shade, adjusting to a range of light according to exposure and climate. They tolerate heavy shade, so are often planted on the north side of buildings or under trees. Thrive in moist, well-drained soil. Easily propagated by rooting cuttings in a jar of water.

Uses
Popular foliage plants for dark places in warm climates; suitable for container culture.

japonica p. 92
Usually less than 10 ft. high, with opposite leaves, slightly toothed, glossy, dark green, more or less oval, 4–8 in. long. Small male and female flowers, borne on different plants, bloom in spring. Half-inch berries, mostly scarlet, on female plants. Variegated cultivars have gold dots or splotches on leaves. Indispensable throughout the South, of limited use to zone 7.

Bambusa
Bam-boo'sa. Bamboo
Gramineae. Grass family

Description
The true bamboos constitute a large genus of often gigantic, woody, hollow-stemmed grasses native to warm regions of the Old World, where they have been grown for ornament and

construction for centuries. Plants form dense clumps, with polished stems and short-stalked, tough, bladelike leaves. Flowers are rare in cultivation.

How to Grow
For part to light shade. Grows best in rich, moist, well-drained soil that is not too acid. Propagate by division of clumps or by stem layering in spring.

Uses
Hedges, accents, screening in warm climates. Container culture.

glaucescens *p. 256*
Hedge bamboo. Stems 3–20 ft. high, to 1½ in. in diameter, with branches at each node down to ground level. Leaves narrow, lance-shaped, to 6 in. long. Less commonly cultivated than its lower-growing, fancy-leaf forms. Zone 8.

Begonia
Bee-go′ni-a
Begoniaceae. Begonia family

Description
An immense genus of shade-loving tropical herbs grown for their showy flowers and foliage. Leaves alternate, often brightly colored or with colored veins, oblique in general outline. Flowers red, pink, orange, yellow, or white, slightly irregular, waxy, single or double, the male and female separate. Widely diversified by breeders, begonias are found in a multitude of horticultural forms. Those listed below are versatile and widely available plants for outdoor culture.

How to Grow
There are suitable begonias for a wide range of light conditions, from part to light, toward moderate and full shade. All need protection from intense summer sun and afternoon light; they enjoy even more shade in hotter and southerly climates or where moisture is not plentiful. On the other hand, without adequate light, especially in the North, begonias may grow leggy and flowering will be sparse. Hardy begonia needs more shade than wax begonias or tender tuberous forms, which prefer bright, indirect light or morning sun. Any begonia raised in a protected or shaded environment should be gradually adjusted to a change of light.

All begonias, when in active growth, require plenty of fertilizer (such as liquid manure), moisture, warmth, and good air circulation. Most are not cold-hardy; set plants out after the last spring frost and bring in tubers or take cuttings before first hard frost of autumn, otherwise you have to start over with nursery stock in spring.

Pests and Diseases
To prevent problems with begonias, it is probably best to start with healthy plants and grow them under the best of conditions in combination with other plants. Gardeners may also choose to use traditional sprays to combat the whiteflies, mealybugs, gray mold, and leaf spot that begonias sometimes fall prey to. In either case, remove or bury diseased or infested plant material and clean pots and tools thoroughly before continuing with survivors or replacements.

Propagation
Begonias are easily grown from cuttings, seeds, bulbils, and division of the tubers. To make a stem cutting, cut below joint with sharp knife, and insert in moist sand at room temperature. Some forms may be propagated by inserting stalk of a leaf in sand, soil, or water.

Tuberous species may be also be propagated in spring by cutting up the tubers like seed potatoes, leaving an eye on each cut; dust with charcoal and cover lightly with peat. As with mature tubers, keep warm and moist and, when sprouted, plant in potting soil.

Another method, especially for *B. grandis,* is to use bulbils that sprout at intersection of leaf and stem. Spread these tiny propagules over surface of potting mixture, press down, and cover with glass. Bulbils will soon produce young plants. To grow from seeds, place in groove of a bent card and tap lightly over potting mixture to sow evenly. Press gently — but do not cover — into a fine potting medium. Give light, keep warm, and preserve moisture by covering flat with sheet of glass or plastic. Water from below. When large enough to handle, transfer seedlings to individual pots to grow on.

Tuberous Begonias
B. × *tuberhybrida* may be purchased as dormant tubers, with cultural requirements similar to any tender bulb. These should be sprouted in early spring, in shallow flats of peat, with adequate moisture and bottom heat. Pot on in a rich medium after they have sprouted. To carry tubers from one year to the next, allow plants to ripen off and rest at the end of the growing season, withholding water and fertilizer. To prevent

tubers from desiccation during dormancy, leave in their pots or pack lightly in moss or sawdust and store in a cool dry place. Resume active culture after new growth begins.

Uses
Superb plants for summer bedding, hanging baskets, lathhouses, and container culture. Wax begonias are also excellent foliage plants.

grandis p. 198
Hardy begonia. A smooth, branching perennial, 1–2 ft. high. Leaves red on the underside, more or less oval, with toothed lobes. Flowers large, summer-blooming, male and female separate. The hardiest of all cultivated forms, perennial *B. grandis* will survive winter in the North, withstanding temperatures of 0 degrees F, provided the soil is mulched so that the tuberous roots do not freeze. China and Japan. Zone 6.

× *semperflorens-cultorum* p. 169, p. 170
Wax begonia. A group of hybrids and cultivars, usually 8–12 in. high, with bronze to green leaves. Flowers white, pink, or red, 1 in. wide, blooming continuously outdoors in summer. An excellent foil for many summer bedding plants, the cultivar 'Gin' has attractive bronze leaves and white flowers with bouncy yellow stamens. Many other varieties with single or double blossoms, some with large flowers, others have numerous clusters of small flowers. South America. Tender perennial grown as a tender annual.

× *tuberhybrida* p. 199   *Pictured above*
Tuberous begonia. Stems fleshy, erect or spreading, to 18 in. high. Flowers large, in a wide range of colors from white to red, to 4 in. in diameter. Flowering in summer, dormant in winter. Modern varieties of tuberous-rooted begonias come in numerous sizes, colors, and forms. Carnation, rosebud,

and camellia begonias are named for their resemblance to other flowers. A group of hybrids and cultivars from species native to the Andes. Tender bulb.

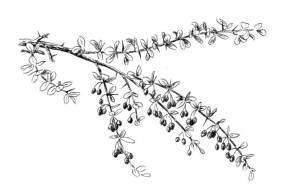

Berberis
Ber'ber-iss. Barberry
Berberidaceae. Barberry family

Description
Almost 500 species of evergreen or deciduous shrubs, all more or less spiny, most native to the north temperate zone. Yellow flowers bloom in spring. Leaves are small and simple, turning to scarlet, orange, or yellow in the fall. Many species have brightly colored late berries.

How to Grow
Barberries are suitable for part to light shade and are easy to grow in ordinary garden soil, even in urban conditions. Shear hedges in spring and occasionally thin out oldest growth.

Uses
Hedging, background, and filler in shrubberies and foundation plantings.

julianae p. 93
Barberry. An upright evergreen shrub, 6–8 ft. high. Leaves 1½–3 in. long; dark green above, pale beneath. Flower clusters 2 in. wide, berries bluish black. The hardiest of the evergreen species and one of the most popular. Makes a mounded specimen or an impenetrable hedge. China. Zones 6-8.

thunbergii 'Atropurpurea' p. 93   *Pictured above*
Barberry. Deciduous shrub, usually 4–6 ft. high. Leaves ½ to 1½ in. long, purple in this cultivar. Though the shrub is quite shade-tolerant, the leaves lose their bronze cast if light is in-

adequate. Berries bright red. More widely cultivated than almost any other shrub, and available in many cultivars, including dwarf forms. Japan. Best in zones 4–8.

Bergenia
Ber-gen′i-a
Saxifragaceae. Saxifrage family

Description
About 12 Asiatic perennial herbs, several of which are grown in borders for glossy, cabbagey foliage and early pink or white flowers. Grows in dense clumps or colonies from thickened rootstocks. Leaves mostly basal, thick and fleshy, half-evergreen. Flowers large, in nodding panicles or racemes. Many hybrids and cultivars available.

How to Grow
Prefers part to moderate shade. The more shade, the less moisture is needed. Prefers humus, but adaptable to most garden soils. Increase by division of established clumps. Species can also be grown from seeds.

Uses
Edgings, ground cover, accent, excellent for larger mixed borders.

cordifolia 'Profusion' *p. 218*
Heartleaf bergenia. To 18 in. high. Leaves 12–18 in. long, leathery, with wavy margins. This cultivar has especially large clusters of pinkish white flowers. Prey to slugs. Most widely grown species on the East Coast. Zone 3.

crassifolia *p. 218   Pictured above*
Siberian tea. To 18 in. high. Similar to *B. cordifolia* but with leaf blade extending down the stalk. Flowers rose-pink or lilac,

clusters well above the foliage. Well known on the West Coast. Zone 3.

'Margery Fish' *p. 136*
Hybrid bergenia. From 9–18 in. in height. Flowers are 12–18 in. high, ¼–½ in. wide, pink in this variety. There are many other cultivars in the same class: 'Abendglut' or 'Evening Glow' grows to 9 in. high; flowers crimson-purple, usually semidouble. 'Morganrote' or 'Morning Blush' 18 in. high, pink flowers. 'Silberlicht' or 'Silver Light' 12 in. high, white flowers with a pale pink calyx. 'Sunningdale' 12 in. high, with carmine flowers on red stalks. All hardy to zone 3.

Bignonia
Big-known′i-a
Bignoniaceae. Trumpet-creeper family

Description
A single species of evergreen or semi-evergreen woody vine native to the South.

How to Grow
Plant cross vine in part shade and rich, moist, well-drained soil.

Uses
A showy vine, ideal for trellises and fences throughout the South, climbs by sticky discs and tendrils. Control vigorous growth and maintain good coverage with regular pruning. Supporting structures should be sturdy to hold up this lush evergreen.

capreolata *p. 245* *Pictured above*
Cross vine. Woody vine, climbing to 50 ft. high. Leaves are evergreeen, compound, with each leaflet 4–6 in. long. Flowers 2 in. long, reddish orange, from April to August, funnel-shaped

and slightly irregular. Fruit a long, narrow, slightly flattened pod. Zone 7.

Browallia
Brow-wall'i-a
Solanaceae. Potato family

Description
A genus of mostly tropical American herbs, several widely grown, mostly blue-flowered, something like a petunia only smaller and more delicate.

How to Grow
Enjoys part to light shade, needing protection from afternoon sun in the South. Purchase nursery-grown plants or start seeds indoors; they require light and a temperature of 65 degrees to sprout. Transplant when weather has warmed. Browallias need a warm growing season and plenty of moisture. Seed-grown plants may not bloom until fall where summer is short, but plants may be brought indoors for winter color.

Uses
An excellent plant for summer bedding, containers, lath-houses, hanging baskets on shaded porches.

speciosa **'Blue Bells'** *p. 170*
Smooth-branching, about 1 ft. tall, somewhat kneeling or tumbling. Leaves are simple, small, and green. Flowers 2 in. wide, with the tube 1 in. long, violet-blue. The cultivar 'Major' has dark blue flowers; white forms also exist. South America. Tender annual.

Brunnera
Brun'er-ra
Boraginaceae. Borage family

Description
A large cousin of forget-me-not, brunnera is native to the Caucasus and Siberia.

How to Grow
Shade-loving, brunnera needs at least afternoon shade or continous dappled shade, otherwise it wilts. Performs best in moist soil, but can survive drier sites.

Uses
Shady borders, ground cover.

macrophylla *p. 136*
Siberian bugloss. 12—18 in. high perennial. Leaves are large, heart-shaped, basal, with fuzzy stems. Flowers blue, small, starlike, in loosely branched clusters; spring-blooming. Several cultivars have variegated leaves. Zone 4.

Buddleia
Bud'lee-a. Butterfly bush
Loganiaceae. Buddleia family

Description
A genus of about 100 species of shrubs, primarily from the tropics, that attract a profusion of butterflies when they bloom in late summer.

How to Grow
The species listed below will grow in afternoon shade. Demands well-drained soil and is somewhat drought tolerant. Flowers appear on the last year's wood, so prune lightly as soon as bloom is past. Protect during winter with a late mulch over the crown; any winter-killed stems or tips should be cut back neatly in early spring. Propagated by root cuttings.

Uses
Specimen in mixed borders and wildlife plantings.

alternifolia 'Argentea' *p. 94*
Butterfly bush, summer lilac. Deciduous shrub, 10–20 ft. high. Leaves lance-shaped, 1–4 in. long, green above, grayish beneath; in this cultivar, silky-haired and silvery. Flowers fragrant, bell-shaped, lilac-purple, 4-lobed, ½ in. long in short, dense, leafy clusters to ¾ in. in summer. A beautiful plant, with arching or pendulous branches. China. Zone 6.

Caladium
Ka-lay'di-um
Aracea. Arum family

Description.
About 15 species of stemless tropical bulbs, native to South America. With their large, colorful, heart- or arrow-shaped leaves, caladiums offer lush seasonal foliage. There are dozens of named varieties to choose from.

How to Grow

Shade-loving plants, caladiums enjoy bright, indirect light to a moderately shaded spot. Purchase plants in leaf or dormant tubers. Culture is similar to tuberous begonias; start indoors in an all-purpose soil mix in early spring, keep warm and moist in a 5-in. pot, then set outdoors in urn, or sink in garden when weather has warmed. Caladiums like heat, moisture, and fertile soil. When the leaves die down, the soil should be allowed to dry out and the plant ripen and rest. Store dormant tubers in a cool, dry place to carry on through winter. Propagate by separating clumps of tubers.

Uses

Containers, foil for summer flowers, filler in immature beds. Tropical in provenance, in northern climates caladiums fit more easily into formal settings as display and accent plants; never out of place in a Victorian pot on a wrought-iron stand.

'June Bride' *p. 199*

About 1½ ft. tall, with white leaves about 10 in. long. Hybrid. Tender bulb. Not hardy north of zone 10.

'White Queen' *p. 200*   *Pictured above*

Grows about 1½ ft. tall, with whitened leaves 8–12 in. long. Hybrid in origin. Tender bulb; strictly for summer display north of zone 10.

Calceolaria

Kal-see-o-lay′ri-a
Scrophulariaceae. Figwort family

Description

A very large genus of tropical American herbs or shrubby

plants, collectively called slipperworts for their slipper-shaped, showy flowers.

How to Grow
Garden calceolarias prefer part to light shade and moist soil. In areas with mild winters and cool summers they may be grown as perennials. Soil must be well-drained. Divide in spring or grow from seed. Sow in flats in spring and grow on in a cold frame for flowering plants the following year.

Uses
Potted plant and bedding. Mixed borders in mild climates.

'John Innes' *p. 137*
Calceolaria. The garden calceolaria is a dwarf tufted plant that grows to 6 in. high. Bright yellow flowers ½–1 in. long, 2-lipped, pouchlike, in irregular clusters. South America. Zone 7.

Callicarpa
Kal-li-kar'pa. Beautyberry
Verbenaceae. Verbena family

Description
A large genus of shrubs, grown for their beautiful clusters of fruit in fall.

How to Grow
Beautyberries enjoy part to light shade and rich soil. Because flowers appear on new growth, prune in spring to within 6 in. of the ground. Stems may be winter-killed, but the crown often survives to put forth new shoots.

Uses
Fall interest in the shrub border.

americana *p. 94*
French mulberry. Deciduous shrub, 5–8 ft. high, with opposite leaves 4–6 in. long. Small pinkish flowers in compact bunches in spring. Berries round and violet. A white-fruited variety, *lactea,* is also offered. Maryland to Texas and Oklahoma, and the West Indies. Zone 7.

Caltha
Kal'tha
Ranunculaceae. Buttercup family

Description
About 20 species of marsh or swamp perennial herbs, growing in the north temperate and arctic zones. Grown for their mats of glossy leaves and wealth of buttercup-like spring flowers.

How to Grow
Grows well in part shade and prefers rich, moist soil. Propagated by division or seeds and easily transplanted.

Uses
Choice, spreading plant for damp wildflower gardens.

palustris p. 137 Pictured above
Cowslip, marsh marigold. 1–2 ft. high, the leaves more or less heart-shaped. Flowers 2 in. wide, bright yellow, with glossy, lacquered texture, several together. The most popular cultivar is 'Flore Pleno', with double blooms. Zone 4.

Calycanthus
Kal-ee-kan'thus
Calycanthaceae. Sweet-shrub family

Description
Four species of deciduous shrubs native to the southeastern U.S. Plants entirely aromatic, with large dark flowers.

How to Grow
Carolina allspice enjoys part to light shade and thrives in rich, well-drained soil with plenty of moisture. Prune after flow-

ering. Propagate by layers, suckers, division, or seeds. Control spread into other plantings by pulling out suckers.

Uses
Fragrant addition to thickets, screens, and informal shrubberies.

floridus p. 95   *Pictured above*
Carolina allspice, common sweet-shrub. A densely hairy shrub, 4–8 ft. high, with glossy leaves 3–5. in long. Purple-brown flowers, 2 in. wide, have fruity fragrance, bloom in spring. Bark and wood redolent of cinnamon and cypress. Virginia to Florida and Mississippi. Zone 5.

Camellia
Ka-mee′li-a
Theaceae. Tea family

Description
Asiatic evergreen shrubs or small trees, widely grown for their waxlike, very showy, long-lasting flowers. The leaves are alternate. The flowers are nearly stalkless, 5-petaled or double, in shades of pink, red, and white with prominent yellow centers.

How to Grow
Camellias flower best in part to light shade. Container-grown camellias are easily transplanted into moist, well-drained, acid soil, with mulch around the roots. Don't plant them too deep. Fertilize with Epsom salts (magnesium sulfate) for good green foliage. Generally, prune plants lightly after flowering, cutting back to a new set of buds. Specimens in formal shapes will require selective pinching and thinning of new growth as well.

Propagated from cuttings of current season's growth or by seed.

Uses
Pot specimen in colder areas, small flowering trees or formal hedges in warmer climates.

japonica 'Rev. John G. Drayton' *p. 95*
Evergreen shrub or small tree, 20–25 ft. high, with shiny, dark green, oval leaves 3–4 in. long. Flowers 3–5 in. wide in winter; in this cultivar they are double and pink. Several hundred cultivars are grown in the U.S., with single or double flowers ranging from white to dark red. Zone 8.

sasanqua 'Showa No Sakae' *p. 96*
Sasanqua camellia. Evergreen shrub, 6–10 ft. high. This variety has rose-colored blossoms from fall to winter, 2–3 in. wide or smaller. There are dozens of cultivars with different colored flowers, from white and pink through rose and red and bicolors. Sasanqua camellias have smaller leaves and flowers, bloom earlier, and are somewhat less hardy than Japanese camellias. Zone 8.

Campanula
Kam-pan′you-la. Bellflower.
Campanulaceae. Bellflower family.

Description
Bellflowers comprise an important group of annuals, biennials, and perennials that come in a wide variety of shapes and sizes. Principally native to southeastern Europe and the Mediterranean. Common to all is the handsome bell-shaped flower, typically blue, but also white, pink, violet, or purple.

How to Grow
The species listed below enjoy part to light shade, ordinary garden soil, and moisture. Cut faded flowers off to keep the plants vigorous and tidy. Guard against slugs, which may devour leaves. Propagate perennials by division, cuttings, or seeds. Grow C. *medium* from seeds; sow in cold frame in fall, set out in the spring. Canterbury bells begin to bloom 6 months after germination.

Uses
Borders and cutting gardens.

latifolia p. 138
Great bellflower. Perennial, 2–4 ft. high. Flowers purplish blue, solitary, 1½ in. long. Species self-seeds and does not usually need support. *Var. macrantha* has flowers nearly twice as large. Zone 4.

medium p. 171   *Pictured above*
Canterbury bells. 2–4 ft. high. Flowers violet-blue, solitary or in loose clusters, 1 in. wide and 2 in. long. A wide variety of forms are available. Biennial to annual.

persicifolia var. *alba* p. 138
Peach-leaved bellflower. Perennial, 2–3 ft. high. Flowers white, 1½ in. long, in showy terminal clusters. Other varieties have blue, larger, or double flowers. Zone 4.

Cardiocrinum
Card-ee-o-kry′num
Liliaceae. Lily family

Description
Three species of bulbous herbs, ranging from the Himalayas through China to Japan. Funnel-shaped, lilylike flowers and heart-shaped leaf bases.

How to Grow
Enjoys dappled or light shade and prefers a cool, moist, humus-rich soil. Plant the bulbs shallowly, because roots do not form above the bulbs.

Uses
Naturalizing and accent.

giganteum p. 200
An immense lilylike, bulbous-rooted plant, to 12 ft. high.
Leaves grow in a basal rosette and scattered along the stem,
the lower ones 12–18 in. long. Flowers funnel-shaped, drooping, fragrant, nearly 6 in. long, white tinged with green outside
and reddish purple stripes inside; summer-blooming. Himalayas. Zone 7.

Carex
Cay'rex. Sedge
Cyperaceae. Sedge family

Description
The sedges are an enormous genus of over 2,000 species of
grasslike plants, most grown for their ornamental foliage.
Most form low to medium tufts of leaves and have minute
green flowers atop slender grasslike stalks.

How to Grow
The species below grow best in part to light shade and fertile,
moist, garden soil. Increase by division. Durable and easy to grow.

Uses
Generally borders, waterside plantings.

conica 'Variegata' p. 257
Miniature sedge. Tufted, to 6 in high. Leaves dark green,
silver-edged, to 12 in. long. Flowers yellow. A tidy, compact plant for edging or the rock garden. Japan and Korea.
Zone 5.

grayi p. 257
Gray's sedge, morning star sedge. Tufted perennial, to 2 ft.
high. Leaves narrow, to 18 in. long, bright green. Seedheads

unusual, triangular, borne in summer and autumn. Well suited
for specimen use or woodland naturalizing. Northeastern U.S.
Zone 3.

pendula p. 258   Pictured on p. 316
Drooping sedge. Mound-forming perennial to 2 ft. high, evergreen except at northern limits of hardiness. Leaves narrow,
to 18 in. long, bright green, arching. Terminal flower spikes,
gray-green, pendulous, on stalks well above foliage. Old
World. Zone 5.

Ceratostigma
Ser-rat-o-stig'ma
Plumbaginaceae. Plumbago family

Description
Small genus of perennial herbs or low shrubs, several grown
as border plants for their blue flowers.

How to Grow
Prefers part to light shade and moderately fertile, loose soil.
Propagate by spring division or cuttings. Late to emerge in
spring, so take care not to damage dormant plants.

Uses
Borders, massing for fall interest.

plumbaginoides p. 219
Leadwort. Low or semiprostrate, to 12 in. high. Alternate
leaves, hairy on margins. Tubular flowers deep blue, to ½ in.
wide, in loose heads with stiff bracts, blooming in autumn
when foliage tinged with russet. China. Zone 5, with winter
protection.

Cercis
Sir'sis. Redbud
Leguminosae. Pea family

Description
A small group of attractive shrubs or small deciduous trees
grown for their showy spring flowers. Their early bloom, before they leaf out and when many plants are still dormant,
makes them exceedingly useful in the landscape.

How to Grow

Redbuds flower satisfactorily in part to light shade and are easy to grow in open, dry, sandy, well-drained soil. Select site carefully as they resent transplanting. In some parts of the country, a vascular wilt and a cancer disease trouble redbuds. Drought may increase the chance of infection; deep irrigation and mulching during dry spells is beneficial in disease-prone areas. Prune young trees lightly and selectively after flowering to train mature shape.

Uses

Specimen trees, woodland plantings. Excellent canopy for spring-flowering bulbs and woodlanders.

canadensis p. 81   Pictured above
Eastern redbud. A small, round-headed tree, not usually over 35 ft. high, often half that height. Leaves broadly oval or nearly round, heart-shaped at the base, 3–5 in. long, pointed at the tip. Flowers ½ in. long, rosy-purple, in clusters 1–2 in. wide, very numerous, often borne on mature trunks and branches. There are white and double-flowered cultivars as well. Seed-pods resemble flat beans. New York to Florida and Texas. Zone 4.

Chaenomeles

Kee-nom'e-lees. Flowering quince
Rosaceae. Rose family

Description

Popular garden shrubs with beautiful early spring bloom. Flowers bloom before or with the unfolding leaves. All are from eastern Asia.

How to Grow

Flowering quinces will grow in part shade and adapt to a wide range of soils, provided drainage is good. Plants will not survive heavy pruning but can be lightly shaped and pruned in early spring before growth starts. Do not shear plants. May be propagated from semihardwood cuttings or by layering.

Uses

Informal hedges, shrub borders, rock gardens, accent plant, or espalier. Hard, aromatic fruits can be made into preserves.

speciosa 'Toyo Nishiki' *p. 96*

Flowering quince. These spiny shrubs grow 6–10 ft. high, with a handsome branching structure. Oval to oblong, 2–3 in. leaves are shiny, dark green, and finely toothed. The fruits are yellowish green. Flowers are 1–2 in. wide, in close clusters; and in this vigorous cultivar, white, pink, and carmine. There are many other garden varieties, ranging from white through pink and orange to deepest red. 'Phyllis Moore' has double pink flowers. Best in zones 5–8.

Chasmanthium

Kas-man'the-um
Gramineae. Grass family

Description

Five species of native perennial grasses, all strong-growing plants.

How to Grow

Chasmanthiums grow well with part to light shade and prefer moist, well-drained, loamy soil. These grasses self-sow and can be invasive.

Uses

Best for natural areas. Showy ornamental spikes can be cut in late summer for dried arrangements.

latifolium *p. 258   Pictured on p. 319*
Northern sea oats, river oats, wild oats. Grass to 5 ft. tall,
leaves 9 in. long by 1 in. wide. Flowers on slender, drooping,
flat, 8-in. clusters on graceful stalks in summer. Zone 5.

Cheiranthus
Ky-ran'thus. Wallflower
Cruciferae. Mustard family.

Description
Perhaps a dozen perennial herbs, scattered from Madeira to
the Himalayas, one the widely cultivated and sweet-scented
wallflower.

How to Grow
Wallflowers will grow well with shade in the afternoon and
prefer cool weather. Can be grown as biennials in mild-winter
areas from direct seeding in early fall, but they need cold to
trigger flowering. To grow as hardy annuals for spring bloom,
start seeds indoors in midwinter. Shift seedlings to 4-in. pots,
set in cold frame, and cover on very cold nights. After danger
of frost is past, plant in well-drained soil.

Uses
Walls, rockeries, and as a cut flower.

cheiri *p. 171*
Wallflower. To 2½ ft. high. Leaves narrow. 4-petaled flowers
in yellow, orange, red, purple, or red-brown; 1 in. wide; in
spikes or clusters. Southern Europe. Biennial or tender perennial best grown as a half-hardy annual in cool but moderate
climates.

Chelone
Kel-lo'nee. Turtlehead
Scrophulariaceae. Snapdragon family

Description
A small group of North American herbs, two are garden subjects for moist areas. Flowers usually white or pink and suggesting a turtle with lifted head and open mouth in shape.

How to Grow
Though the species listed below occurs naturally in full sun
beside streams, plants thrive in part shade in ordinary garden

conditions provided soil is rich and constantly moist. Easily propagated by division.

Uses
Damp banks, naturalizing, informal borders.

lyonii *p. 139* *Pictured above*
Pink turtlehead. The most desirable for the garden. To 3 ft. high. Flowers rose-purple, 1 in. long in compact, terminal spikes and opening a few at a time over the course of summer. Zone 4.

Chrysanthemum
Kris-san′the-mum
Compositae. Daisy family

Description
Many important herbaceous garden plants, most from China, Japan, or Europe. Flowers are of all colors except blue and purple, ranging from immense ruffled heads to small button-like affairs.

How to Grow
Though most garden "mums" prefer sun, the species listed here is suited to part shade. Feverfew may be perennial but blooms during the first year, so may be grown as a half-hardy annual. Sow seeds in well-drained soil as soon as the ground can be worked in the spring, and again after midsummer. Thin to 18 in. apart. Self-seeds once established. It prefers a cool growing season and low humidity. Like the rest of the genus, it needs good air circulation and is shallow-rooted, requiring moist soil and regular feeding. Nipping off the young growing

tips a few times in early spring promotes more blooms and a more compact plant.

Uses
Borders and flowerbeds. Excellent for late bloom.

***parthenium* 'White Stars'** *p. 172*
Feverfew. 2–3 ft. high. Flowerheads many, to ¾ in. wide. The leaves are alternate, somewhat divided, and pungent. This cultivar has cushionlike, yellow disk flowers and ruffled, short white rays. Many other cultivars; disk flowers are typically yellow and buttonlike; white ray petals may be more daisylike, or lacking altogether. Sometimes offered as *Matricaria capensis*. Southeastern Europe to the Caucasus. Perennial, often grown as a half-hardy annual. Zone 5.

Chrysogonum
Kris-sog'o-num. Green-and-gold
Compositae. Daisy family

Description
An herbaceous perennial native to the eastern United States.

How to Grow
Grows well in part to light shade in moderately rich soil with good drainage. Not reliably winter-hardy; will probably be damaged in the extremes of its range if there is no snow cover. Propagate by seeds or division.

Uses
Ground cover.

virginianum *p. 219*
Green-and-gold, golden star. 4–10 in. high with opposite, long-stalked, bluntly toothed leaves. Flowerheads solitary or few, 1½ in. wide, yellow. Plants flower for a long period in spring and summer, especially where summers are cool. Zone 5.

Cimicifuga
Sim-mi-siff'you-ga
Ranunculaceae. Buttercup family

Description
A small genus of tall, rather showy, summer-blooming herbs native to the north temperate zone.

How to Grow
Black snakeroot enjoys part to moderate shade and prefers moist soil that is not especially acid. May need staking.

Uses
Well suited to the wild garden or the shadiest part of the border.

racemosa p. 139
Black snakeroot, black cohosh. Herbaceous perennial, up to 6 ft. high. Large, thrice-compound leaves. Flowers small, white, crowded in a dense, branched cluster, the main spike 1–3 ft. long. Native to Virginia, North Carolina, and Tennessee. Marginally hardy to zone 3; best in zones 4–7.

Cirsium
Sir'si-um
Compositae. Daisy family

Description
One of a large genus of thistles, a few of which are of garden interest.

How to Grow
Easy to grow in part shade and any garden soil. Sow seeds in early spring. Prefers cool weather.

Uses
Adds interesting texture to mixed beds.

japonicum p. 172 *Pictured above*
Plumed thistle. To 2½ ft tall with lobed and spiny leaves. Flowers 1–2 in. wide, in dense, solitary heads, rose-red,

tubular, with bristles. Japan. Short-lived, best grown as a hardy annual.

Clematis
Klem'a-tis
Ranunculaceae. Buttercup family

Description
About 270 species of long-lived herbs, and sometimes woody vines, widely distributed in East Asia, the Himalayas, and North America.

How to Grow
Though most clematis prefer full sun, the small-flowered species listed here thrives in part to light shade. Clematis prefers rich but well-drained soil. Add dolomitic lime, leaf mold, and sand when planting; never allow plants to become too dry. To help keep root run cool and moist, mulch and underplant with a shallow-rooted ground cover, plant on the north side of a low wall, or place flat stones at base of plant. Provide a stable support when plants are set out, since stems are brittle and break easily in the wind.

Hard pruning and regular feeding during the growing season pay off with luxuriant foliage growth and heavy flowering. In late winter or early spring, young plants may be cut back to within a few inches of the ground or to 2–3 buds; established plants to 12–18 in. To rejuvenate old entangled growth, crop back entirely in late autumn or spring; it should come back and bloom with renewed vigor in the same year. Propagated by layering or by softwood cuttings.

Uses
An excellent, long-lived flowering vine for trellises, fences, arbors, walls, tree stumps, and other surfaces. It is a superb, fragrant candidate for a structure on a northern or eastern exposure.

paniculata p. 246
Sweet autumn clematis. Vigorous, deciduous perennial vine with clouds of small, white, vanilla-scented flowers in late autumn. Fluffy, pinwheel-shaped seedheads follow. Leaves have 3 leaflets, egg-shaped, 1–4 in. long, leathery, staying dark green long after most trees have lost their leaves. The quality of the foliage alone is good reason to plant it on chainlink fences and other objects that need clothing. Also listed as

C. maximowicziana or *dioscoreifolia robusta*. Northern Asia. Zone 5.

Cleome
Klee-o′me. Spider flower
Capparaceae. Caper family

Description
Two hundred known species, chiefly tropical, one a showy familiar annual.

How to Grow
Suitable for part to light, dappled shade; needs and enjoys more shade in southerly climates. Where summers are long and warm, sow seeds in early spring; seeds will sprout when the soil warms. Elsewhere, start seeds indoors 8–10 weeks before the last spring frost and set out in the garden 2–3 weeks before that last frost. Needs plenty of space, so thin seedlings. Prefers warm weather and may self-sow once established.

Uses
Lends an airy tropical accent to annual beds and mixed borders, naturalizing schemes, and the rough half-cultivated areas of a large yard.

hasslerana p. 173   *Pictured above*
Spider flower. 4–5 ft. high, bushy. Leaves compound, slightly sticky, with 3–7 leaflets arranged finger-fashion. Flowers 2–3 in. long, rose-purple, pink, or white flowers clustered in loose, spidery wheels at the top of stems. Tropical America. Half-hardy annual.

Clerodendrum
Clare-o-den'drum
Verbenaceae. Vervain family

Description
A group of over 450 species of evergreen or deciduous trees or shrubs, mostly native to the Eastern Hemisphere, many featuring showy flowers and fruits.

How to Grow
The species described below is suitable for part to dappled shade and prefers moist, well-drained soil. Prune in early spring.

Uses
Shrub borders in mild climates.

trichotomum *p. 97*
Harlequin glorybower. Deciduous small tree or large shrub, 10–15 ft. high, with large, heart-shaped leaves. Fragrant white flowers in summer. Colorful, bright blue berries accompanied by red bracts persist into fall. China and Japan. Zone 7.

Clethra
Kleth'ra
Clethraceae. Summer-sweet family

Description
About 30 species of shrubs with fragrant white or rosy flowers.

How to Grow
Natural understudies, clethras enjoy part to full shade and moist, acid soil.

Uses
Fragrant shrubs for thickets and borders.

alnifolia 'Pink Spires' *p. 97   Pictured on p. 326*
Sweet pepperbush. A deciduous shrub, 3–8 ft. high. Leaves
oblong, pointed, 2½–5 in. long. Erect clusters, 5 in. long, of
very fragrant pink flowers in summer. 'Rosea' has flowers of
the same color; the species is typically white. Maine to Florida
and Texas. Zone 4.

Clytostoma
Kly-tos'to-ma
Bignoniaceae. Trumpet-creeper family

Description
Eight species of South American evergreen woody vines, one
cultivated in mild climates for its showy bloom.

How to Grow
The species below grows in any garden soil in part to light
shade. Slow-growing until thoroughly established. Prune after
flowering to remove old canes, encourage new growth to keep
on support, and control size. Propagated by cuttings of last
season's wood.

Uses
Vigorous, evergreen flowering vine for sturdy arbor or trellis
in warm climates.

callistegioides *p. 246*
Violet trumpet vine. To 8 ft. high. Evergreen leaflets grow in
pairs; they are glossy, oblong, and up to 4 in. Flowers in pairs,
3 in. long, light purple or pale lavender, streaked darker inside.
Blooms in spring. Sometimes known as *Bignonia speciosa* or
B. violacea. Latin America. Zone 8.

Coleus
Ko'lee-us
Labiatae. Mint family

Description
About 150 species of foliage plants of the Old World tropics.

How to Grow
Coleus can be grown in a range of light, from morning sun
to deep shade. Start seeds indoors 10 weeks before last spring
frost, providing 70–75 degrees F bottom heat, and raising this
to 80 degrees if germination does not occur in 10 days. Do
not cover the seeds with soil. Cover pots with plastic wrap.

After last frost, plant in moderately shady site outdoors. Keep moist. Pinch off flowers to promote bushy plants. Favorite varieties are easily carried over by taking cuttings, which take root in any potting medium. Prefers warm weather.

Uses
Foliage for beds and containers, filler in flower arrangements. Good for children's gardening projects.

× *hybridus* *p. 173*
Garden coleus. To 3 ft. high with square stems and opposite leaves, very showy: variously toothed, scalloped, or fringed; in greens, creams, pinks, reds, and maroon combinations. Tender perennial usually grown as an annual or bedding plant.

Collinsia
Kol-lin′si-a
Scrophulariaceae. Snapdragon family

Description
Twenty-five species of attractive herbs, most natives of western North America.

How to Grow
This species grows well in part shade. It prefers good drainage and cool nights. Sow seeds in spring, after warm weather has arrived. Not heat-resistant.

Uses
A pretty flower for wild gardens.

grandiflora *p. 174*
Bluelips. 8–15 in. high. Leaves opposite. Flowers ¾ in. long, in small clusters at the sides and top of stems, irregular and 2-lipped. Upper lip is purple or white, lower blue or violet. Native British Columbia to California. Half-hardy annual.

Comptonia
Komp-to′ni-a. Sweet fern
Myricaceae. Bayberry family

Description
A single, highly aromatic shrub found in sandy or rocky soil throughout eastern North America. Despite its common names, it is not a true fern.

How to Grow

Sweet fern enjoys part shade and needs well-drained, sandy, acid soil. Not widely available and difficult to establish. Collect seeds from the wild and sow in a container; transplant carefully, keeping rootball intact. Little pruning needed, and then only to groom.

Uses

Fragrant, low shrub for sandy banks, also naturalizing and wildlife plantings in lean soil.

peregrina *p. 98   Pictured above*

Sweet fern or shrubby fern, sweetbush. A hairy shrub, to 5 ft. tall, but often much shorter. Leaves are alternate, narrow, much divided, with leaflets scalloped on edges, generally suggestive of fern fronds; fragrant when crushed, 4–5 in. long. Flowers inconspicous, green, in catkins. Seeds small, burrlike nutlets. Also known as *Myrica asplenifolia.* Zone 3.

Consolida

Con-sol′id-da
Ranunculaceae. Buttercup family

Description

About 40 species of annuals native to central Europe and Asia, 2 fairly commonly cultivated. They are related to and sometimes confused with *Delphinium;* flowers are similar but have fewer petals.

Uses

Bedding plants for the back of the garden or against a fence. Cut flowers.

How to Grow
Suitable for part shade. Since seedlings are so frost-hardy, sow seeds in raised beds with heavy soil, in fall in areas with mild winters, and in very early spring elsewhere. When plants are 12–18 in. high, provide mulch of dried grass clippings to keep roots cool. Difficult to transplant unless started in peat pots. Tall varieties need support. The species below prefer cool weather.

ambigua p. 174
Rocket larkspur. 1–2 ft. high, with erect branches. Flowers 1¼ in. long, violet, rose, pink, blue, or white. Blooms in late spring to summer. Many cultivars are available, some to 5 ft. high. Southern Europe. Hardy annual.

orientalis p. 175
Larkspur. Similar to the above, but with branches more horizontal. North Africa, southern Europe. Also sold as *Delphinium consolida*. Hardy annual.

Convallaria
Kon-va-lair′ee-a. Lily-of-the-valley
Liliaceae. Lily family

Description
About 3 species of rhizomatous perennial herbs native in Eurasia or eastern North America. An intensely fragrant cut flower, lily-of-the-valley is a mainstay of perfumery.

How to Grow
Thrives in part to full shade; flowering will be better with adequate indirect light. Prefers moist, fertile soil enriched annually with organic matter, but tolerant of leaner conditions.

Propagate from divisions of local, well-established colonies. Thin plantings when flowering becomes sparse.

Uses
Ground cover, among bulbs, naturalized in grass under trees and in woodlands as well as difficult dark areas close to buildings in cities.

majalis *p. 220 Pictured on p. 330*
Lily-of-the-valley, muguets-des-bois. Tongue-shaped, basal leaves are medium green and come up with the slender spires of white, bell-shaped flowers in midspring. Typically, flowers are ⅜ in. wide, waxy, very fragrant. Bright red berries are attractive but sparse. Cultivars include 'Rosea', with pink flowers, and 'Aureo-variegata', with yellow-striped leaves. Zone 4.

Coreopsis
Ko-ree-op′sis.
Compositae. Daisy family

Description
About 100 species of annual and perennial herbs, most with yellow flowers.

How to Grow
Thrive in ordinary well-drained garden soil. Divide in spring or fall.

Uses
Meadow gardens, summer borders, cut flowers.

verticillata 'Golden Shower' *p. 140*
Threadleaf coreopsis. Drought-tolerant native perennial 2–3 ft. high with slender threadlike leaflets. Daisy-form yellow flowerheads nearly 2 in. wide in summer. Species is usually shorter. Other cultivars are light yellow 'Moonbeam', and deeper gold 'Zagreb'. Southeastern U.S. Zone 4.

Cornus
Kor′nus. Dogwood
Cornaceae. Dogwood family

Description
An important genus of some 45 species, all trees and shrubs except the bunchberry. Native of north temperate zones. They

are grown for their ornamental attributes, including overall form, showy spring floral displays, bright summer berries, handsome autumn foliage, and in some species, the color of their twigs and bark for winter interest. Leaves are usually opposite, smooth-margined, and veined. The typical dogwood "flower" consists of about 4 snowy-white bracts surrounding a central boss of small, greenish, true flowers.

How to Grow

Most dogwoods enjoy part, light, or dappled shade, and are easy to grow in any good garden soil. Adequate moisture and attention to winter-hardiness is critical, as most woody species set flower buds in summer for bloom the following spring; these must survive the winter if plant is to bloom. Dogwoods are distinctive in their bearing. Prune selectively, only to enhance natural character and after flowers go by. Avoid shearing and other radical styles. Propagated by hardwood cuttings, layering, or by seed. Unfortunately, some natives are prey to insect and disease problems, notably the fungus anthracnose. Consult a local extension agent before planting a native dogwood.

Uses

Versatile small trees and shrubs for shade, accent, mixed borders, thickets for wildlife, and shrub borders. Bunchberry is a choice herbaceous ground cover. All have at least two seasons of interest.

canadensis p. 220

Bunchberry. A low woodland plant, stems to 6 in. high above the creeping, woody rootstock. Incised, deep green leaves pointed, 2 in. long, whorled. Stems topped by flowerhead with 4–6 pointed, white bracts of creamy texture. Shiny red berries follow. This native woodlander likes humus-rich, moist soil; where conditions are to its liking, it is a highly ornamental and worthwhile subject. Eastern North America. Zone 2.

florida p. 82   *Pictured on p. 332*

Flowering dogwood. A showy tree, up to 30 ft. high, often spreading wider. Flowers 3–4 in. across, the bracts cupped, faintly striped, and neatly notched rather than pointed, produced in abundance before the leaves emerge in early spring. Leaves oval, 3–5 in. long, consistently coloring red or purplish for a magnificent autumn show. Narrow scarlet berries in summer and fall. Flowerbuds are flat gray buttons. Cultivars with pink or red flowers, double flowers, variegated foliage, and of weeping habit are available. The most popular pink is rubra, commonly called the red flowering dogwood. Flowering dogwoods need excellent drainage but are not tolerant of extended drought and can be prey to anthracnose. Eastern U.S. Zone 5.

kousa p. 83   *Pictured above*

Kousa or Japanese dogwood. The Asiatic counterpart of our native flowering dogwood. It is a smaller tree, about 20 ft. tall, and blooms about 2 weeks later. The 4 white bracts are pointed, about 2 in. wide, and unfold after the leaves have expanded. These are followed by raspberry-sized compound fruits, and good scarlet fall color. New flower buds are pointed. Mature trees have sycamore-like exfoliating bark. Enormous variation within the species has resulted in a plethora of named cultivars with different growth habits, larger or pink flowers, variegated leaves. More trouble-free than the native and apparently immune to anthracnose. Japan and Korea. Best in zones 5–8.

mas p. 84

Cornelian cherry. A hardy shrub or small tree to 25 ft. high. In this species, flowers lack the hallmark white bracts. In early spring the naked twigs are crowded instead with short-stalked, small, ¾-in.-wide tufts of minute golden tassels flowering well before the leaves appear. Leaves oval or elliptic, 3–4 in. long, reddish in fall. Fruit edible, the size of a cherry, ⅝ in. long, scarlet, ripening in late summer but best left to the birds. Tolerates urban conditions and is generally pest-free. Eurasia. Best in zones 5–7.

racemosa p. 98
Gray dogwood. Shrub, 8–15 ft. high, with gray twigs. Leaves elliptic or narrowly oval, 2–4 in. long, tapering at the tip, but wedge-shaped at the base. Flowers white, the cluster branched, not flat-topped, 2 in. wide. Conspicuous fruit is white on red stalks, borne in summer. Likes more shade than other woody species listed here, and tolerates wet to dry soil. Eastern U.S. Zone 4.

Cosmos
Kos′mus
Compositae. Daisy family

Description
A genus of showy summer- and fall-flowering annuals and perennials from the Americas, primarily Mexico.

How to Grow
Plant cosmos in part to light shade in any well-drained soil. Cosmos are quite drought resistant. Start seeds outdoors after the last frost or indoors 5–7 weeks earlier. Space the plants 1–3 ft. apart depending on their ultimate height. Stake the tall varieties if necessary and plant them out of the wind. Cut off faded flowers to prolong bloom. Self-sows. Of such easy culture, cosmos is often suggested for a child's first garden.

Uses
Plant cosmos at the front or back of the border, depending on its height, or in large massed plantings. Excellent cut flower.

bipinnatus p. 175
Plants can grow up to 8 ft., but usually reach 3–4 ft. Habit is open, branching, with bright green lacy foliage. The 3- to 6-in.-wide daisylike flowers are single, double, or crested, in light, airy clusters. They have white, pink, crimson, or lavender petals, often notched or frilled, with yellow centers. Tender annual.

Cotoneaster
Ko-to'nee-as'ter
Rosaceae. Rose family

Description
About 50 species of deciduous or evergreen shrubs or small trees native to the Old World temperate zone. Chiefly grown for their spreading habit, glossy foliage, and showy fruit.

How to Grow
The species named below is suitable for part shade and prefers neutral to slightly acid, well-drained soil. Once established, tolerates drought and wind but may be prone to spider mites and lace bug in dry summers. Prune only to shape and control their size. Grow new plants from cuttings or by layering. Large specimens are difficult to transplant.

Uses
Ground cover, on top of and against retaining walls and steps.

divaricatus p. 99
Spreading cotoneaster. This upright deciduous shrub grows 3–7 ft. tall and has wide-spreading branches. The ¾-in. leaves are pale green underneath and turn orange-red in fall. The pinkish flowers are ¼ in. wide. The profuse and showy berries are bright red, turning plum. Handsome and easy to grow. China. Zone 5.

Crinum
Kry'num
Amaryllidaceae. Amaryllis family

Description
Perhaps 130 species of bulbous or thick-rooted lilylike herbs, mostly tropical, a few cultivated for their showy flowers.

How to Grow
Suitable for part to light shade in warm climates. These handsome plants, sometimes called crinum lilies, are grown outdoors chiefly in the South, although some can be wintered over up to warmest reaches of zone 7 with a good mulch of straw and manure. They are naturally rich feeders and do best in good soil with plenty of water. They dislike moving and may not flower for two or three seasons after being lifted. When left alone they are apt to make large, striking clumps. Most species produce small offsets from base of the bulblike root; these root easily in warm, moist soil.

Uses
Showy accents and potted plants for warm climates.

americanum *p. 201*
Swamp lily. Leaves few, long and narrow. Flowers white, 3 in.
wide, the tube 3–4 in. long, segments long and narrow. Stalk
of flower cluster 1½–2 ft. long, usually arising before leaves
appear. Late spring to summer blooming. Florida to Texas.
Zone 9.

bulbispermum *p. 201   Pictured above*
Common crinum. A vigorous plant, to 3 ft. high. Leaves long
and narrow, the margins roughish. Flowers pink or white, in
late spring, about 12 to a cluster, to 4 in. wide, the tube long
and curved. Native to South Africa. Zone 8; with winter protection up to zone 7.

× *powellii* *p. 202*
A cross of *C. bulbispermum* and *C. moorei,* with a globular,
long-necked bulb, and about 20 narrow leaves, to 4 ft. long.
Flowers curved, 3 in. long, reddish green at base, with 6–8
flowers in a terminal umbel that stands 2 ft. high. Summer.
Hybrid origins. Zone 8.

Crocus
Kro′kus
Iridaceae. Iris family

Description
A genus of about 80 species of popular garden plants, ranging
from the Mediterranean region to southwest Asia. They are
usually stemless plants arising from a bulblike corm with a

showy flower. The genus includes the familiar spring-blooming garden hybrids and the economically important saffron crocus, *C. sativus*. Both species listed here bloom in autumn.

How to Grow
Plant the small corms 3–4 in. deep in light, dappled shade of deciduous trees with warm, well-drained soil where they may self-sow. Avoid planting among dense ground covers. Crocus naturalizes well in lawns; with autumn species like those listed below, cease mowing as soon as buds emerge from soil in late summer. Most crocuses need cold winters.

Uses
Naturalizing under deciduous trees, rock gardens.

longiflorus p. 202
Autumn crocus. Leaves present at autumn flowering time. Blooms 2¾–5½ in. long, lilac to purple, yellow throat. Southern Europe. Zone 5.

medius p. 203
Autumn crocus. Leaves appear after flowers in autumn. Flowers 4–10 in. long, lilac to deep purple, throat with purple veins. Northwest Italy and southeast France. Zones 6–7.

Cyclamen
Sy′kla-men
Primulaceae. Primrose family.

Description
About 15 species of perennial herbs with tuber-corms and heart-shaped, marbled leaves, showy flowers with distinctive reflexed petals, native in Europe and Asia Minor. Hybrids are very popular florists' pot plants, grown for their handsome flowers. The species listed here is relatively hardy.

How to Grow
Cyclamen enjoy shade and adjust to a wide range of light according to climate, moisture, and exposure, from part sun in cooler, moister northern climates to moderately full shade in the South. They need good loam enriched with organic matter, adequate moisture, and good drainage. From zone 7 southward, they can be grown as hardy perennials, provided the situation is free of alternate freezing and thawing. North of zone 7 they may overwinter in pots in a cold frame or a cold greenhouse.

Uses
Rock gardens, shaded borders. Containers in cold climates.

hederifolium p. 203
Sowbread. Plant is 3–6 in. high. Tuber to 6 in. in diameter, globular but flattened on top. Leaves heart-shaped, to 5½ in. long, marbled above, plain green or red beneath. Flowers to 1 in. long, pink or white, with a crimson blotch in late summer to autumn. South Europe. Zone 7.

Cyperus
Sy-peer'us
Cyperaceae. Sedge family

Description
About 600 species of annual and perennial grasslike herbs, a few of garden interest. *C. papyrus* is the paper plant of antiquity.

How to Grow
Most *Cyperus* prefer rich, moist soil and enjoy part to light shade. They will also grow in shallow pools or in pots placed on stands in deep water. Propagate by division or by detaching the leaf crown, which, in moist sand or water, will send up new plants from most of the axils. Papyrus can be potted and submerged in outdoor ponds in summer and wintered over in a greenhouse.

Uses
Pools, waterside plantings, and damp spots in warm climates. Container culture northward.

alternifolius p. 259   *Pictured above*
Umbrella plant. Semiaquatic ornamental grass. Stems usually several, slender, 2–4 ft. high, essentially leafless but with

brownish sheaths. At top of each stem an umbrella-shaped cluster of leafy bracts gives rise to flower spikelets. Look for 'Gracilis', a smaller, more slender form. African tropics. Zone 9.

papyrus *p. 259*
Paper plant, papyrus. Rhizomatous, evergreen, aquatic sedge, stems 6–8 ft. high, essentially leafless but with sheaths. Drooping threadlike leaves to 18 in. long at tip of stem. Terminal cluster of flower spikelets umbel-like, borne in short stems just above the whorl of leaves. Africa. Zone 10.

Cyrtomium
Sir-toh'mee-um
Polypodiaceae. Polypody family

Description
About 10 species of evergreen ferns, most native to the Old World.

How to Grow
The tender fern described below prefers light shade and moist, well-drained soil containing plenty of organic matter.

Uses
Mass plantings, borders, in combination with broad-leaved evergreens in warm climates.

falcatum *p. 271*
Holly fern. Glossy, deep green fronds, 24–30 in. high. 'Compactum' is lower-growing than the species. 'Rochfordianum' has fringed leaf margins. Zone 10.

Daphne
Daf'nee
Thymelaeaceae. Daphne family

Description
A genus of Eurasian shrubs, some evergreen. A few species are grown for their intensely fragrant small flowers. All parts are poisonous.

How to Grow
The species listed below enjoy part to light shade. Prefers loose, fertile soil, neutral to slightly alkaline with excellent drainage.

Little pruning required. Trim off any winter-burned leaves of the evergreen species in spring. Propagate from fresh seeds or summer cuttings.

Uses
Fragrance in border or rock garden. *D. mezereum* can be forced for late winter bouquets.

mezereum *p. 99*
February daphne. An upright deciduous shrub, to 5 ft. high. Leaves oblong, 2–3 in. long, wedge-shaped at base. Flowers in clusters, 1½ in. wide, blooming before the leaves unfold, lilac-purple or rosy purple, and very fragrant. Poisonous fruit is scarlet. Eurasia. Zone 6.

odora *p. 100   Pictured above*
Fragrant or winter daphne. An evergreen shrub, to 4 ft. high. Leaves oblong to elliptic, 2–3 in. long and tapered at ends. Flowers rosy purple, fragrant, in dense terminal clusters 1 in. wide in early spring. Cultivar 'Aureo-marginata' has yellow-bordered leaves. Japan and China. Zone 7.

Decumaria
De-koo-mare'ee-a
Saxifragaceae. Saxifrage family

Description
Two known species of woody vines with clusters of white flowers, related to *Hydrangea*.

How to Grow
Enjoys part to light shade and prefers fertile, moist soil. Propagated by cuttings in late summer. Prune lightly to train and groom after flowering.

Uses
Suitable as a wall cover in mild climates.

barbara p. 247
Climbing hydrangea, wood-vamp. Stems, climbing by aerial roots, to 30 ft. high, covered with peeling, shreddy bark. Leaves opposite, oval, glossy, half-evergreen. Flowers small, white, in clusters at the ends of stems. Native of southeastern U.S. Zone 7.

Deschampsia
Des-kamp'se-a. Hair grass
Gramineae. Grass family.

Description
50 species of annual or perennial temperate-zone ornamental grasses.

How to Grow
Thrives in part, light, to moderate shade, in moist but well-drained soil. Cut flowerheads before seedheads ripen. Propagate by division or seeds.

Uses
Perennial borders, specimen use, or naturalizing.

caespitosa p. 260
Tufted hair grass. Mound-forming evergreen perennial to 2 ft. high. Leaves dark green. Summer inflorescence an open, feathery panicle to 20 in. long, 8 in. wide, very graceful; color varies from silvery to gold to green and purple; many color selections have been made. Zone 5.

Dianthus
Dy-an'thus. Pink
Caryophyllaceae. Pink family

Description
A large genus of annuals, biennials, and perennials, mostly Eurasian, that includes an important group of ornamentals. Single or double flowers are white, pink, salmon, red, or wine colored with sweet, clovey perfume. The species listed here is a biennial. Perennials are equally prized for their handsome foliage, which is typically grassy with a tinge of blue, gray, or silver.

How to Grow
Sweet William grows in any ordinary, well-drained soil in part
to light shade. (As a rule the genus prefers sun and a limey or
slightly alkaline soil.) In mild climates, sow seeds outdoors in
the fall. Elsewhere, to get first-year bloom, purchase plants or
start seeds indoors about 8 weeks before last frost and transplant to garden in early spring. Exposure to cold will help
ensure same-season bloom. Plants prefer cool weather and
tend to reseed if the situation is to their liking.

Uses
Old-fashioned sweet William is excellent as a cut flower, summer bedder, and filler in immature borders. Compact varieties
make a cheerful edging and dress up beginner's rock gardens.

barbatus p. 176
Sweet William. 1–2 ft. high. Flowers fragrant, ⅓ in. wide and
numerous, packed in dense rounded heads at the top of stems.
Red, rose-purple, white, or varicolored, and sometimes double-
flowered. Many cultivars available, including 'Nanus', a dwarf
variety, and 'Auriculiflorus', with lobed petals. Eurasia; sometimes naturalized in eastern U.S. Biennial or short-lived perennial, often grown as an annual.

Dicentra
Dy-sen'tra
Fumariaceae. Fumitory family

Description
A small genus of slender herbs from Asia and North America
which includes some excellent plants for the shaded garden.
Fleshy rootstocks and light green feathery leaves. Flowers are
heart-shaped or long-spurred, strung along a gracefully nodding stem arising from the rosette of foliage.

How to Grow

These are shade-loving plants, needing protection from afternoon sun, and thriving in light and dappled shade. Generally easy to grow in fertile, moist soil with plenty of organic matter. Increase by division in early spring.

Uses

Bleeding hearts are useful in borders, rock gardens, and among spring bulbs. Dutchman's-breeches is a choice specimen for a wildflower nook.

cucullaria p. 140

Dutchman's-breeches. Flowering stalk 5–8 in. high. Flowers white, tipped with yellow, ¾ in. long, looking like small pairs of bloomers, neatly hung out to dry. Plant in well-prepared humusy soil in a shady wind-free place. Prefers cool temperatures and may die back after bloom in warm climates. Native to eastern woodlands. Zone 4.

'Luxuriant' p. 141   *Pictured on p. 342*

Hybrid bleeding heart. 12–18 in. high. Leaves basal, fine textured. Flowers dark reddish pink, heart-shaped, 1 in. long, loosely arranged on stem. 'Bountiful' has red flowers. More heat-tolerant and free-flowering than species. Hybrid origin. Zone 4.

spectabilis p. 141

Common bleeding heart. 1–2 ft. high. Flowers white or rose, 1½ in. long, hanging formally from one side of the 9-in.-long stem. Needs moist, well-drained soil. Hot or dry weather may cause foliage to flag, in which case cut to the ground after flowering. Asia. Zones 3 or 4.

Digitalis

Di-ji-tay′lis
Scrophulariaceae. Snapdragon family

Description

Handsome, sometimes poisonous or medicinal herbs, including some showy garden perennials, biennials, and the annual listed here. Slightly fuzzy leaves are coarse and medium green, forming a basal rosette of leaves. Flowers on long, sometimes one-sided spikes and shaped more or less like small bells.

How to Grow

Easy to grow in ordinary well-drained garden soil in part to light shade with adequate moisture. The annual probably does best with morning sun and afternoon shade. Propagate perennials by division and annuals and biennials by seed. Expect some winter-kill in cold climates that experience extreme fluctuations of temperature and moisture.

Uses
Shady borders.

grandiflora p. 142
Yellow foxglove. Hairy, to 3 ft. high. Flowers to 2 in. long, buff yellow with brown freckles in the bell. Grows best in a moist, rich soil. Remove faded flowers unless reseeding is desired. Europe and western Asia. Zone 4.

purpurea 'Foxy' p. 176   *Pictured above*
Annual foxglove. 2½–3½ ft. Flowers large, 2–3 in. long, in shades of white to yellow, pink to magenta. Start seeds indoors 8–10 weeks before the last frost. Harden off seedlings and set out 2–3 weeks before last frost; early transplanting lets good vegetative frame develop before warm weather forces bloom. Bred from the Mediterannean species. Does best in relatively cool, moist climates, especially in coastal New England, Washington, and Oregon. Heavy-flowering biennial or short-lived perennial which blooms the first year from seed.

Dirca
Der′ka. Leatherwood
Thymelaeaceae. Daphne family

Description
A small genus of North American shrubs with attractive dark foliage and charming habit of a miniature tree.

How to Grow
Enjoys part to light shade, easy to grow in moist soil. In drier sites, amend the soil with organic matter. Shade is important to keep the foliage dark. Little pruning needed. Propagation is difficult but the aspect of this small plant earns it an important niche.

Uses
Specimen in mixed borders and small gardens.

palustris p. 100
Leatherwood, wicopy, rope bark. A tough-wooded but pliable shrub, 3–5 ft. high, the leaves elliptic, 2–3 in. long, short-stalked. Pale yellow spring flowers ornamental at close range. Eastern North America. Zone 5.

Disporum
Dy-spor′um
Liliaceae. Lily family

Description
A genus of perennial woodland herbs native to North America and Asia. Creeping rootstocks, leaves somewhat downy, nearly stalkless, alternate. Flowers bell-shaped.

How to Grow
Shade-lovers for part, light, dappled toward moderately full shade. The species below perform best in dry, well-drained, humus-rich soil. Easily propagated by seed or by division in spring.

Uses
Woodland gardens, dry shade.

flavum p. 142   *Pictured on p. 345*
Fairy-bells. 2–3 ft. high. Leaves shiny, leathery. Flowers 1 in. long, yellow. Zone 4.

sessile 'Variegatum' *p. 143*
Japanese fairy-bells. 1¼–2 ft. high. Leaves white-striped, oblong, to 4 in. long. Flowers creamy white, small, usually solitary or in groups of 2 or 3, in spring. Japan. Zone 5.

Dodecatheon
Do-deck-kath′-ee-on
Primulaceae. Primrose family

Description
Beautiful North American wildflowers comprising perhaps 14 species, a few of which are cultivated in the wild or rock garden.

How to Grow
The species below prefers part to light shade and rich, sandy soil high in organic matter and well-drained. Needs moisture during growing season and drier conditions when dormant. Standing water in winter can be fatal to crown. Easily propagated by division.

meadia p. 143
Shooting-star. 1–2 ft. high. Leaves to 1 ft. long, forming a basal rosette. Flowers 1 in. long, rose-pink or lavender, whitish at the base with turned-back petals suggesting a falling star. Foliage dies down after flowering. Zone 5.

Elaeagnus
Eel-ee-ag′nus
Elaeagnaceae. Oleaster family

Description
A genus of about 40 species of handsome shrubs and trees from the north temperate zone. Several are cultivated for their silvery foliage and ornamental fruit. The small flowers are fragrant but not showy.

How to Grow
Enjoys part to light shade and tolerates much more shade. Easy to grow in a variety of adverse conditions. Withstands wind, drought, and urban conditions. May be sheared into hedges.

Cut back side shoots in spring to encourage colorful new growth. Propagated from cuttings, by layering, or from seeds.

Uses
Hedges, windbreak, screen. Suitable for urban and seaside gardens.

pungens 'Variegata' *p. 101*
Thorny elaeagnus. This usually spiny, spreading shrub grows 15 ft. high. The 5-in.-long evergreen leaves have wavy margins, white or yellowish white and silvery underneath. The drooping silvery white flowers are fragrant and bloom in fall. The fruit is brown at first, then red. Japan. Zone 7.

Enkianthus
En-ki-an'thus
Ericaceae. Heath family

Description
Asiatic shrubs, some cultivated for their yellow-orange flowers and fine red color in the fall.

How to Grow
Plant in part to light shade, in a well-drained, moderately acid soil like that needed for rhododendrons. Do not move established plants. Little pruning needed. Propagated by seeds or cuttings.

Uses
Handsome, versatile shrub for large borders, woodland plantings.

campanulatus *p. 101*
Deciduous shrub, useful at 8–12 ft.; ultimately 30 ft. high. Alternate leaves, 1–3 in.-long. Drooping clusters of ½-in. long bell-shaped flowers, yellow with red veins, cover the bush in midspring. Japan. Zone 5.

Epimedium
Ep-i-mee'di-um
Berberidaceae. Barberry family

Description
Twenty species of rather woody perennials from the north temperate zone. They have clumps of finely toothed, heart-

shaped 1- to 3-in. leaves that are light green, often tinged with red in autumn. The flowers bloom in clusters in spring, sometimes hidden under the leaves and squarish in configuration. Both the flowers and the leaves appear on thin, wiry stems. The plants spread slowly by underground stems.

How to Grow
Epimediums enjoy shade, from part to light, toward full. May even grow under needled evergreens provided water can be supplied. They like rich, moist, slightly acid soil, but tolerate dry conditions well. Cut back plants in early spring to encourage compact growth. Propagate by division. At limits of their hardiness range, evergreen species need winter protection.

Uses
Under trees and shrubs, rock garden, front of borders, for ground cover. Among the finest of perennial ground covers for shade.

× *rubrum* *p. 221*
Red epimedium. To 12 in. high. Flowers small, bright pink to crimson with white spurs. Bronze-purple autumn foliage. Sometimes sold as *E. alpinum*. Zone 5.

× *versicolor* 'Sulphureum' *p. 221*
Persian epimedium. Robust, to 12 in. high. An excellent cultivar with graceful pale yellow petals, and darker yellow spurs. Foliage persistent but not evergreen in the North. Zone 5.

× *warleyense* *p. 222*
Warley epimedium. 9–12 in. high. Flowers small, with 8 orange sepals and 4 spurlike yellow petals. Zone 5.

× *youngianum* 'Niveum' *p. 222*   *Pictured above*
Snowy epimedium. 8–10 in. high. Flowers tiny, pendulous, held well above foliage, white. Slow-growing, but a beautiful border specimen. Zone 5.

Euonymus
You-on′i-mus
Celastraceae. Bittersweet family

Description
About 170 mostly Asian species of deciduous or evergreen trees, shrubs, or woody vines. Grown for their showy fruits and evergreen leaves. Leaves are smooth, opposite. Inconspicuous flowers are borne in spring. Fruit a capsule, inedible, often lobed or brightly colored, opening to show red or orange seeds late in the season.

How to Grow
The species listed below enjoy part to moderately full shade. The genus grows well in ordinary soil in any exposure, but not all are hardy. Where fruiting display is desired, plant several together for good berry production. Prune in early spring to remove twiggy old growth, enhance outline, invigorate plantings. Propagate from seeds or cuttings. Some forms get euonymus scale; avoid mass plantings of susceptible types and control with horticultural oil sprays.

Uses
Varied group of woody landscape plants. Allowed to sprawl, the trailing stems of winter creepers make a deep ground cover; given support, they will climb. 'Matanzaki' is a choice shrub, offering fall and winter interest.

fortunei 'Silver Queen' *p. 223   Pictured above*
Winter creeper. A mounding form selected for ground cover, growing to 2 ft. high and 3 ft. wide, with green and creamy-white leaves. Species is a trailing or climbing evergreen vine with rooting branches to 12 in. high and 20 ft. long, with

small oval leaves, greenish white flowers, nearly round, pale pink fruit. Zone 4.

fortunei radicans 'Variegata' *p. 247*
Winter creeper. Trailing or climbing evergreen vine to 12 ft. high. Leaves ovalish or broadly elliptic, glossy, variegated white, to 1 in long. Flowers greenish white. Fruit nearly round, pale pink. Best evergreen vine for the North. China. Zone 5.

japonica 'Matanzaki' *p. 102*
Japanese euonymus. An evergreen shrub, to 15 ft. high or more. Leaves elliptic, narrow, 1–3 in. long, bluntly toothed. Flowers greenish white. This showy cultivar has nearly round, bright red fruit and variegated leaves with a creamy gold border. The species typically has pinkish fruits with orange aril, green leaves. Japan. Zone 7.

Eupatorium
You-pa-toe'ri-um
Compositae. Sunflower family

Description
A genus of some 500 species of chiefly tropical American herbs, a few reaching temperate regions and grown in gardens for their showy flowerheads.

How to Grow
Grow in ordinary garden soil and light shade. Propagate by division in spring.

Uses
This species is a mainstay in autumn gardens, wild or formal.

coelestinum *p. 144*
Mist flower, hardy ageratum. Herbaceous perennial, to 2 ft. high. Leaves thin, coarsely toothed. Flowerheads numerous, small, light blue to violet blue. Can be invasive; spreads quickly in sandy loam, more slowly in thicker soils. Zone 5.

Eustoma
You-sto'ma
Gentianaceae. Gentian family

Description
A small genus of North American prairie herbs, the species below cultivated in the garden for its large showy flowers.

How to Grow
Suitable for afternoon to light shade. Blooms reliably the first year if seeds are started very early indoors and transplanted outdoors after last frost. Heat-resistant if planted in moist, well-drained soil. Prefers warm weather.

Uses
Spectacular cut flower.

grandiflora *p. 177   Pictured above*
Prairie gentian. 2–3 ft. high. Flowers pale purple with dark purple blotches at the base, usually in a branched panicle, the corolla nearly bell-shaped, flaring, 2 in. long and wide. Cultivars have pink, white, or lavender flowers; dwarf varieties available. Also called *Lisianthus russellianus*. Nebraska to Colorado, south to Texas and Mexico. Biennial grown as a half-hardy annual.

Exacum
Ecks′a-kum
Gentianaceae. Gentian family

Description
A genus of 20 species of herbs or subshrubs from the Old World tropics, the species below is a widely grown bedding plant.

How to Grow
Persian violets thrive in a range of light conditions, depending on climate, exposure, and moisture, from part to light toward full shade. Seeds need light and temperatures of 60–65 degrees F to germinate. Start indoors 8 weeks before last frost. Prefers moist, well-drained soil and warm weather.

Uses
Containers, bedding.

affine *p. 177*
Persian violet. 1–2 ft. high. Leaves opposite and small, plant is compact and free-flowering. Flowers bluish to mauve, ½ in. wide, with pointed petals. Native to South Yemen. Cultivar 'Atrocaerulum' has dark lavender flowers. Biennial grown as a tender annual.

× *Fatshedera*
Fats-hed'e-ra
Araliaceae. Aralia family

Description
A hybrid between two species belonging to different genera, derived from crossing an English ivy or *Hedera* and a Japanese fatsia. The plants have large leaves shaped like the ivy's, colored bright green like those of fatsia.

How to Grow
Fatshedera grows best in part to full shade, needing more shade in hotter and drier situations. Give the plant plenty of moisture, and protect it from hot, drying winds. Regular pruning will encourage compact growth. It is easy to root from cuttings.

Uses
Adaptable landscape shrub for warm climates.

× *lizei* *p. 102 Pictured above*
Fatshedera. Shrub, to 6 ft. high, with large, evergreen leaves often 5–10 in. wide. Flowers small, light green, in dense um-

bels grouped in large, showy, branched clusters that may be
8–10 in. long and half as wide. Blooms in fall. Hybrid origin.
Zone 8.

Fatsia
Fat'si-a
Araliacea. Aralia family

Description
A single evergreen Japanese shrub or small tree, often planted
in the South for its tropical-looking foliage.

How to Grow
This plant does best in full shade. It grows well in nearly every
type of soil but prefers rich, sandy ones that are slightly acid
and thrives with generous doses of fertilizer and water. Protect
from winter sun and wind, which can cause leaf burn. Prune
to maintain shrubbiness. Propagated by semihardwood cuttings.

Uses
Substantial, handsome leaves make this a versatile landscape
shrub for warm climates.

japonica p. 103 *Pictured above*
Japanese aralia. A bushy shrub or small tree, 10–12 ft. high.
Leaves alternate, shiny and stiff, as broad as 12 in. across, and
cut into ovalish, toothed lobes. Flowers whitish, small, in umbels, many of which are grouped in large, very showy,
branched clusters. Blooms in fall. Fruit black, ¼ in. in diameter.
There is a form with variegated leaves. Often offered as *Aralia
japonica*. Zone 8.

Ficus
Fy'kus. Fig
Moraceae. Mulberry family

Description
More than 800 species of chiefly tropical trees, shrubs, and vines, including the common fig and many ornamentals.

How to Grow
The shade-loving vine listed below enjoys part to full shade, depending on moisture, climate, and exposure. It grows best in fertile soil with good drainage. Prune *F. pumila* to keep young growth vigorous and to prevent development of mature leaves and branches, which are coarse and detract from the trim effect. Generally free of pests and easily rooted from cuttings, but not suitable for hot south- or west-facing walls.

Uses
The species listed below makes outstanding coverage for the walls of courtyard gardens in mild climates. In cold climates, a popular hanging plant for greenhouses and seasonal display outdoors.

pumila p. 248
Creeping or climbing fig. Evergreen vine to 40 ft. high, clinging by sucking disks. Alternate leaves dense, very numerous. Young stems grow neat and flat against walls, have small leaves. East Asia. Zone 9.

Filipendula
Fill-i-pen'dew-la
Rosaceae. Rose family

Description
A small genus of herbs, all from the north temperate zone. About 5 species grown for ornament. Divided, feathery to palmate leaves and large terminal clusters of numerous small white or pink flowers in summer. Similar to astilbes in aspect and use, and sometimes sold as *Spiraea,* a close relative.

How to Grow
Both species listed below thrive in part to light shade, moist soil, and are easily propagated by division of the clumps in spring.

Uses
Fine texture and color in summer borders and beds.

palmata *p. 144*
Meadowsweet. 2–4 ft. high. Rose-pink flowers ⅜ in. across, in 6-in. plumes. Also sold as *F. purpurea* or *Spiraea gigantea.* Japan. Zone 4.

rubra *p. 145* *Pictured above*
Queen-of-the-prairie. A stout but graceful herb, 4–7 ft. high. Flowers magenta, ⅜ in. across, in a fine-textured cluster. Eastern North America. Zone 3.

Fothergilla
Foth-er-gil′la
Hamamelidaceae. Witch hazel family

Description
A small genus of North American shrubs, sometimes called witch alder, related to witch hazel. They have lovely, fragrant flowers, small, white, packed in showy spikes. Leaves coarse, toothed, alternate, coloring orange to red in autumn.

How to Grow
Fothergillas prefer part to light shade and adequate moisture for best flowering. They prefer acid, sandy, well-drained, loamy soils, but are otherwise adaptable and pest-free. Pruning is seldom needed or desired. Propagated by softwood cuttings in the summer.

Uses
Shrub borders and informal hedges.

gardenii *p. 103*
Dwarf fothergilla. A low shrub, to 3 ft. high, the broadly wedge-shaped leaves 1–2 in. long, dark green, bluish white

and hairy on the underside. Flowers white, the spikes oblongish and 1 in. long, blooming before the leaves unfold. Virginia to Georgia. Zone 5.

major p. 104
Large fothergilla. A shrub, 4–10 ft. high, the nearly round or ovalish leaves 2–5 in. long, pale and a little hairy on the underside. Flowers white, the clusters 1½–4 in. long, blooming with the unfolding of the leaves. North Carolina to Alabama. Zone 5.

Galax
Gay'lacks
Diapensiaceae. Galax family

Description
A single perennial evergreen herb from eastern North America.

How to Grow
Needs part to full shade and moist soil. Optimum growth requires moderately acid soil with abundant peat moss or other organic matter. Increase by spring or fall division.

Uses
Spreading evergreen ground cover for moist areas; leaves used in flower arrangements.

urceolata p. 223
Galax. A stemless herb growing from a clump of scaly rhizomes. Leaves in ground-hugging clusters, about 6 in. high, are nearly round and green, but bronze with age. Tiny flowers white in spikelike racemes on slender stalks two or three times taller than foliage. Also sold as *G. aphylla.* Zone 5.

Galium
Gay'li-um. Bedstraw
Rubiaceae. Madder family

Description
Weak, almost weedy perennial herbs with fragrant flowers.

How to Grow
Galium requires part to full shade and moist, well-drained, slightly acid soil to keep foliage shiny green into fall. If location

is too hot or sunny, plants becomes stunted and may die down. Easily divided in spring.

Uses
Filler and ground cover in informal plantings, rock gardens, and among spring bulbs.

odoratum *p. 224   Pictured above*
Sweet woodruff. To 1 ft. high. Shiny green, stalkless narrow leaves growing in tiered whorls on arching to prostrate stems, fragrant when dried. Flowers white, tiny, in clusters. Formerly known as *Asperula odorata*. Eurasia. Zone 5.

Gardenia
Gar-dee′ni-a
Rubiaceae. Madder family

Description
A genus of 200 species of tropical Old World shrubs and trees with fragrant white flowers and glossy evergreen leaves.

How to Grow
Gardenia enjoys part to light shade and needs moisture-retentive, acid soil, to which peat or other organic matter has been added. Yellow leaves indicate soil is too alkaline. Mulch to help retain moisture and keep roots from being damaged by shallow cultivation. Plants may be attacked by aphids, scale, mealybugs, and spider mites; fragrant flowers over a long season may justify the effort. In cold climates, overwinter potted specimens in a greenhouse or sunroom. Propagated by softwood cuttings.

Uses
Luxuriant and fragrant bloom over a long season in warm climates. Specimen plant for containers in colder areas.

jasminoides p. 104 *Pictured above*
Gardenia. Evergreen shrub, 4–6 ft. high. Leaves 3–4 in. long, thick and glossy. Fragrant white flowers 2–3½ in. wide bloom spring to summer. Popular cultivars include 'Mystery', an upright shrub with large double flowers; 'Radicans', a low creeping shrub with small flowers; and 'Veitchii', 3–4 ft. high, a very good bloomer from spring to fall. China. Zone 8.

Gaultheria
Gaul-theer′ri-a
Ericaceae. Blueberry family

Description
Beautiful evergreen shrubs, some herblike, most of the 100 species from the Andes, a few from eastern Asia and North America.

How to Grow
Needs part to moderately full shade and acid soil. Gaultheria does not transplant easily from the wild, so it is better to plant nursery-grown stock. Propagated by cuttings of half-ripened wood or by seeds; seeds are minute and seedlings grow slowly.

Uses
Ground-hugging evergreen for wildflower nooks or rock gardens.

procumbens p. 224
Wintergreen, teaberry. A prostrate, herblike, evergreen woody plant, the stems half underground, the tips upright and to 4 in. high. Alternate leaves ovalish, purplish when plant is in

fruit, 2 in. long. Urn-shaped flowers tiny, solitary in leaf axils, nodding, white or pinkish, in late spring to early summer. Fruit scarlet, pea-size, redolent of wintergreen. Eastern North America. Zone 5.

Gelsemium
Gel-see'mi-um
Loganiaceae. Buddleia family

Description
Two or three evergreen woody vines native in eastern Asia and eastern North America.

How to Grow
Suitable for part to light shade; needs fertile, well-drained soil. Somewhat drought tolerant. Propagate by seeds or cuttings.

Uses
Versatile vine for trellis, fence, lampposts, ground cover.

sempervirens p. 248   Pictured above
Carolina jasmine. Evergreen, climbing 10–20 ft. high. Shiny 2–4 in. long leaves. Covered with clusters of fragrant bright yellow flowers in spring. All parts of the plant are poisonous. There is also a double-flowered form. Zone 7.

Geranium
Ger-ray'ni-um. Cranesbill or hardy geranium
Geraniaceae. Geranium family

Description
About 300 species of hardy perennial, biennial, or (rarely) annual herbs. Generally low-growing, cranesbills have thin stems and toothed, lobed, or dissected leaves forming mounds of foliage

and blooming in spring. The flowers are white, pink, or rose to blue and violet. Some have bright foliage color in autumn.

Confusingly, the Latin genus *Geranium* does not include the common garden geranium, which is related, but classed in the genus *Pelargonium*.

How to Grow
The species listed below are best grown with morning sun or light shade; most need protection from intense heat, drought, and afternoon sun. Soil should be rich, well-drained, and moist. Divide clumps in spring or fall or grow from seeds to increase stock. Some will self-sow. Bigroot cranesbill likes more shade than the other two species listed here, but flowering will be sparse without adequate light. Where summers are hot and dry 'Johnson's Blue' requires moist soil and afternoon shade.

Uses
Ground cover, borders, wild or rock gardens.

'Johnson's Blue' *p. 145*
Cranesbill. To 2 ft. high. Flowers profuse, 1½–2 in. wide, petals blue with darker blue veins. Long flowering season beginning in early summer. Probably a hybrid of *G. pratense* and *G. himalayense*. Zone 4.

macrorrhizum *p. 225*
Bigroot cranesbill. Aromatic perennial, 12–18 in. high. Leaves nearly evergreen, deeply parted. Flowers magenta or pink, 1 in. wide, in early summer. Cultivars include 'Album', with white flowers and red calyxes, and 'Ingwersen's Variety', a pale pink. Southern Europe. Zone 5.

maculatum *p. 146*　*Pictured above*
Wild geranium. 12–20 in. high. Flowers 1 in. wide, pale lilac. Eastern U.S., especially in rocky woods. Zone 5.

Hakonechloa
Hack-oh-nee-cloh'a
Gramineae. Grass family

Description
A genus of low-growing, rhizomatous grasses recently introduced into cultivation from Japan. One species is widely available here.

How to Grow
Prefers part to light shade, preferably under limbed-up deciduous trees. Will tolerate moderately full shade. Needs fertile,
well-drained garden soil. Propagate by division.

Uses
Accent, ground cover, mixed border.

macra 'Aureola' *p. 260*
Golden variegated hakonechloa. Slowly spreading deciduous
perennial to 18 in. high. Graceful arching habit. Leaves to 8
in. long, narrow, bright yellow with fine green stripes. Autumn
foliage buff-colored, handsome. Inflorescence a delicate open
panicle, blooming in late summer. Zone 5.

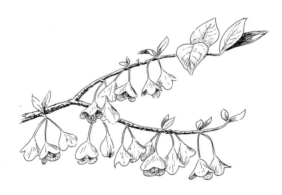

Halesia
Ha-lee'zi-a
Styracaceae. Storax family

Description
Five species of handsome, medium-sized trees from the southeastern U.S. and one from China. Prized for their white, bell-
shaped flowers in spring.

How to Grow
Halesias thrive in part, light, or dappled shade. They grow best along stream banks, in acid, moist but well-drained soil. Hardy, pest-free, and seldom in need of pruning.

Uses
For edges of woodlands, specimen trees. Spectacular against taller evergreens.

carolina *p. 84   Pictured on p. 361*
Silverbell tree, snowdrop tree. Round-headed, deciduous tree, usually reaching 30–40 ft. high. Leaves 2–4 in. long, yellow-green in fall. Numerous drooping clusters of white flowers in spring. Attractive bark is gray with off-white stripes. The related mountain silverbell, *H. monticola,* is a larger tree with larger flowers. Both native to the South. Best in zones 5–8.

Hamamelis
Ha-ma-mell′is. Witch hazel
Hamamelidaceae. Witch hazel family

Description
A small genus of shrubs and small trees native to North America and East Asia. Ornamental hallmarks are its fragrant flowers in the off-seasons and brilliant fall foliage. The leaves are alternate, oval to round, more or less wavy-toothed. Four-petaled flowers are yellow or reddish, crumpled in bud, unwinding like watchsprings. Curious, explosive seedpods pop open, propelling 2 shiny black seeds a considerable distance.

How to Grow
Witch hazels are suitable for a range of shade, from part to moderately full; of the two species listed below, *H. virginiana* can tolerate more. Needs adequate indirect light for good flow-

ering and fall color, however. Easy to grow in ordinary or moist garden soil and quite pest-free. Prune lightly, selectively to control size if garden is small or shape branching structure.

Uses
Valuable in shrub borders, as naturalized thickets or backgrounds in mixed borders, specimens.

× *intermedia* 'Arnold Promise' *p. 105*
Hybrid witch hazel. Deciduous shrub or small tree, to 20 ft. high. Leaves 3–4 in. long, turning yellow to red in fall. Flowers on bare twigs, winter to spring. This popular cultivar has fragrant yellow flowers. Another variety, 'Jelena', has copper-colored flowers and orange-red fall color; 'Ruby Glow' has coppery-red flowers and orange-red foliage in fall. All are choice hybrids derived from two Asian species, *H. japonica* and *H. mollis*. Zone 5.

virginiana *p. 105* *Pictured on p. 362*
Common witch hazel. Deciduous shrub, somewhat rustic and coarse in aspect, growing about 20 ft. high and about as wide. Leaves 4–6 in. long, toothed, yellow in fall. Flowers fall- or winter-blooming, fragrant, bright yellow, ¾ in. long, and long-lasting. Native to eastern North America. Zone 4.

Hedera
Hed'er-ra
Araliaceae. Aralia family

Description
Evergreen woody vines from northern Eurasia and northern Africa, generally called ivy. One is perhaps the best-known and most used climbing vine, and a mainstay in shade gardens.

How to Grow

Ivy thrives in shade, light to deep, where summers are hot or where winters or overexposure to sun will scorch foliage. It grows well in a rich, moist soil, though ivy will tolerate unpromising conditions surprisingly well. Aerial rootlets cling to masonry, brick, and tree bark. Ivy will hide a chain-link fence, but it does not twine and must be first trained into the links. Prune heavily or shear for desired habit and compact growth. Cut back as needed to keep ivy off wooden structures and out of gutters and drains, where it will cause problems. Easy to grow from cuttings or simply half-burying young stems with whiskery rootlets in damp mixture. Common ivy can be invasive in some sites; where soil is drier, poorer, and winters longer and colder, it may take several years to establish. Hardiness varies according to cultivar.

Uses

Versatile plant, perhaps best known as a clinging vine on brick or masonry. It will grow on trees quite handsomely, but may dangerously obscure dead limbs. Ground cover under trees where grass cannot be maintained. Deep roots help control soil erosion on slopes. Fancy-leaved cultivars are less aggressive and ideal in containers, as specimen or accent plants.

helix 'Baltica' *p. 249   Pictured on p. 363*

English ivy. Evergreen vine, creeping or climbing to 50 ft. high. Juvenile leaves 3- to 5-lobed, about 3 in. long; leaves on flowering branches of mature plants are larger, squarish, not lobed. Berries are tiny, round, and black. This vigorous cultivar is a hardy form with medium-sized triangular leaves and white veins. Other garden varieties include 'Buttercup', with brighter green foliage; 'Glacier' and 'Goldheart', both variegated; the widely planted, glossy-leaved 'Hibernica'; 'Ivalace', a bushy spreader for small areas; and 'Thorndale', said to be hardy to 20 degrees below zero. All these are hardy to zone 6. 'Needlepoint', 'Deltoidea', 'Fan', and 'Dragon's Claw' are among the fancy-leaved cultivars that are well suited to the South.

Helianthus

He-li-an'thus. Sunflower
Compositae. Daisy family

Description

A genus of 150 species of coarse, sturdy annuals and perennials, most from North America. They are very diverse in size and character since they hybridize readily in their natural surroundings; some are spreading, invasive plants. The leaves are hairy, sticky, and coarsely toothed. The daisylike flowers are mostly yellow or gold and range in size from 3 to 12 in. followed by great heads of edible seeds enclosed in woody husks, much loved by birds, bats, mice, and schoolchildren.

How to Grow
Sunflowers are of limited use to northern shade-gardeners, but they are well suited to part shade in hotter climates. They need light, dry, well-drained soil. They are drought resistant and grow best in warm to hot weather. Sow seeds outdoors after all danger of frost has passed. Seedlings sown outdoors grow quickly. Depending on the variety, space the plants 1–4 ft. apart. Tall varieties may need to be staked.

Uses
Informal areas, quick screens, and bird and wildlife plantings. An excellent plant for an edible flower garden, or for children to grow. Smaller varieties suitable for container culture, cutting, and autumn arrangements when dried.

annuus p. 178
Common sunflower. To 12 ft. high. Flowers in heads to 1 ft. or more across, white, many shades of yellow, orange, chestnut, maroon, or bicolored, the disk flowers purplish brown. Native Minnesota to Washington and California. Hardy annual.

annuus × *hybrida p. 178*
Hybrid varieties of common sunflower include a much broader range of colors, from cream, yellow, and gold through mahogany and burgundy, and include bicolors and double forms. They are generally smaller, more branching, and with smaller flowers than the seedhead types, well suited for ornamental use. Hardy annual.

annuus 'Italian White' *p. 179*
This cultivar grows only about 6 ft. high, with flowerheads also smaller than the species; cream-colored petals and a chocolate eye. Good for cutting. Hardy annual.

Helictotrichon
Hel-lick-toe-try'kon
Gramineae. Grass family

Description
About 30 species of perennial grasses native to Eurasia and North America, a few grown for ornament.

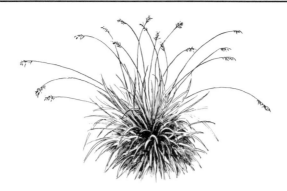

How to Grow
Grow in part to light shade. Soil should be well drained and not too acid. Established plants tolerate dryness. Cut back in late winter to groom and rejuvenate, or "comb" out dead leaves. Not well suited to the South.

Uses
Handsome in groups or specimen clumps.

sempervirens *p. 261   Pictured above*
Blue oat grass, avena grass. To 2 ft. high. Clump-forming perennial. Foliage blue, glaucous, with narrow blades 1 ft. long, stiff and arching. Flowering stems to 3 ft. long, one-sided with few spikelets, held well above the leaves in summer. Evergreen except at northern limits of hardiness. Frequently listed as *Avena sempervirens*. Europe. Zone 4.

Helleborus
Hell-e-bore'rus
Ranunculus. Buttercup family

Description
A small genus of Eurasian herbs with thick, fibrous roots and divided evergreen leaves. Flowers are showy, nodding, very long-lasting in the garden. Some are the source of drugs; the root of *H. niger* is a violent poison.

How to Grow
Shade-loving, hellebores enjoy part, light, to moderately full shade, depending on climate and moisture. The genus prefers moisture but will adapt to most garden soils. Hellebores form clumps and also spread by self-sowing. If handled carefully, brittle roots may be successfully divided in late summer. Pest-

free, long-lived perennials where conditions are to their liking. A translucent cover over plants in winter will help prevent damage from snow, ice, and rain. *H. orientalis* is the easiest species to grow and most shade-tolerant of the species listed here.

Uses
Wildflower nooks, in bulb beds, in rock gardens, naturalizing.

lividus p. 146
Hellebore. To 24 in. high. Evergreen. Flowers nodding, nearly 2½ in. wide, greenish yellow, borne in a profuse cluster of 15–20 flowers in spring. At temperatures below 5 degrees F, foliage becomes tattered. Also sold as *H. corsicus*. Zone 8.

niger p. 147
Christmas rose. To 12 in. high. Flowers nearly 3 in. wide, white or pinkish green. Depending on locality, plant blooms in late fall, Christmas, or early spring, sometimes under snow. With winter protection, hardy to zone 4.

orientalis p. 147 Pictured above
Lenten rose. To 18 in. high with a cluster of 2–6 flowers, 2 in. wide, cream, purplish pink, or greenish white fading to brown in early spring or winter on a branched, leafless stem. Zone 5.

Hemerocallis
Hem-mer-o-kal′lis
Liliaceae. Lily family

Description
About 15 species of perennial flowers, native from Central Europe to Japan. Fleshy roots send up narrow, sword-shaped,

arching leaves from the base of the plant. Clusters of funnel or bell-shaped flowers appear atop taller upright stalks in late spring to fall, depending on variety. Flowers may be single or double, funnel- to trumpet-shaped, and sometimes ruffled. Colors include off-white, yellow, gold, orange, pink, and red. There are also small-flowered and dwarf forms. Among the best of herbaceous perennials.

How to Grow
Daylilies are easy to grow. They are suitable for part to light shade, often needing protection from intense sun in hot climates or on southern exposures. In most locations they will need 4–6 hours of sun for best flowering and overall performance.

Daylilies flower freely and resist disease. They adapt well to many locations, prefering moist but well-drained soil. Individual flowers last only a day, but others follow on branched stems; some may flower a second time in the season. By selecting different varieties it is possible to have flowers from late spring until fall. Increase by division of clumps. Whenever growth gets too congested, divide and replant in late summer or early spring. Removal of gone-by flowers and dead stalks improves appearance of large-flowered hybrids. To avoid such chores in large plantings, choose species and smaller-flowered varieties. Evergreen varieties are better suited for the South, but with protection may survive further north.

Uses
Versatile for beds, borders, massed plantings, edgings, naturalizing in open areas or slopes, where they will help control erosion. Choice varieties suitable as ground cover. Flowerbuds of some species used in Chinese cookery.

aurantiaca p. 204
Spreading, 3 ft. tall and summer-blooming. Flowers burnt-orange to salmon, 4 in. across. China. Zone 7.

fulva p. 204
Tawny daylily, cornlily. To 5 ft. high. Leaves 2 ft. long. Flowers to 5 in. long, orange-red, often with dark lines, blooming in summer. May crowd out choice cultivars if planted in the same bed. Eurasia and naturalized in eastern U.S. Zone 3.

Hybrids *p. 205 Pictured on p. 369*
Hybrid daylilies. There are many hybrid varieties, evergreen and deciduous, varying in height from 2½ to 3½ ft. Flowers range from 2 to 7 in. wide, in shades of cream, yellow, orange, salmon, rose, pink, to mauve and lavender. Some are bicolored

or have ruffled petals; some are fragrant; most have one or more bursts of flowering between early June and late September. Compact varieties have flower stalks 12–18 in. high, tall cultivars reach 36 in. or higher. Evergreen varieties are hardy to zones 6 or 7, depending on variety and climate. Generally, hybrids survive winters to zone 4.

'Hyperion' *p. 205*
Introduced in the 1920s, this cultivar is still one of the best performers, 4 ft. tall with lemon-yellow, medium-sized, mid-season flowers of good substance, and graceful foliage. Long the standard by which other yellows are judged. Zone 4.

Heuchera
Hew'ker-a. Alumroot
Saxifragaceae. Saxifrage family

Description
About 40 species of attractive North American perennial herbs, chiefly from the Rocky Mountain region.

How to Grow
Coral-bells is well suited to part shade. In hotter climates, it grows best in light shade. It requires fertile, well-drained soil with lots of humus. In winter, good drainage is important and plants may need mulching. Grow from divisions or seed in spring; divide every 3–4 years, discarding old, woody rootstocks.

Uses
Front of borders, raised beds, atop retaining walls, rock gardens. Sprays of bloom have an airy texture, excellent in arrangements.

sanguinea p. 148
Coral-bells. Best known and easiest to grow. Tidy rosettes of small leaves, lobed and crisp, stems 1–2 ft. high. Small, bell-shaped red flowers with long-flowering season, beginning in early summer. Most coral-bells are cultivars or hybrids of this species; there are pink and white varieties, and a mixture may be grown from seed. Native to the Southwest. Zone 4. (Closely related *H. americana* and *Heucherella* are better suited for the South.)

Hibiscus
Hy-bis′kus
Malvaceae. Mallow family

Description
An important genus of more than 250 species of herbs, shrubs, and trees. Gardeners have long favored the shrubs for their showy flowers.

How to Grow
The species listed here needs good drainage and is suitable for afternoon or light shade. Vigorous growth can be promoted by pruning ⅓ of the older stems out each spring. Light nipping of remaining stem tips in spring and summer promotes more flowers. Propagate by seeds or softwood cuttings taken in summer.

Uses
Late, showy bloom makes it valuable in the shrub border or larger garden.

syriacus 'Althea' p. 106
Rose-of-Sharon, shrub althea. A deciduous shrub, 5–15 ft. high, with ovalish leaves 2–5 in. long, sharply toothed, and often late to leaf out. Flowers 3–5 in. wide and very showy, candy-pink with a darker eye and prominent yellow stamens in this cultivar. Species varies from red, purple, violet, or white, broadly bell-shaped. Some other popular cultivars are 'Diana', with large white flowers; 'Helene', whose white flowers have a reddish purple base; 'Blushing Bride', with double pink flowers; and 'Collie Mullens', with double lavender flowers. Bloom summer to fall and the only really hardy shrubs of the genus. China. Zone 5.

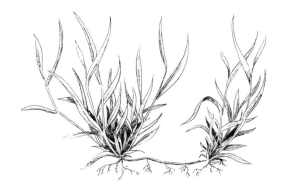

Holcus
Hol'kus
Gramineae. Grass family

Description
Perennial grasses native to Eurasia, closely related to oats *(Avena)* and bent grass *(Agrostis)*.

How to Grow
Leaf colors are best in part or light shade. Grows well in fertile, moist, well-drained soil. Will brown out in dry soil. Propagate by division.

Uses
Suitable for ground cover or border-edging.

mollis **'Albo-variegatus'** *p. 261 Pictured above*
Variegated velvet grass. Creeping rhizomes and spreading stems to 12 in. high. Leaves striped green and white, hairy. Often listed as *H. mollis 'Variegatus'*; the similar *H. lanatus 'Variegatus'* has erect rather than spreading stems and is suited for specimen use or borders. Zone 5.

Hosta
Hos'ta
Liliaceae. Lily family

Description
About 25 species of herbaceous perennials, all from China, Korea, and Japan. Numerous cultivars are grown for their handsome basal leaves; they have white, lilac, or blue flowers in midsummer. Some are fragrant. Hosta species hybridize and sport readily, and hundreds of fancy-leaf selections have been

named. Hostas are superb, versatile plants for the shady garden and easy to grow.

How to Grow
Hostas prosper in a range of light conditions, from east-facing borders to the light, dappled shade of deciduous trees to moderately full shade. Though many will survive quite dark corners, overall performance will be more satisfactory with good indirect or morning light. Fine specimens that improve with age, a clump of hostas can grow in the same place for 20 years or more; on the other hand, many readily forgive uplifting, dividing, and transplanting better than most herbaceous perennials. Hostas do best in moist soil, but need good drainage, especially in winter. Seek control of leaf-eating slugs and snails with baits or traps; root-eating voles with cats or traps; and blights with fungicide. Adequate light, air circulation, and mixing with other plants will go a long way toward healthy culture.

Uses
Versatile tribe of ground covers, border and edging plants, massed under trees, or accents. Excellent for skirting latticework around porches or wherever an herbaceous foundation planting is desired. Some small varieties make choice rock garden subjects.

fortunei **'Aureo-marginata'** *p. 225*
Fortune's hosta. Perennial, 2 ft. or more high. Leaf blades to 5 in. long, egg-shaped, green with yellow or gold border. Flowers lilac to violet, to 1½ in. long. Blooms in midsummer. Zone 4.

'Ginko Craig' *p. 226*
Ginko craig hosta. About 10 in. high. Among the best of the hybrids for ground cover, with medium-sized, dark green, white-margined lance-shaped leaves. Zone 4.

'Krossa Regal' *p. 226 Pictured on p. 372*
Krossa regal hosta. To 3 ft. high. Leaf blades silvery blue,
boldly veined, in basal cluster. Flowers lavender, trumpet-
shaped, 2–3 in. long, at top of stalk to 5 ft. high, blooming
in late summer. Zone 4.

lancifolia *p. 227*
Narrowleaf hosta. Perennial, 2 ft. high. Leaf blades 4–6 in.
long, lance-shaped or narrower, often with a long point. Flowers violet, to 2 in. long. A fast-growing, resilient hosta that
forms a cascading mound of leaves. Blooms in late summer.
Zone 4.

sieboldiana *p. 227*
Siebold plantain lily. To 2½ ft. high. Great rosettes of oval to
heart-shaped, 10–15 in. long, blue-gray, puckered leaves.
Flowers pale lilac, to 1½ in. long, on a stalk generally shorter
than the leaves, but nevertheless decorative. Blooms in midsummer. Cultivar 'Elegans' is a sumptuous plant with even
larger leaves. Foliage of 'Frances Williams' has gold margins.
Mature clumps are outstanding specimens. Zone 4.

Hydrangea
Hy-dran'jee-a
Saxifragaceae. Saxifrage family

Description
Deciduous shrubs and woody vines, cultivated for their showy
flower clusters in summer. Most garden sorts are Asiatic or
North American.

How to Grow
Hydrangeas enjoy part to moderate shade and rich, moist,
well-drained soil. The climber, usually propagated from seed,
is a notoriously slow starter and may need irrigation regularly
in its early years. Expect it to take off in earnest in its third
or fourth year. Mature growth may need light pruning.
   Oakleaf hydrangea, the shrubby species listed here, is propagated by suckers or layering. It benefits from light pruning
to maintain size and shape and remove any winter-killed
branches. Space container-grown plants 6 ft. apart for hedges.

Uses
Climbing hydrangea clings well to brick or masonry or tree
trunks. *H. quercifolia* is well-suited to mixed borders, informal
hedges, massing.

anomala petiolaris p. 249
Climbing hydrangea. Woody deciduous vine climbing by aerial
rootlets, to 50–60 ft. high. Leaves broadly oval, rounded or
heart-shaped at base, 2–5 in. long. Flower clusters loose,
white, 6–12 in. wide, in summer. Nice golden autumn foliage
color. May be sold as *H. petiolaris*. China and Japan. Zone 4.

quercifolia p. 106
Oakleaf hydrangea. A coarse-textured shrub, to 6 ft. high,
with hairy, reddish twigs and flaky bark. Large oak-shaped
leaves with 3–7 toothed lobes, often turning a rich reddish
purple in fall. Showy upright clusters of flowers, white in June,
turning pink or tan later in the summer and persisting into
autumn. Named cultivars like 'Snowflake' and 'Snow Queen'
have larger, heavier flower clusters. Native to southeastern
U.S., and tolerant of heat. Zone 5.

Ilex
Eye'lecks
Aquifoliaceae. Holly family

Description
About 400 species of valuable evergreen and deciduous shrubs
and trees from temperate and tropical regions. Many are grown
for their ornamental leaves, showy fruits, and pleasing shapes.
The leaves are alternate, sometimes spiny-toothed. Male and
female flowers, borne on separate plants, are white, yellow, or
greenish, inconspicuous. Generally, both sexes must be grown
together to produce berries, which form on female plants.
Fruits are usually red, black, sometimes yellow, and showy.

How to Grow
Hollies are excellent broad-leaved evergreens for part to light
shade. The genus thrives in moist, well-drained, slightly acid
soil. Keep balled and burlapped or keep container-grown
plants moist until planting; water freely the first year or two.
Evergreen species are slower growing and more difficult to
establish than deciduous ones, but are more valuable as ornamentals. They need careful siting, to protect leaves from
harsh winter sun in northern areas and from afternoon sun
in the South. Of the species listed here, Japanese holly enjoys
the most shade. Like other deciduous hollies, winterberry holly
needs adequate indirect light to flourish.

Pruning
As specimens, hollies need only light, selective pruning, at
most, to groom and shape. Some are useful as hedges; pruning

young plants early on will force them to put out extra stems. Thereafter, one pruning in spring before new growth begins and a moderate follow-up later in the season should suffice.

Uses
Versatile group of woody plants for hedges, screens, specimens, borders, foundation plants, and boughs for winter arrangements. Evergreen hollies make good food and cover for wildlife.

× *attenuata* 'Fosteri' *p. 107*
Foster's hybrid hollies. A varied group of evergreen shrubs or small trees, 10–25 ft. high, depending on variety and pruning regimen. Most have small, light green, lightly toothed, narrow leaves and small scarlet berries. This hybrid group includes 'East Palatka', 'Foster's', and 'Savannah' hollies. All are prized for their narrow form and are popular as foundation plants, hedges, and specimens. Well suited to the South. Hybrid in origin. Zone 6.

***cornuta* 'Rotunda'** *p. 107*
Chinese holly. Dense-branched, spiny-textured, evergreen shrub or tree, usually 8–15 ft. high, but in this dwarf male (berryless) form only about 18 in. tall. The angular, lustrous leaves have 3 spines at the tip and 1 or 2 along the sides. Once established, tolerates heat and dryness better than most hollies. The closely related female cultivar 'Burfordii' can reach 20–25 ft.; it has bright green wedge-shaped leaves with only a few spines at the tip. Red berries, ½ in. wide, are produced without fertilization so it is not necessary to have a male tree nearby. Too large for most foundation plantings, it is best used as a large specimen shrub or pruned into a small tree. China. Zone 7.

***crenata* 'Helleri'** *p. 108*
Japanese holly. An extremely handsome dwarf female evergreen shrub with small, fine-toothed leaves. Fruit black, not showy. There are other cultivars with compact, spreading, or upright growth form. The species ranges 5–10 ft. high. Insists on slightly acid soil; don't plant near concrete or where soil may contain other alkaline construction debris. Often used in foundation plantings and hedges. Japan. Zone 6.

× *meserveae* *p. 108*
Meserve holly. A class of evergreen shrubs, 8–12 ft. high, resembling *I. aquifolium* but with twigs deep purple and leaves purplish green. 'Blue Princess' has dark, blue-green leaves and numerous berries; 'Blue Prince' has a compact, pyramidal

shape and no berries. 'Blue Maid' is hardy and fast-growing, and 'Blue Angel' has small, crinkled, shiny leaves and dark red berries. 'Blue Stallion', a tall male, is a suitable pollenizer for the entire group. Meserve holly is probably the best evergreen holly for Northern areas. Cross of a European with a Japanese species. Zone 5.

verticillata *p. 109   Pictured above*
Winterberry. A deciduous, usually spreading shrub 5–15 ft. high, grown mostly for its bright red fruits, which are more profuse than in any other holly, borne in early winter on the bare stems and persisting until songbirds eat them. Leaves are 1½ to 3 in. long, toothed but not spiny. Tolerant of poor drainage. 'Chrysocarpa' has yellow fruit. Eastern North America. Zone 4.

Impatiens
Im-pay′shens
Balsaminaceae. Balsam family

Description
Nearly 500 species of tender, succulent plants, widely distributed in Asia, tropical Africa, and North America, including an important group of warm weather annuals which flower heavily in the shade. Simple leaves, alternate, opposite, or whorled. Flowers slightly irregular, spurred, solitary or clustered, and typically white, pink, salmon, or red. Some cultivars have showy or variegated leaves. Seedpods, when ripe, explode at a touch.

How to Grow
All 3 species prefer warm weather. Flowering will be more satisfactory if plants are grown in well-drained, fertile soil with plenty of moisture and regular fertilizing during flowering.

I. balsamina and *I. wallerana*

Old-fashioned impatiens and their modern descendants *(I. wallerana)* are shade-loving plants, adapting to a range of light from morning sun to nearly full shade. Where summers are hot, this species needs at least light to moderate shade. *I. balsamina* is well suited to part or light shade.

These annuals are easy to grow from purchased bedding-size plants, cuttings, or seed. Start seed indoors 6–8 weeks before last frost at 70–75 degrees F. Do not cover seeds with soil; they need light to sprout. Stretch clear plastic over the flat and plant seedlings outdoors 2 weeks after danger of frost is past.

New Guinea impatiens

The New Guinea group enjoys more light, prospering with light or less than half-shade in the north, and thriving with more shade in sunnier and hotter climates. The New Guineas must be started from cuttings or nursery-grown seedlings.

Uses

Endless possibilities for bedding, containers, urns; filler in immature borders. Larger ones make excellent annual hedges. Informal masses of *I. balsamina* lend a old-fashioned, Victorian flavor to summer flower beds. An easy and exciting plant for a child's garden.

balsamina *p. 179*

Garden balsam, lady's slipper. 24–30 in. tall, and stiff in habit. Flowers 1–2 in. wide, some very double or camellia-flowered, in salmon pink, old rose, scarlet, yellow, purple, or white. Subtropical India and China. Tender annual.

'New Guinea' *p. 180*

Very showy 1–2-ft.-high plants. Leaves bicolored or variegated and substantial in texture and appearance. Flowers extra-large, typically red to pinkish purple. New Guinea. Tender annual.

wallerana p. 180   Pictured on p. 377
Impatiens, patience plant, sultana. Brittle, 1–2 ft. high plants.
Flowers solitary or 2–3 on a short, slender stalk, 1–2 in. wide.
Bright scarlet in original form, but hybrids are red, pink, orange, salmon, purple, white, or variegated. Some forms are
compact or dwarf. Tanzania to Mozambique. Tender perennial, often grown as a summer annual.

Imperata
Im-per-a′ta. Blood grass
Gramineae. Grass family

Description
A genus of ornamental grasses recently introduced into cultivation in the U.S.

How to Grow
Suitable for part to light shade and prefers reasonably fertile,
moist, well-drained garden soil. Increase by division.

Uses
Mass plants in a border, or use mature clumps for accent. This
variety is especially striking if sited so that nothing else inter-
feres with sun shining through foliage; red leaves seem to glow
intensely when backlit.

cylindrica rubra p. 262
Japanese blood grass. Tufted perennial grass of upright, open
habit, to 12 in high. Leaf sheaths cylindrical, blades flat. Leaves
deep red throughout the growing season. Japan. Zone 5, with
protection. Reliably cold-hardy to Zone 6.

Iris
Eye′ris
Iridaceae. Iris family

Description
Over 150 species of herbaceous perennials, mostly from the
north temperate zone. Irises have stout rhizomes or bulbous
rootstocks; narrow, often sword-shaped leaves; and showy
flowers. There are thousands of horticultural varieties.

How to Grow
Most garden irises prefer sun and sharp drainage. The exceptional species listed below prefers humusy, moist soil in part

shade. Plant rhizome slightly exposed, with leaves pointing in the direction you wish plant to grow. Rhizomes may rot if they are covered. *I. cristata* is mat-forming and does not require frequent division. It may also be propagated by seed and is prey to slugs.

Uses
Borders and rock gardens.

cristata *p. 148   Pictured above*
Crested iris. 4–6 in. high. Rhizomatous species with narrow, bladelike, light green leaves. Flowers lavender-blue with yellow crest, outer segments 1½ in. long, faintly fragrant, in mid- to late spring. White and light blue horticultural varieties available. Spreads to form wide clumps. Native to the Southeast. Zone 4.

Itea
It′ee-a
Saxifragaceae. Saxifrage family

Description
A small genus of shrubs or trees cultivated for their showy flowers and autumn leaves.

How to Grow
Virginia sweet spire adapts to varying amounts of shade, preferring part to light, but tolerating moderately full shade. It is easy to grow in well-drained, moist soil. Tolerates heat if moisture is plentiful. Lightly prune to groom specimen plantings if needed. Propagated by cuttings taken in late spring or by division in spring or fall.

Uses
Best naturalized or as a specimen in large shrub borders.

virginica p. 109
Virginia sweet spire. Deciduous shrub, 4–8 ft. high with graceful arching branches. Spreads to form colonies. The leaves are
oval, 2–4 in. long, bright red in fall. Upright clusters 4–6 in.
long, of small, white, fragrant flowers, blooming from late
spring to early summer. 'Henry's Maroon' has rich garnet-
colored foliage in autumn. Native New Jersey to Florida and
Texas. Zone 5.

Jasminum
Jas'mi-num
Oleaceae. Olive family

Description
The jasmines comprise 200 species of climbing or spreading
shrubs or vines widely cultivated for their attractive fragrant
flowers and neat compound leaves. Chiefly tropical and subtropical natives of Eurasia and Africa.

How to Grow
Most garden jasmines are tender plants preferring loamy soil,
sun, and a warm climate. The species listed below is suitable for part to light shade and is somewhat cold-hardy,
more so if given a protected niche. Prune lightly to shape and
train after flowering; blossoms are produced on wood of previous season. Propagate by layers and cuttings of nearly ripe
wood.

Uses
Winter jasmine is perhaps best trained as a vine against or
over a wall or a rock.

nudiflorum p. 110
Winter jasmine. Deciduous, semi-shrubby scrambling plant by
nature, 4–5 ft. high, with stiff, arching 4-angled branches.
Leaves opposite, dark green, with 3 oval leaflets 1 in. long.
Flowers yellow, ¾–1 in. across, solitary along branches of
previous season, appearing in winter or spring before the
leaves. China. Zone 7, or protected niches in zone 6.

Kalmia
Kal'mi-a.
Ericaceae. Heath family

Description
Shrubs, mostly with small, narrow, evergreen leaves, from North America. Mountain laurel is an exceptionally handsome plant in bloom, one of the choicest broad-leaved evergreen shrubs for cold climates.

How to Grow
Kalmias enjoy part, light, to moderately full shade, and require moist, peaty, acid soil. They can tolerate rather dry, exposed places once established, but they will need a permanent mulch of oak or beech leaves — and more close attention and watering when young. Nurseries propagate by seed; gardeners usually acquire plants as container stock in spring.

Uses
Excellent shrub for wild or formal plantings or accent. Old specimens develop interesting lines and can often be trained as garden bonsai.

latifolia p. 110 *Pictured above*
Mountain laurel, calico bush. Round-topped shrub, usually growing 7–15 ft. high, though occasionally becoming a small tree. Leaves evergreen, oval, alternate or sometimes whorled, 2–4 in. long. Confection-like flowers are pointed and darker in bud, opening to round cups or disks, rose to white, nearly red in some cultivars, ¾ in. across, in larger terminal clusters 4–6 in. wide. Blooms in late spring. Look for 'Silver Dollar', a large-flowered white, and 'Ostbo Red', an exceptional dark-flowered cultivar. New England to Florida and Louisiana. Zone 5.

Kerria

Ker'ri-a
Rosaceae. Rose family

Description
One Chinese species, a deciduous shrub, grown for its yellow
flowers and green stems in winter.

How to Grow
Kerria will thrive in part to full shade and is easy to grow in
ordinary garden soil. Tolerant of urban conditions and of poor
if well-drained soil. Prune the shrub after flowering; thin old
stems at the base every few years to maintain vigor and bright
stem color. Propagate by divisions or cuttings.

Uses
Mass plantings, hedges, especially where choice is limited by
poor growing conditions. Better in natural clumps than formal
rows or pairs.

japonica '**Pleniflora**' *p. 111   Pictured above*
Japanese rose. Deciduous shrub with slender green branches,
growing 4–6 ft. high. Medium-sized, narrow leaves. Bright
gold double pompons of flowers, 1½ in. wide, in spring. 'Shan-
non' has larger flowers. Zone 5.

Kirengeshoma

Keer-en-gay-show'ma
Saxifragaceae. Saxifrage family

Description
One or two perennial rhizomatous herbs native in Japan and
Korea and related to *Hydrangea*.

How to Grow

Does best in part, light, or moderately full shade, where soil is moisture-retentive and high in organic matter. Abundant additions of well-rotted, sifted compost or peat moss will improve growth.

Uses

Choice conversation piece for the shady border.

palmata p. 149
To 4 ft. Opposite leaves are lobed and toothed, resembling a maple's. Nodding, butter-yellow, bell-shaped flowers to 1½ in. long, borne in clusters. Zone 5.

Lamiastrum

Lay-mee-as'trum
Labiatae. Mint family

Description

One low-growing perennial herb, native to Europe and planted as a ground cover.

How to Grow

Lamiastrum is a durable, even rampant grower for almost any soil in part to moderate shade. Though prey to slugs, it is otherwise pest-free. Increase by cuttings or division.

Uses

Excellent ground cover for dry shade; also useful for obscuring old foliage. Similar to *Ajuga*.

galeobdolon 'Herman's Pride' *p. 228*
Yellow archangel. Herbaceous ground cover to 12 in. high. Opposite leaves are heart-shaped, small, with a pungent odor. This variety has silvery leaves veined with green. Dense clusters of yellow turtle-headed flowers in spring. 'Variegatum' has silvery leaves with green-spotted margin. Zone 4.

Lamium

Lay'mium. Dead nettle
Labiatae. Mint family

Description

About 40 species of Old World herbs with opposite leaves, square stems and clusters of small 2-lipped flowers. Like other ground covers in the mint family, can be weedy if not managed intelligently.

How to Grow
Lamium is easy to grow in ordinary moist garden soil in shade. Propagate by division or cuttings.

maculatum 'White Nancy' *p. 228*
Spotted dead nettle. A spreading herbaceous ground cover, about 9 in. high. This popular cultivar has small opposite silver leaves with green margins, white flowers, and is more restrained in its spread than the species. 'Beacon Silver' is much like it, with pink flowers. The species is taller, more vigorous, with a narrow white median stripe on the leaves and purplish blossoms. There are many other cultivars. 'Aureum' has yellow foliage with a white stripe; 'Chequers', with violet flowers, is best for the South. Zone 4.

Leucothoe
Lew-koth′o-ee
Ericaceae. Heath family

Description
Ornamental shrubs grown for their handsome dark foliage, graceful habit, and attractive fragrant early flowers. Evergreen species are low-growing and especially handsome, with thick leaves that turn red or bronze in winter.

How to Grow
The two evergreen species listed here prefer part to full shade, tolerating even more if other conditions are excellent. Leucothoes need moist, acid, peaty soil, or sandy loam with plenty of humus added. Prune carefully and lightly; cut back a few of the oldest canes at base of plant in spring to encourage new

suckers to replace them. Propagate by division, cuttings, seeds, or underground runners. Protect from drying by winter sun and wind. In some locations leaf spot diseases are a problem.

Uses
Shrubberies, foundation plantings, mixed borders. They grow well in open woods, and sprays make beautiful winter bouquets.

axillaris p. 111
Coast leucothoe, dog hobble. 4–5 ft. high shrub with arching branches. Leathery, pointed leaves, 2–4 in. long. White flowers in clusters between leaf and stem, 1–2 in. long, in spring. Native Virginia to Florida and Mississippi. Zone 6.

fontanesiana p. 112   Pictured on p. 384
Drooping leucothoe, fetter bush. 6-ft.-high shrub with slender, arching branches. Smooth stems and long-tipped leaves. White flowers in drooping 3-in.-long clusters along the branches in spring. Native Virginia to Georgia and Tennessee; hardiest of the evergreen leucothoes and slower-growing than *L. axillaris*. Cultivar 'Rainbow' has bright white, pink, and coppery new growth. 'Scarletta' has reddish purple leaf coloration. Zone 5.

Ligularia
Lig-you-lay′ri-a.
Compositae. Daisy family

Description
Handsome Eurasian herbs cultivated for their showy flower heads and large, sometimes variegated leaves.

How to Grow
These plants are easy to grow and do well in ordinary to moist garden soil. Exposed to intense sun and heat, the foliage flags. Morning light is acceptable in coolest climates; light shade is even better. Not a good choice for hot climates. Propagate by cuttings or division.

Uses
Specimens in borders, or massed in island beds.

✕ *przewalskii* 'The Rocket' *p. 149*
Rocket ligularia. Distinctive, outsize perennial, 4–6 ft. high. Leaves alternate, triangular to round, sharply toothed, stems blackish purple. Flowers yellow, ½ in. wide, in spikes 12–18 in. long. Zone 4.

Ligustrum
Ly-gus'trum. Privet
Oleaceae. Olive family

Description
A genus of 50 species of evergreen or deciduous shrubs, rarely trees, all from the Old World. Popularly used as hedging, since most species tolerate shearing, pollution, wind, and drought.

How to Grow
Privets are suitable for part to light shade. They are easy to grow and will adapt to any soil condition except constant wetness. They grow fast and transplant easily. Prune to shape at any time; remember that heavily trimmed plantings may need more frequent fertilizing and watering. Flowers and berries will of course be scant on manicured hedges. Propagated from softwood cuttings which root easily.

Uses
Small leaves and overall vigor make privet a versatile shrub for hedges, screens, and topiary. The species listed below is often grown in containers.

japonicum p. 112
Japanese privet. This evergreen shrub grows 7–10 ft. high. The 3–4-in.-long leaves are leathery and smooth, somewhat linear and glossy. The flowers are white, pungent, in 5-in. clusters at the ends of twigs in spring; blue-black berries follow in late summer or fall if flowers remain. Sometimes sold as *L. coriaceum,* the cultivar 'Rotundifolium' has lower, more compact growth, with lustrous dark green leaves that are more numerous than those on the species and nearly circular in outline. Japan and Korea. Zone 7.

Lilium
Lil'i-um
Liliaceae. Lily family

Description
An important ornamental genus of showy, summer-flowering bulbs. There are about 100 species native to the north temeprate zone, and a great many hybrids and cultivars. Leafy-stemmed, perennial herbs with one to many showy trumpet-shaped flowers, growing from scaly bulbs. These peerless creatures bloom for a few weeks in summer; the season may be happily extended by planting a variety of early to late types.

How to Grow

Lilies are excellent garden subjects, for the most part long-lived, thrifty, easy-going plants once established, and utterly rewarding in flower. All like well-drained soil, year-round moisture, and a cool, moist root-run provided by mulch or shade. Hybrids are generally easier to grow than species.

Siting

The lilies listed here are suitable for part to light shade. The martagon lily enjoys even more. All need protection from afternoon sun; flowers tend to bleach in overbright and hot situations and will not last as long. Prevent disease by placing lilies where there is good drainage, adequate air circulation, and enough light. Staking of taller, heavier-flowered varieties may be avoided by planting against a west-facing wall or fence.

Planting

Newly purchased bulbs should be solid, nearly dormant, and onionlike, showing little or no new roots or sprouts. Plant in fall or spring, setting them at least 3 times their diameter in depth; the exception is *L. candidum*. Bulbs should be handled as if they were transplants, and planted as soon as possible after purchasing or digging, or they will dry out or begin tormented growth out of the soil. In spring, do not walk on brittle new shoots or damage them with cultivating; plants may survive but you will lose the year's bloom.

Propagation

Once lilies are established, they do not need moving unless they become overcrowded or to increase stock. At end of summer or in the fall after frost, lift clumps gently with a spading fork, separate, and replant entire plant if in growth, bulbs if dormant. If moving whole plants, top stems by about a third, handle carefully during transition, replant to a similar depth, and water in as needed; many are surprisingly resilient if transplanting operation is speedy.

Enthusiasts also propagate lilies by bulb offsets, bulb scales, and in some species by seed or bulbils, incipient bulbs which grow in the leaf axils. These propagules can be grown on in nursery set-ups, under lights, in cold frames, and in greenhouses. Though it will take several years to obtain a flowering plant with most of these methods it is often a worthwhile project, for one learns a lot about individual types in the process and bulbs are often expensive.

Pests and Other Challenges

Good culture will prevent most problems. However, some lilies are susceptible to viral diseases spread by aphids; stunted plants or plants with yellow-streaked foliage should be culled and buried deeply in a remote corner. Discourage rodents by planting bulbs in buried cages of coarse hardware cloth, or keep cats. Lilies have a mixed reputation as garden plants south of zone 7, but the candidum hybrid is suitable for zone 8.

Uses
Outstanding perennial with suitable types for borders, sheltered nooks, at the foot of walls, rock gardens, naturalizing, cutting gardens, among ferns.

'Bellingham' *p. 206*
Pink American hybrid. 4–8 ft. high. Flowers 4–6 in. wide, nodding, lipstick-pink with darker freckles, long stems, summer-blooming. Others in this class may be red, pink, orange, and yellow. Derived from *L. parryi* and *L. pardalinum.* Zone 4.

'Black Dragon' *p. 206*
Bicolored Aurelian hybrid. 5–8 ft. tall. Flowers 6–8 in. long, wine-colored in bud, opening to sweetly, heavily scented, slightly nodding, white-lined trumpets in summer. Sepia-colored anthers, yellow throat, and burgundy crease on the petal backs further decorate the lush blooms. May also be classed as a Chinese or trumpet hybrid. Derived from several Asiatic species; others in this group may have blooms white, greenish white, yellow, orange, pink, and gold. Zone 4.

'Cascade' *p. 207*
Madonna lily. Candidum hybrid. 3–4 ft. tall. Flowers 4–5 in. wide, held close to stalk, narrow-petaled, outward-facing, pure white with golden anthers. Fragrant, summer-blooming. Plant candidum lilies shallowly, only 1 in. below the ground. Zone 5.

'Enchantment' *p. 207*
Red Asiatic hybrid. Plants grow 2–5 ft. high. Flowers 4–6 in. wide, upfacing and of a bright nasturtium red-orange with darker freckles and anthers. Early to midsummer. A popular lily, easy to grow, and vigorous. Similar 'Connecticut Lemonglow' has yellow blooms. Others may be white through yellow, orange, pink, lavender, and red, or combinations thereof, with or without spotting. Derived from Asiatic species. Zone 4.

'Golden Showers' *p. 208*
Yellow Aurelian hybrid. 4–6 ft. high. Golden flowers 8 in. wide, flared and slightly nodding with brown anthers. Summer-blooming. Zone 4.

'Imperial Silver' *p. 208*

White Oriental hybrid. Plants 2-½–7 ft. tall. Flowers fragrant, 8–10 in. wide, flat, and more outward-facing, with chestnut-stippled petals and anthers of the same color. Summer-blooming. The group varies greatly in form and color; most have freckled faces. Derived from Asiatic species. Zone 5.

'Jamboree' *p. 209*

Red Oriental hybrid. Plant 4–6 ft. tall. Flowers 6–8 in. wide, outward-facing with reflexed petals. Cherry-red with darker spots on inside, fading to a softer pink to white with mid-stripe on edges and backs. Summer-blooming. Zone 5.

martagon var. *album* *p. 209*

Turk's-cap lily, martagon lily. 4–6 ft. high. 2-in. flowers in late spring, drooping, segments turned back, white in this form. Typically, the species is purplish pink and dark-spotted; many horticultural varieties exist in these colors. Native to Eurasia. Zone 4.

parryi *p. 210*

Lemon lily. 4–6 ft. high. Flowers held more or less horizontal, funnel-shaped, fragrant, to 4 in. long, lemon-yellow, with or without maroon spots. Summer-blooming. California. Zone 7.

philadelphicum *p. 210*   *Pictured above*

Wood lily. 2–3 ft. high. Flowers erect, cup-shaped, to 4 in. long, orange-red with darker spots, in late spring to summer. Eastern North America. Zone 5.

superbum *p. 211*

Turk's-cap lily. 5–8 ft. high. Flowers drooping, segments reflexed, to 3 in. across, orange-red and dark-spotted, in summer. Eastern U.S. Summer. Zone 5.

washingtonianum *p. 211*
Washington lily. 4–6 ft. high. Leaves to 6 in. long. Flowers horizontal, funnel-shaped, fragrant, to 4 in. wide, white, often purple-spotted, summer-blooming. California. Zone 7.

Liriope
Li-ri'o-pe. Lilyturf
Liliaceae. Lily family

Description
Asiatic herbs with grasslike appearance and texture, evergreen in milder climates.

How to Grow
Enjoys part to full shade. Prefers fertile, moist, well-drained soil amended with organic matter; may tolerate occasional drought and seaside conditions once established. In cold-winter areas, foliage may become tattered or brown, but roots will probably survive; shear back clumps in spring to groom and promote regrowth. Prey to slugs and snails. Increase by division.

Uses
Ground cover.

***muscari* 'John Birch'** *p. 229   Pictured above*
Lilyturf. 18 in. high. Spreads to form thick mats of arching, straplike leaves, with creamy margins. Spikes of tiny blue flowers in summer followed by round black ornamental fruits in fall. Other forms may have purple or white flowers and green leaves. Zone 6.

Lobelia
Lo-bee′li-a
Lobeliaceae. Lobelia family

Description
A large genus of perennials or annuals popular for their showy spires of flowers in summer. Both species listed below are native to damp sites in eastern North America.

How to Grow
Lobelias need moist soil and part to light shade. Increase by dividing clumps in spring or fall. *L. cardinalis,* though perennial, is not long-lived but tends to self-sow. A dark background of ferns helps display its brilliant flowers. In the northern extent of its range, it does best in a moist, mulched, partly shaded wild garden with a few hours of sun. In warm climates, however, plant may rot in wet winters; to improve survival, keep leaf litter and mulch off the foliage. *L. siphilitica* may be prey to rust.

Uses
Borders, wild gardens, edgings.

cardinalis p. 150   Pictured above
Cardinal flower. Herbaceous perennial, 3–6 ft. high. Stems are topped with clusters of scarlet flowers, 1½ in. long, in summer. Zone 3.

siphilitica p. 150
Blue or great lobelia. Herbaceous perennial, 2–4 ft. high. Stems topped with clusters of blue flowers 1 in. long in late summer. Zone 5.

Lobularia

Lob-you-lair′i-a

Cruciferae. Mustard family

Description

A small genus of about 5 species of Mediterranean herbs, related to and sometimes classed as *Alyssum*. The plants listed below are perennials generally treated as annuals, low-growers admired for their carpets of small but numerous fragrant flowers in spring and summer.

How to Grow

Needs well-drained soil and part shade. Grows easily from seed sown in spring or fall or small bedding plants purchased before they have spent themselves in flowering in their flats. Self-sow under good conditions. Prefers cool conditions. If plants flag in midsummer, shear back foliage; a second flush of bloom often recurs when moister, cooler conditions return.

Uses

Fragrant plant for edging, containers, bedding. Kneels nicely over walls and the rims of ornamental pots. Good filler in a new rock garden.

maritima *p. 181*   *Pictured above*

Sweet alyssum. Generally less than a foot high, many-branched, spreading plant with narrow green leaves. Flowers pungent, numerous, tiny, usually white, lilac to pink, or purple, in gumdrop-shaped clusters ¾ in. wide. Cultivars may be more compact, have variegated leaves, or larger or double flowers. Hardy annual.

maritima 'Rosie O' Day' *p. 181*

Sweet alyssum. Similar in all respects to the species, except more free-flowering, with rosy-purple blooms. Hardy annual.

Loropetalum
Lor-o-pet′a-lum
Hamamelidaceae. Witch hazel family

Description
One species of Chinese shrub with evergreen leaves and fragrant white flowers.

How to Grow
Suitable for part to full shade. Prefers moist, well-drained acid soil rich in organic matter, but can withstand some dryness. Loropetalum is probably best when its natural habit is preserved, although it can survive severe pruning. Propagated by cuttings taken in summer.

Uses
Specimen, hedge, or foundation shrub.

chinense p. 113
Grows 6–12 ft. high, naturally in a casual, rounded shape but often rigidly pruned. Leaves are 1–2 in. long, ovalish. Clusters of small fragrant flowers 1 in. long line the stems in spring. Zone 7.

Lunaria
Loo-nay′ri-a
Cruciferae. Mustard family

Description
Two Eurasian herbs with satiny, parchmentlike round pods, which have inspired most of the plants' common names.

How to Grow
The species described below tolerates part to light shade, and more in hotter climates. It thrives in average to moist soil and

prefers cool weather. Sow seeds outdoors in early spring, or, where winters are mild, in fall. Rarely blooms the first season, but is quite winter-hardy and will live over to bloom in mid-spring the following year. Leave a few plants to reseed.

Uses
Chiefly grown for the unique silvery seed pods which are excellent in dried bouquets. The fragrant, somewhat weedy plant is also an easy candidate for naturalizing on shady banks.

annua *p. 182   Pictured on p. 393*
Honesty, moonwort, moneyplant, satin pod. 18–36 in. high. Flowers fragrant, purplish, to 1 in. long. Cultivar 'Alba' has white flowers, and there is also a form with variegated leaves, and another with purplish foliage. Native to South Europe; naturalized in North America. Biennial.

Lupinus
Loo-pine′us
Leguminosae. Pea family

Description
A genus of many species, widely distributed; mostly annuals and perennial herbs cultivated for the spikes of showy pealike flowers in the full spectrum of color, as well as their handsome compound leaves.

How to Grow
The species listed below enjoy shade in the afternoon; as a rule, the genus prefers sun. Lupines need at once excellent drainage and moist soil. They prefer cool weather and are not a good choice for areas with hot or dry summers. Aphids may be a pest. Where conditions are good, colonies will reseed and naturalize.

Gardeners have traditionally grown lupines from seed. In cooler climates, nick seeds with a file (they have a tough coat) and grow in flats 8–10 weeks before last frost; transplant to garden after danger of frost has passed. Where winters are mild, sow seeds in a well-groomed spot in fall. Increasingly, plants are available from nurseries; though you may not be able to tell what colors their flowers will be, small immature plants make more successful transplants than large pot-grown specimens.

Uses
Borders, naturalizing on moist banks. Before opening and elongating, the conical flowerheads resemble a pineapple in shape, lending interesting texture and accent to more mounding or vertical drifts of other perennials and effectively prolonging their own flowering season.

'Russell Hybrid' *p. 151*
Lupine. Perennial, 2–3 ft. high. Flowers in late spring, showy, like those of sweet-pea; ½–1 in. wide; white, red, pink, orange, yellow, blue, and purple — or any combination thereof. The pretty flowers are packed into dense, regular spires that punctuate handsome clumps of soft, blue-green palmate leaves. Particular colors may be obtained by purchasing plants in bud at a nursery; seed packages should contain most of the range. This group of British hybrids are perhaps the finest garden plants and certainly the most famous. Zone 5.

subcarnosus *p. 182*   *Pictured on p. 394*
Bluebonnet. 8–10 in. high. Flowers ½ in. long, unquestionably blue with a white or yellow beauty mark on the keel and typical lupine leaves. A rangier, wilder plant than the hybrids, and similar to *L. texensis,* the Texas bluebonnet, which is darker but likewise a native of that state. Hardy annual.

Luzula
Looz'you-la
Juncaceae. Rush family

Description
About 80 species of wood rushes of wide natural distribution, typically in rich, moist woodlands. Dense, tufted perennial ornamental grasses of fine to medium texture, both species listed below are stoloniferous. Leaves soft, flat, with hairy margins. Flowers in dense clusters of varying shapes.

How to Grow

Enjoys part, light, medium, to full shade. Prefers humus-rich, woodsy soil, but adapts to many garden soils. Cut back foliage in late winter if it becomes unsightly. Increase by seeds or division.

Uses

Ground cover, under trees and shrubs if moisture is adequate. Snowy wood rush is equally suitable for borders or rock gardens.

nivea p. 262

Snowy wood rush. Semi-evergreen of upright, arching habit, to 2 ft. high. Flowers in spring showy, white, in roundish umbels. Europe. Zone 4.

sylvatica p. 263

Greater wood rush. Strong-growing, forming bright green mounds to 12 in. high. Flowers in spring, rusty brown, in nodding terminal clusters held well above foliage. Europe and Asia Minor. Zone 5.

Lysimachia

Ly-si-mack′i-a. Loosestrife
Primulaceae. Primrose family

Description

About 165 species of widely distributed perennial herbs, a few grown for ornament. All are erect but creeping *L. nummularia*. Wheel- to bell-shaped, small but often numerous, usually white to yellow flowers, sometimes in clusters. Both species listed below are perennials native to Europe, naturalized in eastern North America, summer-blooming.

How to Grow
The species listed below prefer reasonably moist, well-drained sites in part to light shade; the ground cover likes even more shade. Will tolerate less moisture with more shade. Increase by division in spring or fall.

Uses
Moneywort is a good ground cover for moist soil. Garden loosestrifes, with showier floral displays and upright habit, are suitable for damp borders and naturalizing.

nummularia *p. 229   Pictured on p. 396*
Moneywort, creeping Jennie. Prostrate, to 2 in. high, with trailing stems that root easily at the joints. Leaves opposite, nearly round, ¾ in. wide. Solitary yellow flowers appear between leaf and stem. The golden-leaved cultivar 'Aurea' though less vigorous prefers more shade, needing protection from afternoon sun. Zone 4.

punctata *p. 151*
Yellow loosestrife. 2–3 ft. high. Flowers 1 in. wide, in whorls between stem and leaves, yellow, upfacing bell-shaped. Zone 5.

Machaeranthera
Ma-kee-ran'the-ra
Compositae. Daisy family

Description
A small genus of herbs, including one showy ornamental, found in western North America and closely related to *Aster*.

How to Grow
This species is suitable for part shade and needs well-drained soil with near-neutral pH. It grows best in cool, dry climates, but will have 4–6 weeks of color in warmer, humid environments. Start seeds indoors in early spring; break dormancy by mixing seeds with moist peat moss and refrigerating at 40 degrees F for 2–3 weeks. Transplant hardened-off seedlings after danger of hard frost is past, or sow seeds outdoors in early spring or fall.

Uses
Showy annual for part shade and drier soils.

tanacetifolia *p. 183*
Tahoka daisy. 1–2 ft. high. Flowerheads to 2 in. wide, lavender-blue, the rays slender and pointed. Half-hardy annual.

Magnolia
Mag-no′li-a
Magnoliaceae. Magnolia family

Description
About 125 species of trees and shrubs native to North America, Central America, and Asia. Many are grown for their spectacular spring flowers, handsome foliage, and graceful habit. Leaves are alternate, simple, often leathery, usually large. Flowers are likewise regular, ample, solitary and showy, with 6–20 petals in soft colors. Deciduous species like those listed below usually bloom before leaves appear. Fruits are knobby, interesting cones that split open to reveal scarlet seeds, adding autumn interest in the landscape. Downy, pointed flowerbuds are produced the season previous to bloom, a subtle attraction in winter.

How to Grow
The magnolias listed below enjoy part to light shade. They thrive in deep, well-drained soils, rich in organic matter like peat moss or leaf compost. Usually propagated by softwood cuttings taken in early summer. The saucer magnolia grows surprisingly well in urban conditions, though it may host scale insects. Plant balled-and-burlapped or container-grown plants in spring, cover with mulch, irrigate during drought, and avoid further soil disturbance.

Magnolias have fleshy, shallow roots and resent careless cultivation and handling. Once established, they have few pests except unknowing gardeners. Digging-in bulbs around the base may damage the brittle roots. Casual, heavy, or autumn pruning butchers the form. These primordial, statuesque beauties need little improvement via clippers. Prune lightly after flowering, only to remove damaged wood. Fall pruning, of course, would remove the next spring's flowers.

Uses
The genus offers a versatile repertoire of large landscape plants. The two species listed below are delightful accent or mixed border plants in smaller schemes both formal and informal. In larger settings, magnolias are splendid massed or mixed with other trees, planted along paths and streets, or in shrub borders.

× *soulangiana* p. 85
Saucer magnolia. A large shrub or small tree, a pink to lavender cloud when in bloom, maximum size about 30 ft. tall and equally wide, often grown with several trunks. Deciduous leaves broadly oval, slightly soft and hairy beneath. Flowers cup-shaped, 6 in. across, purplish to white, scentless or fragrant. There are numerous cultivars; consult local authorities for the best in your area. This small hybrid tree originated in 1820. Zone 5.

stellata p. 85   Pictured on p. 398
Star magnolia. A many-branched, spreading shrub or small tree, to 15 ft. high. Oval leaves 1½–5 in. long, dark green in summer, yellow in fall. Fragrant white flowers, 3 in. wide; petals turn brown if frosted, so plant in a protected area. There are many cultivars. Japan. Zone 4.

Mahonia
Ma-ho'ni-a
Berberidaceae. Barberry family

Description
About 100 species of evergreen shrubs native to North America and Asia. Compound leaves have spine-tipped, leathery leaflets; blue-green in summer, often turning purple with the cold. Terminal clusters of small, fragrant, yellow flowers in spring. Fruit, blue-black, usually covered with a powdery bloom, like a small grape, edible, but mostly eaten by birds.

How to Grow
The plants named below thrive in part to moderately full shade. Plant in ordinary moist soil, sheltered from winter wind

and sun. Mahonias benefit from winter protection in the northern limits of their hardiness range; a heavy snow cover increases their chance of survival. Prune Oregon grape holly lightly in early spring or after the flowers fade, only to remove damaged or awkward growth. On *M. bealei,* remove a few of the older stems each year to promote bushy new growth.

Uses
Low habit and attractive foliage make these valuable specimens for shrub borders, shady corners, wildlife, and foundation plantings.

aquifolium p. 113
Oregon grape holly. 3–6 ft. high. Compound leaves 6–12 in. long, shiny, oval to oblong. Spikes of yellow flowers in spring give way to blue fruit. Leaves turn bronze or purple-red in cold winters. Attractive in all seasons and somewhat drought tolerant. Named cultivars vary in height and leaf color. 'Compacta' grows 2 ft. tall. Pacific Northwest. Zone 5.

bealei p. 114 Pictured above
12 ft. high, with stout, upright habit. Compound leaves are coarse and prickly. Showy clusters of lemon-yellow, fragrant flowers in spring. Birds fond of blue-black berries. The upright stems and stiff leaves give this shrub a striking silhouette. China. Zone 7.

Malcolmia
Mal-col'mi-a
Cruciferae. Mustard family

Description
A small genus of low-growing, compact herbs, with simple leaves and fragrant white, purple, or reddish flowers.

How to Grow

The species listed below is a hardy annual, suitable for part to light shade. Prepare soil in early spring as soon as it is dry enough to work. Sow seeds thinly, then barely cover. Where winters are mild, sow in fall. Prefers cool weather and usually is finished by late summer. Virginia stock self-sows where conditions are to its liking.

Uses

Fragrant edging, old-fashioned flower gardens.

maritima p. 183

Virginia stock. 6–12 in. high. Flowers ¾ in. wide, purplish pink to reddish to white. Mediterranean. Hardy annual.

Malus

May'lus. Apple, crabapple
Rosaceae. Rose family

Description

About 25 species of mostly deciduous trees and shrubs, native to the north temperate zone, with white to pink or carmine flowers, in early spring. Crabapples have showy, small fruits, 2 in. across or smaller on long stems, singly or in bunches, in late summer; colors include purple, red, orange, and yellow. In winter the form of well-pruned trees adds welcome interest to bleak gardens and persistent berries attract songbirds. Eating apples are in this genus, but they need more sun for good fruit production.

How to Grow

The crabapples listed here are suitable for part shade; fruiting will not be spectacular if light is inadequate. These plants do best in moist, acid, well-drained soil and transplant easily in spring. Established specimens tolerate some drought. Not suited for warmer climates.

Pruning
In the first season, begin pruning after flowers go by, and continue as needed to remove small crowded branches, crossing limbs, maverick twigs, suckers, water sprouts, and damaged wood. Aim to thin out, broaden the middle of the canopy. Always cut to an outside bud and use sharp pruners on small twigs. On larger branches, loppers may be adequate; anything thicker than a rake-handle will probably require a bow or pruning saw.

Pests
Crabapples are prone to a variety of diseases and disorders, including apple scab, fire blight, powdery mildew, and cedar apple rust. Insects that trouble flowering crabapples include mites, aphids, and fall webworms. Good cultural practices and choosing vigorous, disease-resistant cultivars will reduce problems.

Uses
Familiar, beloved ornamentals for specimens, massing, wildlife gardens, shade, low screens, hillsides. The edible fruit is enjoyed by birds and if grown organically red ones make beautiful pink preserves.

floribunda *p. 86* Pictured on *p. 401*
Crabapple. Deciduous tree, to 25 ft. high with dark green leaves and broad, round crown. Buds red, flowers pale pink, almost white, 1½ in. wide. Bears small red and yellow fruit every year. Long in cultivation here, a dependable tree with a dense, compact habit. Japan. Zone 4–8.

'Indian Magic' *p. 86*
A relatively new cultivar that can be expected to grow about 20 ft high. Rounded habit, with dark green leaves. Flowers rose-pink, 1½ in wide. Fruits ½ in wide, glossy red changing to orange in late fall, glossy brown in winter, persistent. Sometimes suffers from apple scab, but does not drop leaves as most susceptible cultivars do. Of hybrid origin, from Asian species. Zone 4–8.

sargentii *p. 114*
Crabapple. Deciduous shrub, reaching 12–14 ft. at maturity, spreading twice as broad. Branching is dense, often crisscrossing; judicious pruning of the young tree will help produce

a handsome and controlled older specimen. Leaves medium green, 2–3 in. long, of neat texture. Pink buds open to white flowers, 1 in. wide; bloom may be prolific one year and sparse the next; late-blooming. The small, shiny, dark red fruit is popular with birds. Seed-grown stock varies considerably. 'Rosea' has darker red buds and taller growth, and resists apple scab and fire blight. Japan. Zone 5–8.

Malva
Mal'va. Mallow
Malvaceae. Mallow family

Description
About 30 species of widely distributed herbaceous plants. Mallows are related to *Hibiscus,* but smaller and less tropical in aspect. Plants have finely cut foliage and bear single flowers with notched petals and a satiny texture.

How to Grow
Enjoys part to light shade and prefers dry, well-drained soil and a cool climate, but adaptable and easy. In hot climates, add organic matter to soil and cultivate deeply so roots will grow down to seek moisture. Divide in spring or fall.

Uses
Plant the species listed below in a mixed border or a naturalistic garden. With its lower, looser habit it combines well with many summer perennials.

alcea p. 152   *Pictured above*
Hollyhock mallow. These 2–4 ft. tall plants bear loose spikes of deep pink or white flowers in summer over hairy, divided

leaves. The blooms are 2 in. across; they are more delicate than those of true hollyhock. Europe. Zone 4.

Matteuccia
Ma-too'chee-a
Polypodiaceae. Polypody family

Description
Three species of large ferns found in temperate North America, Europe, and Asia.

How to Grow
Ostrich ferns like light shade and damp soil. They are not suited to warmer climates. Easily transplanted in fall or spring.

Uses
Accent in moist borders, at the foot of rock walls, naturalizing on moist banks.

struthiopteris *p. 272*
Ostrich fern. Large, deciduous, clump-forming fern growing to 4 ft. tall in good conditions. A very showy fern whose giant, feathery plumes grow in great bright green whorls, somewhat formal. Also listed as *M. pensylvanica*. Native of eastern North America. Zone 3.

Matthiola
May-thy'o-la. Stock
Cruciferae. Mustard family

Description
A genus containing 50 species of Old World herbs; the 2 species commonly in cultivation are grown chiefly for fragrance and cutting.

How to Grow
The species listed below is easy to grow and quick to flower. A cool-growing annual, suitable for part or dappled shade, stock cannot withstand heat. Start seeds early indoors so that plants will be at early flowerbud stage before transplanting. Or sow outdoors in very early spring where plants are to grow. Sow thickly and do not thin seedlings; crowding tends to encourage early bloom. Where winters are mild, sow seeds in late summer for winter and spring bloom.

Uses
Exceptionally fragrant flower, redolent of cloves and honey, evening stock is perhaps best planted in clumps in an old-fashioned flower garden or in natural colonies.

longipetala *p. 184   Pictured above*
Evening stock. Low-growing, many-branched, to 1½ ft. high. Flowers ¾ in. wide, scattered, purple to white, fragrant, open in the evening. Spring to summer. Eurasia. Hardy annual.

Mazus
May′zus
Scrophulariaceae. Foxglove family

Description
About 30 species of low, prostrate, perennial herbs native to Asia, Indo-Malaya, or Australasia, 3 of which are commonly grown. They have small toothed leaves and blue or white flowers.

How to Grow
M. reptans prefers a moist location and enjoys part shade. Easy to increase by division. May be invasive in rich soil.

Uses
Ground cover, rock garden subject, between paving stones.

reptans *p. 230*
A ground-covering perennial, to 2 in. high, rooting at the joints. Leaves lance-shaped or elliptic, 1 in. long, coarsely toothed. Flowers small, to ¾ in. long, in profuse, 1-sided clusters, lavender or purplish blue. Blooms in summer. Zone 6.

Meconopsis
Me-ko-nop'sis
Papaveraceae. Poppy family

Description
About 45 species of herbaceous annuals or perennials having alternate, divided, or cut leaves. Sap is yellow. Showy, usually 4-petaled flowers are blue, yellow, or reddish.

How to Grow
Welsh poppies are notoriously difficult to grow and require part to light shade and moist but well-drained soil. The species described below needs rich, humusy conditions. Grow from seed sown in the open in spring.

Uses
Specimen for shady woodland or rock garden.

cambrica p. 152 Pictured above
Welsh poppy. 2-ft.-high, pale green, slightly hairy plants, forming large tufts. Leaves cut feather-fashion. Flowers pale yellow or orange, 2 in. wide, borne solitary and high above foliage. Western Europe. Zone 6.

Menispermum
Men-i-spur'mum. Moonseed
Menispermaceae. Moonseed family

Description
Two species of twining, woody vines with attractive foliage, from North America and Asia. Small white or yellow flowers followed by poisonous berrylike fruits on female plants.

How to Grow
Grows best in partial shade and average soil. Easy to grow from seeds or cuttings. Spreads by underground stems and, though a native plant, moonseed can become very invasive; probably best to experiment by growing it in a large tub sunk to its rim before releasing it in a garden.

Uses
Ground cover in rough areas where little else grows; vigorous quick cover on chain-link fence. Tolerates urban conditions.

canadense p. 250
Moonseed, yellow parilla. Herbaceous vine climbing to 12 ft. high. Leaves shield-shaped, 4–8 in. long, sometimes lobed, soft-hairy beneath when young. Flowers small, white, blooming in late spring, with male and female flowers on separate plants. Fruit black, poisonous. Eastern North America. Zone 5.

Mertensia
Mer-ten'si-a
Boraginaceae. Borage family

Description
Some 40 herbaceous species of low, blue-flowered woodlanders, many showy and native to North America.

How to Grow
Shade-loving, the species described below enjoys part, light, toward moderately full shade and a cool, moist site, rich in organic matter. Division is difficult; propagate plants by sowing fresh seed.

Uses
Excellent ground cover among spring bulbs and in moist woodland settings. The plant provides visual relief from the texture of bulb foliage, and blue flowers of the species are an excellent companion to hotter colors.

virginica *p. 153   Pictured on p. 407*
Virginia bluebells. To 2 ft. high, with pale green, narrow leaves. Flowers sweetly nodding bells, 1 in. long, in clusters, purplish to blue. Plant is dormant in summer when it loses its foliage. Cultivar 'Alba' has white flowers, and a pink form is also available. Native Ontario to Alabama and westward. Zone 4.

Milium
Mill'i-um. Wood millet
Gramineae. Grass family

Description
A small genus of annual and perennial grasses native to North America and Eurasia. The plants grow in loose tufts, with flat leaf blades and lacy flower panicles.

How to Grow
The grass described below is a woodlander and grows best in part to medium shade, though it will subsist with even less light. It thrives in moist, fertile soil. Increase by division or by seeds. May become invasive if flowerheads are allowed to stand and ripen; deadhead to avoid this potential nuisance.

Uses
Ground cover, cut flowers for dried arrangements. Bright, reliable color lights up shaded areas.

effusum 'Aureum' *p. 263   Pictured on p. 408*
Golden grass. Deciduous perennial to 18 in. high, with slowly
creeping rhizomes and open, upright habit. Leaf blades narrow, to 12 in. long, soft, arching, bright yellow or yellow-
green. Flowers yellow, in early summer. Zone 5.

Mimulus
Mim'you-lus
Scrophulariaceae. Snapdragon family

Description
A genus of about 150 herbs and subshrubs, widely distributed,
many native to western North America. Prized for their showy,
2-lipped, often spotted flowers which suggest a monkey's face.
Sometimes called *Diplacus*.

How to Grow
Preferring cool summers, monkey flower is difficult to grow in
most of U.S. except California. Needs light, dappled, or afternoon shade. Good for large cold frames. Sow seeds indoors
in midwinter or very early spring. Set out plants as soon as
danger of frost is past. Water generously. Increase by cuttings
and division. (Can be brought indoors for winter bloom.)

Uses
Bedding, containers.

guttatus p. 184
Monkey flower. To 2 ft. high. Flowers yellow, generally with
red or brown dots on the throat, 2-lipped, 1½ in. wide. Alaska
to Mexico. Perennial grown as a half-hardy annual.

Miscanthus
Mis-kan'thus
Gramineae. Grass family

Description
About 20 species of tall, perennial, Old World grasses, mostly
clump-forming, including some popular ornamental grasses
cultivated in the U.S. Leaf blades have distinct white midrib
and rough margins, feathery flowers.

How to Grow
Miscanthus is suitable for part to light shade and prefers good
soil, moist but not soggy during growing season. Propagate

in spring by dividing the woody roots, using a saw if clumps are sizable. Cut foliage down in late winter. To prevent self-seeding, cut off flower stalks before seeds mature. Giant miscanthus best sited in larger garden. Eulalia grass is well suited to waterside plantings; it may become too vigorous in light soil.

Uses
Specimens, mixed borders. Taller ones are useful for screening.

floridulus p. 264
Giant miscanthus. Coarse-textured, to 10 ft. high, forming clumps. Leaves pale green, elongate, to 3 ft. long. White flower plumes in autumn. Often listed as M. *sinensis giganteus.* Zone 5.

sacchariflorus p. 264
Eulalia grass. Tufted, deciduous grass to 6 ft. high, spreading by rhizomes. Leaf blades to 3 ft. long, 1 in. wide, turning rusty orange in autumn. Flowers silvery, decorative, produced in late summer, effective through winter. Zone 5.

sinensis 'Gracillimus' p. 265   *Pictured above*
Maiden grass. Graceful, fine-textured grass, to 5 ft. high; upright, arching habit; autumn leaves are buff-colored with curled tips; flower plumes, also borne late, are long and feathery. There are many other choice cultivars, including 'Silver Feather', with silvery, earlier flowers, 'Variegatus', with creamy stripes on the foliage, and 'Zebrinus', which grows to 7 ft. and has horizontal yellow bands on the leaves. East Asia. Zone 5.

Mitchella
Mit-chel′la
Rubiaceae. Coffee family

Description
A prostrate, rather woody evergreen perennial, found in woods over most of eastern North America. There is a second species in eastern Asia.

How to Grow
Mitchella prefers partial to full shade and soil slightly acid and rich in leaf mold. Increase by division.

Uses
Ground cover and rock plant for woodsy niches.

repens p. 230
Partridgeberry, twinberry. Opposite, spade-shaped to rounded leaves are only ¾ in. wide, green, sometimes marbled with white. Slender stems root easily at the joints, nearly prostrate, and not more than 2 in. high. Flowers are tiny, white, and funnel-shaped, borne in pairs at the end of short stalks. Their fruits unite into one distinct, showy, red berry with two marks. Zone 4.

Monarda
Mo-nar′da
Labiatae. Mint family

Description
A North American genus of 12 aromatic herbs grown for their brilliant flowers and pleasant if coarse aspect in informal landscapes. The leaves are opposite on square stems; flowerheads

are large, white, red, purplish, yellow, or mottled. Complex, showy affairs, they are borne in tiers on tall stems.

How to Grow
Easily grown in well-drained soil in part shade. Plants spread quickly and can be invasive, more so in moister conditions. Divide in spring as necessary. Wild bergamot will grow in both moist and dry soils and is quite drought resistant once established. Bee balm is susceptible to rust and powdery mildew in some areas.

Uses
Meadows, woodland gardens, borders, herb gardens. Attracts butterflies and hummingbirds.

didyma p. 153   *Pictured on p. 412*
Bee balm, Oswego tea. Herbaceous perennial, 2–3 ft. high, with hairy, aromatic stems and leaves. Scarlet flowers, nearly 2 in. long in vertical tiers. Cultivars 'Cambridge Scarlet' and 'Croftway Pink' are most commonly sold. Zone 4.

fistulosa p. 154
Wild bergamot. Perennial, covered with soft hairs and growing 3–4 ft. tall. The 1½-in.-long flowers are lilac to purple, in vertical tiers. Zones 4.

Myosotis
My-o-so'tis. Forget-me-not
Boraginaceae. Borage family

Description
50 species of annual or perennial herbs, mostly European, but a few through the north temperate zone. Narrow, alternate leaves on low plants; garden varieties are moisture-loving plants prized for their small but numerous, usually blue flowers.

How to Grow
Forget-me-nots prefer part to light shade, moist soil, cool weather, and crowded conditions. Protection from intense or prolonged sun is critical in the South. The perennial is easily divided in early spring or grown from seed; it is sometimes prey to red spider mites and mildew. Where growing season is short, sow seeds of biennial *M. sylvatica* outdoors in early spring. Where winters are mild, sow in the fall for spring color. Self-sows readily where conditions are good.

Uses
Among spring bulbs, ground cover at the edges of woodland and shrub borders, along moist banks and streams. Like their cousin Virginia bluebells, forget-me-nots make an excellent understudy to spring bulbs.

scorpioides var. *semperflorens* *p. 231*
Forget-me-not. 12–18 in. long, more or less prostrate plants form a mat of stems and leaves. Blue flowers have a yellow, pink, or white eye, ⅓ in. wide, borne in loose, 1-sided clusters at the end of the stems. Blooms until frost. Native to Europe, naturalized in eastern North America. Zone 5.

sylvatica *p. 185*
Forget-me-not. 6–18 in. high. Flowers blue, but sometimes pink or white, to ⅓ in. wide, the eye differently colored, often yellow, blooming from spring to summer. Eurasia. Sometimes sold incorrectly as *M. alpestris*. Biennial, usually grown as a hardy annual.

Nandina
Nan-dy′na
Berberidaceae. Barberry family

Description
A single species of evergreen shrub, native to China and Japan, grown for its columnar form, showy berries, and brilliant fall foliage.

How to Grow
Nandina is suitable for part to moderate shade. It prefers a reasonably moist site and is a tough plant in areas where it is fully hardy. Remove a few of the older canes each year to

promote bushy growth. North of zone 7, plant in a protected place and mulch well; the roots may endure even if the top dies back each year. Propagate by seeds.

Uses
Edging, massing, specimen in borders. Compact varieties are suitable for container culture

domestica 'Alba' *p. 115   Pictured on p. 413*
Heavenly bamboo. An attractive shrub, 6–8 ft. high with erect stems. Large compound leaves with small, narrow leaflets arranged feather-fashion. Clusters of small white flowers in spring; showy hanks of white berries ½ in. in diameter, very handsome when ripe and adding fall and winter interest to the shade garden in warmer climates. The species has red fruits. Zone 7.

Nemophila
Nem-off'i-la
Hydrophyllaceae. Waterleaf family

Description
Eleven annuals from North America, a few of garden interest. Some are climbing or trailing plants, all hairy. The leaves are usually cut and the flowers in showy clusters.

How to Grow
The nemophilas are cool-weather wildflowers that do well in northern and high-altitude gardens. They grow quickly and easily, preferring afternoon shade, and will provide a cheerful display of color before heat and humidity set in. In mild climates, sow seeds in fall; elsewhere, sow them in early spring. Thin seedlings to 1 ft. apart.

Uses
Ground cover under spring bulbs, naturalizing.

maculata *p. 185*
Five-spot. Trailing in habit, to 1 ft. long. Bell-shaped, 1½ in. flowers, white with a blue or purple spot at the tip of each petal. California. Hardy annual.

menziesii *p. 186*
Baby-blue-eyes. These trailing plants grow to 1 ft. long. The bright blue flowers are bell-shaped and are 1½ in. wide. There are both white and blue-and-white forms. Hardy annual.

Nicotiana
Ni-ko-she-a'na
Solanaceae. Potato family

Description
Seventy herbaceous species, occasionally shrubby or treelike, mostly tropical, all American except for one found in Australia. Garden varieties, an increasingly popular group of annuals or tender perennials, are prized for their showy, long-blooming flowers which first open at night. The sap has narcotic and poisonous properties; the genus is home to *N. tabacum,* tobacco.

How to Grow
Suitable for part to light shade and prefers moist soil and warm weather. The species described below is easy to grow from seeds started indoors in early spring and transplanted to garden as soon as danger of frost is over. Lime and potash are beneficial soil additives. Water generously during hot, dry weather.

Uses
Fragrant and free-flowering annual for bedding, mixed borders, containers.

alata p. 186 *Pictured above*
Flowering tobacco. To 5 ft. high, erect and slender. Branching stems and large, soft, alternate, simple leaves. Flowers fragrant at night, shaped like small trumpets or funnels, the tube 2–4 in. long, and the funnel 1 in. wide, in clusters at ends of branches. Colors are numerous, including white, pink, mauve, red, maroon, purple, and green. Many cultivars are available, some with larger flowers, and some day-blooming dwarf kinds with showier but less fragrant blossoms. Also called *N. affinis.* South America. Tender annual, perennial in warm climates.

Nierembergia
Near-em-berg'i-a. Cupflower
Solanaceae. Potato family

Description
About 30 species of tropical American herbs or subshrubs.
A few are grown for their attractive, usually white or blue
flowers.

How to Grow
Prefers warm weather and part to light shade. Start seeds
indoors in early spring. If hardened off, seedlings are frost-
hardy and can be set out 2–3 weeks before last frost. Needs
moist, well-drained soil.

Uses
These plants are good for hanging baskets.

***hippomanica* var. *violacea* 'Purple Robe'** *p. 187*
Cupflower. 6–15 in. high. Leaves alternate, somewhat scattered and fine. Flowers numerous, 1 in. wide, violet with yellow
throat in this cultivar and mostly at the ends of twigs. The
hardiest of all cupflowers. Recently introduced 'Mont Blanc'
is a white that grows true from seed. Argentina. Tender perennial where winters are mild, usually grown as a half-hardy
annual.

Oenothera
Ee-no-thee'ra
Onagraceae. Evening primrose family

Description
About 80 species of North American wildflowers, the evening
primroses and the day-blooming sundrops. Cultivated for their
showy, long-blooming summer flowers, usually yellow, sometimes white or rose and poppylike in character. Plants may be
somewhat rangy.

How to Grow
Evening primroses are suitable for part shade and thrive in
warm weather, in sandy, poor to average soil with good drainage. Grow short-lived species like the annual listed below from
seed. Seeds must be started in fall or very early in spring to
bloom the first year. In areas with mild winters, sow outdoors
in fall; elsewhere, sow in early spring. Seeds may also be started
indoors 8–12 weeks before the last frost. Germination takes

21–25 days. Set transplants out in informal patches when ground has warmed.

Uses
Massed plantings, naturalizing, summer filler in informal borders.

erythrosepala *p. 187*
Evening primrose. 2–8 ft. high. Flowers night-blooming, yellow turning orange or red, 3½ in. wide. Biennial grown as a hardy annual.

Omphalodes
Om-fa-lo′dez. Navelwort
Boraginaceae. Borage family

Description
About 25 species of low herbs, native to Europe and Asia. Related and similar to *Cynoglossum, Mertensia,* and *Myosotis.* Flowers blue or pinkish, in loose clusters with white, starlike centers. Basal leaves are ample, long-stalked; stem leaves smaller and fewer.

How to Grow
Cultural requirements according to species and climate. *O. cappadocica* and *O. linifolia* are shade-loving perennials, enjoying part, light, to moderate shade and tolerating even more. Divide in spring or fall to increase stock. Annual *O. linifolia* requires part to light shade and is a good candidate for southern shade gardens. Sow seeds in moist garden soil in spring, or in fall in mild climates. All prefer moist, well-drained soil that is neutral or slightly alkaline, and cool weather, though navelwort tolerates dryer conditions.

Uses
Blue spring flowers for naturalizing in woodsy settings and among bulbs. Choicer perennials may also work well as ground cover or in cool wildflower nooks.

cappadocica p. 154
Navelwort. Rhizomatous perennial, 6–10 in. high. Leaves with silky hairs. Flowers small, bright blue, with markings at the throat. Asia Minor. Needs protection in Northern winters. Zone 6.

linifolia p. 188
Navelwort. To 1 ft. high. Flowers white, ½ in. wide, with long necks. Spain and Portugal. Hardy annual.

verna p. 155   Pictured on p. 417
Blue-eyed Mary, creeping forget-me-not. Perennial, to 8 in. high, main stems prostrate but with erect flowering stems. Leaves pointed, ovalish, with lesser spearlike leaves on flowerstalks. Flowers blue, ½ in. wide, paired in loose clusters. Zone 5.

Ophiopogon
O-fi-o-po'gon. Lilyturf, mondo grass
Liliaceae. Lily family

Description
A small group of grasslike, tuft-forming herbs, native to East Asia. Similar to and easily confused with *Liriope*. *Ophiopogon* has blue fruit.

How to Grow
Mondo grass adapts to a wide range of light conditions depending on moisture, climate, and exposure, from sun to full

shade. It grows well in ordinary soil. Propagate by division. If foliage becomes shabby in winter, cut back hard in early spring to groom and stimulate new growth. Slugs may eat the leaves.

Uses
The species listed below is best used under trees or as a border edging, as a visual substitute for grass.

japonicus p. 231   *Pictured on p. 418*
Mondo grass. A good sod-forming ground cover, 8–15 in. high. Dark green leaves, to 15 in. long, arise from underground stolons; the roots bear small tubers. Pale lilac flowers are almost hidden by foliage. Fruit is pea-size, blue. Dwarf cultivar 'Nana' is about half the size of the species. Popular in the South, where it is evergreen. Zone 7.

Osmanthus
Oz-man'thus
Oleaceae. Olive family

Description
A small group of evergreen shrubs or small trees, primarily Asiatic or Polynesian, with attractive leathery foliage and fragrant white flowers.

How to Grow
Suitable for part shade. Easy to grow from container-grown plants set out in acid soil. This species tolerates heat and heavy pruning.

Uses
Versatile landscape shrub for hedges, espaliers, container and foundation plantings in warm climates.

heterophyllus 'Myrtifolius' p. 115
Holly osmanthus. Shrub, 15–20 ft. high. Unlike the typical species, whose toothed, spiny leaves resemble a holly's, this cultivar has smooth leaves more like a myrtle's, oblong to oval 1½–2½ in. long. Flowers fragrant but small, fall-blooming, white, in clusters 1½ in. wide. Japan. Zone 7.

Osmunda
Oz-mun'da
Osmundaceae

Description
About 10 species of large, decorative ferns, native to temperate and tropical regions of Asia and the Americas. Both species listed below are deciduous and enjoy a wide range in eastern North America from Canada to Florida.

How to Grow
These ferns prefer light shade and acid, wet soil containing plenty of organic matter. They need constant moisture and do not tolerate drought.

Uses
Large vertical plants, adding texture and form to gardens. Also excellent for naturalizing, at the foot of walls and shrubs, moist banks, against structures.

cinnamomea p. 272 *Pictured above*
Cinnamon fern. Clump-forming deciduous fern to 3 ft. tall. Handsome light green fronds surround striking, cinnamon-brown, spore-bearing stalks. Fiddleheads are edible. Eastern North America. Zone 3.

regalis p. 273
Royal fern. Deciduous, clump-forming fern, up to 4 ft. high. Its pronounced, upright habit and widely spaced leaflets give this fern a distinctive look. Rich green fronds turn bright yellow in fall, and spore cases are rich, showy, golden brown. Eastern North America. Zone 2.

Pachysandra
Pack-i-san'dra
Buxaceae. Box family

Description
Five species of low-growing perennial herbs or subshrubs native to North America and East Asia. The trailing ground covers listed here have thick, spoon-shaped leaves with scalloped edges growing in dense whorls and small spikes of white flowers in spring.

How to Grow
Pachysandra is easy to grow in moist, ordinary soil in part to deep shade. To propagate, take cuttings in summer and put in a sandy soil mixture. Water well and shade them. When rooted, plant 8 in. apart for a quick ground cover. The native species needs humus-enriched soil and is vulnerable to southern blight.

Uses
Versatile ground covers for moist shade. The Japanese species can be relied on to make a thick leafy carpet in many unpromising situations, including urban conditions.

procumbens p. 232
Herbaceous ground cover, 8–10 in. high. Evergreen in warmer climates, deciduous further north. Stems trailing to erect, flowers white or purplish, moderately showy in midspring. Zone 5.

terminalis p. 232 *Pictured above*
Semi-evergreen ground cover. Grows to 9 in. high and spreads by underground runners. Leaves thick, dark to medium or yellow-green, glossy, narrower and lighter than the native.

Short spikes of white flowers in spring. 'Silver Edge', with white-margined leaves, is more ornamental but not as vigorous. Zone 5.

Parthenocissus
Par-then-oh-sis′us
Vitaceae. Grape family

Description
A small group of fast-growing, long-lived climbing vines with colorful fall foliage.

How to Grow
Enjoys light shade. Not particular about soil, but grows more vigorously in good conditions. Tolerates drought, heat, salt, wind, urban life. Climbs by holdfasts on tendrils, which may be a nuisance to remove; regular pruning will help keep it off windows and out of gutters. Japanese beetles may eat the leaves of the native species. Easily propagated.

Uses
On masonry walls, trellises, statuary, cover for birds. Scrambles prettily over rocks or other areas which are difficult to cultivate.

quinquefolia *p. 250* *Pictured above*
Virginia creeper, woodbine. Vigorous deciduous vine, to 50 ft. high, growing as much as 10 ft. a year. Compound leaves have 5 pointed leaflets, 2–5 in. long, pointed, arranged like the fingers of a hand. Flowers in summer, followed by blue-black fruits and scarlet leaves. Not dense but leafy, and quick cover. 'Englemanii' and 'St. Paul' are cultivars with smaller leaves. Eastern U.S. Zone 3.

tricuspidata p. 251

Boston ivy, Japanese ivy. Climbs to 60 ft. high and clings firmly. Large, shiny leaves, up to 10 in. long, 3-lobed or divided into 3 leaflets. Deciduous in cold climates, coloring scarlet in fall. Semi-evergreen in mild-winter areas. Outstanding wall climber, with overlapping leaves. The cultivar 'Veitchii', of finer texture, has smaller leaves that are purple when young. China and Japan. Zone 5.

Paulownia
Paul-ow'ni-a.
Scrophulariaceae. Foxglove family

Description
Six species of deciduous Chinese trees. Paulownias are handsome flowering trees but are not long-lived.

How to Grow
Paulownia is suitable for part shade and grows best in rich, well-drained soil, neutral or acid, but adapts to a wide range of soil conditions, except soggy and very dry. Transplant balled or container-grown plants in early spring, in a site protected from wind. Paulownia grows tall rapidly when young, then rounds out; allow space for a tree up to 50 ft. tall and equally wide.

Selection and Maintenance
This species is justly prized for its spectacular spring flowers and rapid growth. However, it may produce weedy seedlings in milder climates; in the northern limits of its range, sub-zero cold may kill flower buds and wood alike. Damaged wood should be removed in spring. Unfortunately, trees which have been cut down are succeeded by a copse of vigorous, large-leaved shoots, growing up to 12 ft. tall in one season. Even

where it is unquestionably hardy, flowers, leaves, and fruits may become a litter problem near buildings, busy walks, or drives.

Uses
Showy lawn specimen or pollarding subject.

tomentosa *p. 87 Pictured on p. 423*
Empress tree. Grows 30–50 ft. high, with thick, stiff branches, rather open in habit and becoming round-topped. Leaves similar to catalpa's, opposite, hairy, more or less oval, varying in size from 5–10 in. on ordinary growth to 2 ft. or more on vigorous shoots. Flowers fragrant, pale violet, 2 in. long, resembling foxgloves and borne in erect clusters, 8–10 in. long, blooming in spring before the leaves come out. China; escaped from cultivation in the eastern states. Zone 6.

Paxistima
Pax-is′ti-ma
Celastraceae. Bittersweet family

Description
Two species of low-growing evergreens native to North America, grown for their neat tufts of small opposite leaves.

How to Grow
Enjoys part, light, to moderately full shade, and prefers well-drained soil. Set out container-grown plants in spring in an area protected from winter wind. Space 8–12 in. apart for hedge or ground cover. Prune in spring or fall; tolerates shearing into forms and hedges. Propagated by seeds, cuttings, or layers.

Uses
Ground cover or low hedge, in east-facing terraced beds, planted steps, front of borders, rock gardens.

myrsinites *p. 233   Pictured on p. 424*
Oregon boxwood. Spreading shrub, 1–3 ft. tall, and 8–10 in.
wide. Branches are stiff. Lush narrow leaves 1¼ in. long,
toothed toward the tip and slightly convex. Small, fragrant,
white to reddish flowers bloom in summer. Zone 5.

Pelargonium
Pel-ar-go'ni-um. Garden geranium
Geraniaceae. Geranium family

Description
A large genus of mostly South African evergreen perennials
of diverse habit. Stems can be trailing, herbaceous, or woody.
Clusters of showy flowers, from pure white to pink, crimson,
and bright scarlet, grow on long stalks above or among substantial, aromatic, usually lobed, often highly ornamental foliage. There are thousands of cultivated varieties in this well-
loved tribe of floriferous plants, usually grown as summer
annuals.

How to Grow
Though many pelargoniums thrive in full sun, the species described below are suitable for part to light shade in temperate
climates; in hotter areas, they actually prefer continuous light
shade. Mediterranean natives, they perform best with clear
cool summer days; in this regard, the Martha Washington
geranium is especially vulnerable to heat and humidity. Garden
geraniums need regular watering but can subsist on a fairly
lean soil. Deadheading will prolong and increase bloom, and
neaten plantings. Pinching out tips early in season encourages
a more compact plant. All thrive in pots and need well-drained
soil.
   Start from purchased plants or cuttings, and set out after
the ground has warmed. Cherished varieties may be easily

carried over the winter as houseplants; take new cuttings early in spring. Some varieties of zonal geraniums are available as seed, and may be grown under lights.

Uses
Versatile bedding plant for topiary, hanging baskets, containers, edgings, window boxes.

× *domesticum* p. 188
Martha Washington geranium. To 18 in. high with crisp, shallowly lobed leaves. Early-blooming flowers 1½–3 in. wide, white, pink, or red, 2 upper petals usually blotched darker, something like a pansy. Needs cool nights to continue flowering. Tender perennial, grown as an annual.

× *hortorum* p. 189   Pictured on p. 425
Common or zonal geranium. Grows 1–3 ft. high as an annual. Flowers 2–2½ in. wide in flat-topped or rounded clusters, red, salmon-pink, white, coral, peach, often bicolored or double. Leaves are typically 3–5 in. wide, lobed and scalloped, with a darker horseshoe-shaped zone, almost chocolate-colored in some varieties. Numerous cultivars. Tender perennial, grown as annual.

Penstemon
Pen-stee′mon. Beard-tongue
Scrophulariaceae. Foxglove family

Description
All but one species in this vast genus of wildflowers and subshrubs are native to North America. Many are cultivated for their attractive foliage and showy, snapdragon-like flowers in a wide variety of colors.

Uses
Bedding, borders.

How to Grow
Penstemons prefer cool weather and are reputedly easier to grow in western North America. The species described here is suitable for part shade and requires protection from afternoon sun in climates where summers are long and hot. Start seeds indoors in early spring. Seeds need light for germination and sprout slowly and unevenly. Transplant seedlings or nursery-grown plants outdoors after last frost into well-drained soil. A pH of 6.5–7.0 gives best results.

'Scarlet and White' *p. 189*
Gloxinia penstemon. 2–3 ft. high. Flowers 2 in. wide, a red
bell with flared lip and white throat. Cultivars such as this are
widely grown on the West Coast and in England, and colors
ranging from white to crimson and blue are also available. Of
hybrid origin, derived from *P. hartwegii* and *P. cobaea.* Tender
perennial usually grow as a half-hardy annual.

Phalaris
Fal'ar-is
Gramineae. Grass family

Description
About 15 species of grasses from the north temperate zone.

How to Grow
Ribbon grass, the species listed below, thrives in a wide variety
of growing conditions. For best results, situate with afternoon,
high, or light shade. In intense sun, the leaves often bleach
out; in full shade the growth will be lanky and sparse. Soil
can be poor and either moist or dry. Clumps spread widely
and rapidly and should be divided when they become crowded.
An old-fashioned favorite, but invasive and must be dutifully
restrained.

Uses
Ground cover or accent plant. Its attractive foliage combines
well with flowers and darker-colored leaves. Tolerates urban
conditions.

arundinacea picta *p. 265*
Ribbon grass, gardener's-garters. Perennial, to 3 ft. high, growing in large mounded clumps. Leaves striped green and white
with pink, 12 in. long, ¾ in. wide. The 4–6 in. seedheads are
loose clusters of white or pale pink and appear on 3 ft. stems.
Zone 4.

Philadelphus
Fill-a-del'fus. Mock-orange
Saxifragaceae. Saxifrage family

Description
About 60 species of North American and Eurasian deciduous
shrubs, widely grown for their citrus-scented white flowers in
late spring.

How to Grow
Mock orange is easy to grow in average garden soil and tolerates part or light shade. Plants tend to become leggy, so prune every year as soon as blossoms go by; flowers appear on the previous year's growth, so late or dormant pruning would greatly reduce bloom. Propagated by cuttings, seeds, layers, and suckers.

Uses
Shrubberies and mixed borders, informal hedge or screen. Cut boughs make a fragrant and sturdy foundation for spring arrangements.

coronarius *p. 116*
Mock orange. Deciduous shrub, to 10 ft. tall, equally wide. Can be kept smaller by pruning. Pointed oval leaves, 1½–4 in. long. Clusters of creamy white, sweet smelling, usually 4-petaled, inch-wide flowers in spring. Zone 5.

Phlox
Flox
Polemoniaceae. Phlox family

Description
About 60 species of perennial and annual herbs, usually hardy, native mostly to North America. Habit varies from erect to kneeling, trailing, or creeping. Lance-shaped leaves and clusters of showy flowers, 5-petaled and regular, with a tubed throat and central eye. Garden favorites with a long season of bloom span the white, pink, salmon, red, and violet to blue color range.

How to Grow
Most phlox are easy to grow and prefer at least part shade and humus-enriched, moist soil with good drainage; the

ground cover *P. stolonifera* needs more shade, especially in hotter climates. Propagate from seeds, cuttings, or divide clumps in spring. The 3 species listed here are hardy native perennials. In late summer heat and humidity, powdery mildew may blemish the foliage of some kinds, but does no long-term harm. Slugs and snails may eat low-growing phlox.

Uses
Many taller varieties are fragrant, showy flowers for wild gardens, naturalizing, borders. Tall ones are excellent cut flowers. Creeping types excellent atop or in planted walls, rock gardens, ground cover.

divaricata '**Mrs. Crockett**' *p. 155   Pictured on p. 428*
Wild sweet William, blue woodland phlox. Perennial, about 12 in. high. Spreads rapidly by creeping stems. Upright stems bear loose clusters of lavender-blue to pale mauve flowers in spring. Leaves opposite and narrow. 'Fuller's White' has white flowers. Part to full shade. Zone 4.

paniculata '**Mt. Fujiyama**' *p. 156*
Garden phlox. This snowy white cultivar shows up well in shade and also grows well in warmer climates. The tribe is one of the best of the taller perennials, with strong stems to 3–4 ft., topped with large, spreading clusters of fragrant flowers which bloom for 2–5 weeks in mid- to late summer. Plants spread to form sizable colonies and attract butterflies and hummingbirds. Remove faded flowers to prevent self-seeding. Other cultivars include cerise-on-pink 'Bright Eyes', cherry-red 'Star Fire', and pastel 'Blue Boy'. Zone 4.

stolonifera '**Blue Ridge**' *p. 233*
Creeping phlox. 6–10 in. high, spreading 1–2 ft. or more where space allows. Loose mats of medium green foliage and clusters of large, soft, blue flowers in midspring for 2–4 weeks. Other cultivars include 'Bruce's White', 'Pink Ridge', and 'Millstream', which has pink petals with candylike red and white rings in the center.

Physostegia
Fi-so-stee′ji-a
Labiatae. Mint family

Description
A small group of North American perennials, one widely cultivated for its pink summer flowers.

How to Grow
Obedient plant is vigorous to the point of invasiveness in full sun and fertile, acid, moist, or even wet soils; in shadier, drier sites its growth is more restrained. The species listed below is suitable for part shade in average garden soil. Easily started in spring by seeds, nursery stock, or throughout the season by division. Cut back plants in early summer to encourage more compact growth and pull out new sprouts which spread by underground runners.

Uses
Naturalizing.

virginiana p. 156
Obedient plant, false dragonhead. Perennial, growing 3–4 ft. tall and spreading at least that far with adequate moisture. Spikes of pink to lavender, snapdragon-like flowers rise above dense, glossy foliage for 3–6 weeks in late summer and fall. Plants may be somewhat floppy or kneeling, in contrast to the flowers themselves which are inserted in neat, squarish ranks on the stalk. Choicer cultivars include 'Alba' and 'Summer Snow', both white; 'Variegata', with leaves edged in cream, and 'Vivid', more compact than the species. Zone 4.

Pieris
Py-ear'is
Ericaceae. Heath family

Description
About 8 species of slow-growing broad-leaved evergreen shrubs or small trees, valued for their graceful spring flowers and shiny foliage.

How to Grow
Thrives in morning sun to light, high shade; tolerant of moderate to full shade. Plant nursery-grown stock in peaty, somewhat sandy, moderately acid soil, well-drained but moist, mulched with leaves. Should be protected from winter wind and sun in northern areas. Prune lightly and selectively after flowering to remove old flowerheads and damaged wood, or to shape plant.

Uses
Versatile landscape plant for entrances, accent specimens, rock gardens, and mixed borders.

japonica 'Wada' *p. 116*
A splendid evergreen shrub, the species growing 3–10 ft. high and taller with age. Leaves are long, narrow, elegant, dark green and shiny when mature, with new growth opening bronze in spring. Flowers mildly fragrant, in graceful, draping clusters 3–5 in. long. Each urn-shaped waxy bloom is a half-inch long and borne in early to midspring; in this cultivar they are pink. Other varieties with rosy blooms are 'Dorothy Wycoff', 'Flamingo', and 'Valley Rose'. Most specimens have flowers the white of mistletoe berries. 'Forest Flame' and 'Mountain Fire' have vivid reddish bundles of new growth. Also sold as *Andromeda japonica*. Japan. Zone 5.

Pittosporum
Pit-toss′por-um
Pittosporaceae. Pittosporum family

Description
More than 100 species of chiefly Australasian evergreen shrubs and trees. Several are widely cultivated in warm climates for their handsome foliage and form; some have attractive flowers and fruit.

How to Grow
Easy to grow in part to moderately full shade in a variety of soils. Pittosporums adapt especially well to sandy soils and hot, dry locations. Watch for aphids and scale insects.

Uses
Informal hedges and landscape use in warm climates.

tobira *p. 117* *Pictured above*
Shrub to 15 ft., lower with pruning. Thick, leathery leaves, 3–4 in. long, on brittle twigs. 2–3 in. wide clusters of small,

fragrant, greenish white to lemon-yellow flowers in early spring. Small hairy fruit. 'Wheeler's Dwarf' makes a cushion 1–2 ft. tall and wide. 'Variegata', to 6 ft., has gray-green leaves with creamy edges. China and Japan. Zone 9.

Polemonium
Po-lee-mo'ni-um
Polemoniaceae. Phlox family

Description
Twenty species of herbs, mostly hardy perennials native to North America, with a few from Europe and Asia. The genus includes species with blue, purple, yellow, or white bell-shaped flowers in loose, branching clusters. Compound leaflets are horizontally arranged on their stem, bearing a fanciful resemblance to a ladder.

How to Grow
Enjoys part to light shade and tolerant of even less light. Easy to grow in moist, humus-enriched, well-drained soil. Very moist soil in summer will prevent foliage tips from browning. Easily started in spring from nursery stock, seedlings, or divisions.

Uses
Front of borders and wildflower nooks.

reptans p. 234
Creeping polemonium. 8–12 in. high perennial with a spreading habit — more kneeling than creeping — and ferny, finely divided leaves. Flowers cup-shaped, light blue, to ½ in. wide, in loose clusters. Eastern North America. Zone 4.

Polygonatum
Pol-lig-o-nay'tum. Solomon's-seal
Liliaceae. Lily family

Description
About 30 species of generally hardy herbaceous perennials distributed throughout the northern hemisphere. Narrow bell-shaped flowers single or in clusters, hang from the axils of the leaves. Though small and white, their carriage and arrangement on tall stems make for a distinctive woodland plant.

How to Grow

Solomon's-seal is easy to grow in part, light, or full shade in moist soil. They need more shade with less moisture and more heat. With adequate shade, tolerates dry soil quite well.

Uses

Wildflower nooks, casual and naturalized plantings among ferns and shrubs.

odoratum var. *thunbergii* 'Variegatum' *p. 157*

Solomon's-seal. Herbaceous perennial with stems 3 ft. tall. Stems arise each spring from thick rootstocks; leaves are borne on upper parts of stems. In this cultivar they have white tips and edges. Smallish white flowers, 2 to a cluster, in spring. Spreads slowly to form an attractive patch of stems that all bend in the same direction, as if combed. Japan. Zone 5.

Polygonum

Pol-lig'o-num. Smartweed
Polygonaceae. Smartweed family

Description

About 150 species of varied herbs found throughout the world. A few are easy ornamentals grown for their clusters of small pink or white flowers. Some are well-known weeds.

How to Grow

The species listed below will thrive in moist soil and part to light shade. Propagate by cuttings, seeds, or division of rootstocks.

Uses

Informal mixed borders. Good for attracting bees.

bistorta 'Superbum' *p. 234*

European bistort. 2–3 ft. high. Basal leaves resemble large paddles. Pink flowers closely set on a 6-in.-long spike. First flush of bloom in early summer, may come back again later in season. Zone 4.

Polystichum

Polly-stick'um
Polypodiaceae. Polypody family

Description

About 120 species of woodland ferns native to temperate areas around the world. Those cultivated are chiefly evergreen.

How to Grow
Christmas fern prefers light to moderate shade and rich, moist, well-drained soil containing plenty of organic matter. Adequate moisture is critical; a stony mulch may help keep root-run cool and damp. Transplants easily. Like many other common ferns, can also be propagated from spores in a moist terrarium in a sterile potting medium.

Uses
Excellent, substantial fern for rock gardens, massing, colonizing half-wild areas, on moist banks, among shrubs.

acrostichoides p. 273
Christmas fern. Evergreen, clump-forming fern. Fronds are 18–24 in. tall, 3–5 in. wide, once-divided, leathery, dark green plumes. Common in moist woods in eastern North America. Zone 3.

Primula
Prim'you-la
Primulaceae. Primrose family

Description
A large genus of 400 low-growing herbs native to the north temperate zone, preferring alpine and cool locations. Many hybrids and cultivated forms exist. They flower in every color, including white, pink, red, orange, yellow to green, blue, violet, brown, and combinations thereof. Showy blooms are carried on leafless stalks above flat rosettes of foliage, in clusters, round umbels, or tiers.

How to Grow
Primroses need humusy, moist soil in light to part shade when they are in active growth, and prefer cool weather. They are not suited to hot, dry climates and should be protected from direct sun wherever they are grown. Red spider mites may plague plants in dry conditions. Many are alpine plants, but those listed below are among the least exacting of the tribe.

Perennials
The longer-lived primroses are excellent for naturalizing and massing under trees and shrubs, borders, rock gardens, along stream banks. Start them from spring-sown seed, nursery stock, or offsets. Established colonies should be divided every 3–4 years in spring to improve vigor and flowering. They like

light, dappled shade, and all but *P. vulgaris* can tolerate constantly moist, even boggy soils.

Annuals
The short-lived species listed below are good candidates for spring bedding, filler, in containers, or among bulbs. They may be grown as half-hardy annuals and propagated under lights, in protected cold frames outdoors, or in cool greenhouses, and set out after the last spring frost. All require good drainage, light, and dappled shade, and perform best in cool, moderate climates.

helodoxa p. 157
Amber primrose. 18–36 in. high. Late-blooming yellow flowers, 1 in. wide. Thrives in boggy soil. Needs protection, or even a cool greenhouse at the northern extent of its range. China and Burma. Perennial, hardy to zone 6 or 7.

japonica p. 158
Japanese primrose. Strong-growing, 8–16 in. high. Midspring flowers of purple, pink, or white, 1 in. wide, glistening, in several whorls on each stalk. Needs ample moisture. Japan. Perennial, hardy to zone 6.

malacoides p. 190
Fairy primrose. 4–18 in. high. Flowers lilac or pink, to ½ in. wide, in several whorls on each stalk. 'Alba' has white flowers, 'Rosea' bright rose-colored flowers. At low elevations in California, will bloom in winter and early spring. In Northern and coastal gardens, blooms in summer. China. Perennial to zone 8; usually grown as a half-hardy annual.

obconica p. 190
German primrose. To 12 in. high. Flowers lilac, pink, red, and white, 1 in. wide, in umbels. Time of bloom is similar to *malacoides*. Leaves can cause mild skin irritation. China. Perennial to zone 8, usually grown as half-hardy annual.

× *polyantha* p. 191
Polyanthus primrose. To 12 in. high. Flowers 1½–2 in. wide, purple, blue, rose, yellow, white, or scarlet, in profuse clusters. Blooms in spring. 'Pacific Giant' strain has large flowers. A long-cultivated group of hybrids derived from *P. elatior, P. veris,* and *P. vulgaris.* The easiest primrose to grow, but short-lived unless divided often. Also grown as a hardy annual, it is cold-hardy to zone 5.

sieboldii p. 158
Japanese star primrose. To 12 in. high. Flowers in crowded
umbels, nearly 2 in. wide, pink or purple, with a different-
colored eye. Prefers moist sites, but more tolerant of occasional
dry spells than most primroses. Dormant in summer. The Barnhaven strain of English hybrids includes plants with pale or
deep pink, purple, or lavender flowers. The species is native
to Japan. Perennial and hardy to zone 5.

vulgaris p. 159   *Pictured above*
English primrose. To 6 in. high. Leaves basal, broadly lance-
shaped, wrinkled, the margins crinkled. Flowers numerous or
solitary, usually yellow, on slender, slightly hairy stalks.
Blooms in spring. There are many double forms and other
colors, including white, purple, blue, lilac, and rose. Europe.
Often called *P. acaulis*. Perennial, cold-hardy to zone 5.

Prunus
Proo′nus
Rosaceae. Rose family

Description
More than 400 species of shrubs and trees, nearly all from
the north temperate zone. Includes plums, cherries, apricots,
peaches, and almonds, as well as many superb deciduous and
evergreen ornamentals with inedible fruit.

How to Grow
As a rule, the genus prefers full sun and reasonably moist,
well-drained soil. However, the evergreen species listed below
enjoys part to full shade. In northern areas, it needs protection
from intense sun and wind in winter. Spread organic mulch
beneath to the drip line of the tree and water deeply and

regularly during drought. Prune weak or crossing branches in early spring. Watch for insect and disease problems and treat them promptly. Stress of any sort increases susceptibility to various insects and diseases; cherry laurel generally live only about 30 years.

Uses
Cherry laurel may be used in mixed borders, shrubberies, informal hedges, or trained as a small tree.

laurocerasus p. 117   *Pictured above*
Cherry laurel, English laurel. Ornamental shrub or small tree, to 20 ft. Leaves 2–7 in. long, evergreen. Small, fragrant, white flowers in short clusters in spring. Small, dark purple fruit. There are many cultivars, differing in leaf and plant shape and in hardiness. 'Otto Luyken' has a compact habit, 4 ft. high with a spread of 6–8 ft., and tolerates deep shade. 'Schipkaensis', an unusually hardy cultivar, has narrow, dark green leaves and usually grows 4–5 ft. high with a wider spread; it is probably hardier than the species. 'Zabeliana' has an especially low, broad habit, reaching 2–3 ft. high and 12 ft. wide at maturity. Southern Europe to Iran. Zone 7.

Pulmonaria
Pul-mo-nay'ri-a. Lungwort
Boraginaceae. Borage family

Description
About 10 species of low-growing European perennial herbs. Garden forms have handsome downy, sometimes mottled foliage. Their spring flowers of blue, white, or rose grow in coiled clusters at the ends of flower stems that unfurl as buds open.

How to Grow
Shade-loving, prospering in moist, ordinary garden soil in part, light, toward moderately full shade, according to available moisture and location North or South. Propagate by division in fall or early spring.

Uses
Borders, among spring bulbs, edging. 'Johnson's Blue', with its vivid flowers, is a fine border plant. 'Mrs. Moon' is excellent foliage or ground cover.

angustifolia *p. 235*
Blue lungwort, cowslip lungwort. 6–12 in. high. Leaves are 6–9 in. high, dark green, narrow, hairy. Flowers are blue, ¾–1 in. long, in nodding heads, in early spring. Zone 4.

saccharata **'Mrs. Moon'** *p. 235   Pictured above*
Bethlehem sage. 8–14 in. high. The species has leaves that are broadly elliptic, mottled white. Flowers white or rosy purple, ¾–1 in. long, emerging before basal leaves. This cultivar has generously dappled leaves and pink flowers that fade to blue. Zone 4.

Reseda
Re-zee′da. Mignonette
Resedaceae. Mignonette family

Description
Fifty to sixty species of Mediterranean herbs, sometimes woody at the base and varying in habit. A few are cultivated for their fragrant blooms.

How to Grow
The species listed below is suitable for part shade. It is a hardy annual preferring rich soil and cool weather. Sow seeds outdoors in early spring and again in late summer to prolong its period of bloom. Thin seedlings early; established plants are difficult to move.

Uses
Informal beds and borders. Excellent fragrant filler in arrangements.

alba p. 191
White mignonette. Erect, 3-ft.-high plant with feathery divided leaves. Greenish white flowers in half-inch wide, spiky clusters. Hardy annual.

Rhododendron
Ro-doe-den'dron
Ericaceae. Heath family

Description
A large, important, ornamental genus of evergreen or deciduous shrubs chiefly from the north temperate zone. Varying in habit from small, almost prostrate shrubs a few inches high to trees 100 ft. tall. Most cultivated are shrubs 3–15 ft. tall. They offer attractive foliage and spectacular spring or summer flowers to cold-climate gardeners.

Leaves are handsome and substantial, oval to elliptic, with smooth margins. Sometimes they are flocked with a feltlike covering or indumentum. Blooms are showy, generally tubular to funnel- or bowl-shaped, and profuse. Two color series dominate the tribe: white through pink to deep rose-pink, and white through yellow and orange to deep burgundy. Many have a contrasting blotch of color or attractive freckling in the throat of the blossom.

The genus *Rhododendron* includes plants called azaleas in common speech. Azaleas are mostly deciduous, with narrow, funnel-like flowers. Rhododendrons are usually evergreen, with larger, bell-shaped flowers borne in rounded clusters at the ends of branches, called "trusses" among fanciers. The distinctions, however, are somewhat blurred. Those cultivated form such a large, interbred tribe, it is best to know both the scientific and cultivar names when acquiring new plants.

How to Grow

Most of the species listed here prefer morning sun or light shade. Evergreen species like more shade than deciduous ones, as a rule, and must be protected from drying winds and direct sun in winter in Northern climates. Deep shade will restrict flowering and may encourage lanky growth, but is tolerated well by some evergreen species. All rhododendrons in the South will benefit from afternoon shade.

Plant nursery stock in spring, carefully positioning crown of plant so that when soil settles, the trunk will not. Provide water to young plants as necessary and mulch to conserve water and reduce the need to cultivate around the plants; rhododendrons are shallow-rooted and may be damaged by such activity.

The genus requires acid, peaty soil with adequate moisture and good drainage. Richly organic soil, mulched to conserve water, fills this seemingly contradictory requirement. If necessary, feed established plants with acid fertilizers formulated for ericaceous plants, following manufacturer's directions.

As plantings mature, prune lightly to shape if necessary, just after flowering. Tip-prune young plants to promote bushy growth or maintain compact forms. Avoid heavy shearing and heading-back, especially with large-leaved species. Propagated by seed, layers, or in the case of evergreens, semihardwood cuttings.

Uses

This versatile group includes suitable plants for borders, foundation plantings, accent, specimen, naturalizing, screens, and massing in light woods. *R. indicum,* North Tisbury, and Robin Hill groups considered ground covers.

austrinum p. 118
Florida flame azalea. Vigorous deciduous shrub, 6–12 ft. high, with medium-sized leaves and fragrant yellow or golden flowers in mid-spring. Native to the Southeast, where it needs afternoon or continuous light, high shade. In the northern extent of its landscape range, part shade would suffice. Zone 7.

canescens p. 118
Piedmont azalea. Common deciduous woodland shrub, 6–10 ft. tall with lightly fragrant pink or white flowers in spring. Spreads by suckers; old colonies can cover several acres where conditions are good. Native to eastern North America and well-suited to the South. Zone 7.

catawbiense *p. 119*
Catawba rhododendron. A magnificent evergreen shrub, 6–
10 ft. high. Leaves 3–6 in. long, shining green above, paler
beneath. Spring flowers lilac-purple, the cluster 6–10 in. wide.
One of the most reliable and cold-tolerant species. Southeast
North America. Zone 5.

indicum *p. 236*
Indicum dwarf azaleas. A group of evergreen azaleas valued
for their late flowering and often spreading form. 'Balsami-
niflorum' (sometimes called 'Rosiflorum') grows only 18 in.
high and has double salmon-pink flowers. 'Flame Creeper', a
semiprostrate shrub, usually to 10 in. high, has orange-red
flowers and small leaves. 'Kozan', a ground-hugging trailer,
has delicate shell-pink flowers. Japan. All zone 6.

mucronulatum 'Cornell Pink' *p. 119*
Korean rhododendron. Deciduous shrub to 8 ft. high, the
branches upright. Leaves narrowly lance-shaped, 1–3 in. long,
somewhat scaly, turning a handsome yellow-bronze in fall.
Flowers slightly hairy on the outside, funnel- or bell-shaped,
1½ in. wide, rosy-purple, produced in profusion before the
leaves unfold. Clusters 6–10 in. wide. One of the easiest, hardiest, and earliest species, flowering with forsythias and
Daphne mezereum. Eastern Asia. Zone 5.

North Tisbury *p. 236*
North Tisbury azaleas. A group of small-leaved, low evergreens. Branches spread horizontally to 4 ft. wide, mounding
to 15 in. high in 10 years. Give them room to spread or they
will mound excessively. 'Alexander' has bright red flowers and
fine-textured foliage turning bronze in winter. 'Joseph Hill'
has creeping branches and rich red flowers in early summer.
'Pink Pancake', 10 in. high, has bright ruffled flowers. 'Late
Love', the last to flower, has rosy-pink blooms in summer.
Hybrid origin. Zone 6.

PJM Hybrid *p. 120*
PJM rhododendrons. A group of evergreen, rounded shrubs,
3–6 ft. high. Small leaves turn a purplish-bronze in fall. Flowers in 3–5 in. clusters in varying shades of vivid lavender-pink,
magenta, or blue-purple in midspring. One of the hardiest
broad-leaved rhododendrons and more tolerant of harsh exposures in cold climates. Derived from native and exotic species. Zone 4.

Robin Hill *p. 237*
Robin Hill azaleas. A group of shrubby evergreen ground covers, growing ultimately 12–15 in. high and spreading 1½–2½ ft. wide. Leaves as long as 2½ in., and flowers predominantly in soft pastel colors. 'Betty Ann Voss' has pale pink, double hose-in-hose flowers and dark green foliage. 'Mrs. Hagar' has vibrant pink double flowers resembling miniature camellias. 'Hilda Niblett' has soft pink flowers with deep rose markings. 'Sir Robert' has large ruffled flowers ranging from white to pale salmon-pink, and forms a mound 2 ft. high. Derived from Asian species. Zone 6.

Rhododendron 'Snow' *p. 120*
Kurume hybrid azalea. One of a group of evergreen hybrids, generally dense, slow-growing, upright shrubs, 6–10 ft. at maturity, with small, glossy leaves. This cultivar has large, single white flowers in spring as wide as 4 in. across. The tribe is characterized by small, profuse, single or double flowers, mostly in intense colors from white to pink and from salmon to red and purple. Other popular varieties are shell-pink 'Coral Bells', deep red 'Hino-crimson', and cherry-red 'Hinodegiri'. Japan. Will grow throughout the South. Zone 7.

Rhododendron 'Toucan' *p. 121*
Exbury hybrid azalea. One of a group of deciduous, upright-growing azaleas, to 4 ft. high, with leaves yellow, orange, and red in fall. Flowers, borne in trusses 3 in. in diameter, bloom in spring. This cultivar has large, butter-yellow blossoms with a darker splotch. Other named varieties may have pink, cream, orange, rose, or red blooms. Hybrid origin. Zone 5.

Rhodotypos
Ro-doe-ty'pos
Rosaceae. Rose family

Description
A single species of hardy Asiatic shrubs related to *Kerria* and grown for its white flowers and shiny black berries.

How to Grow
Easy to grow in any garden soil, jetbead will tolerate pollution and a wide range of light conditions, from sun to heavy shade. Prune older specimens after flowering to shape and invigorate. Propagated by seeds or cuttings.

Uses
Border or foreground shrub.

scandens p. 121
Jetbead, white kerria. A handsome shrub, 4–6 ft. high, with opposite, short-stalked, doubly-toothed leaves that are more or less oblongish, 3–4 in. long. Flowers pure white, borne in spring, nearly 2 in. wide, the 4 petals suggesting a wild rose. Shining black fruits follow. Zone 5.

Ribes
Ry'beez
Saxifragraceae. Saxifrage family

Description
A large genus of sometimes prickly shrubs, most from the temperate regions, and horticulturally important because it includes currants, gooseberries, and several shrubs grown for ornament.

How to Grow
Alpine currant is suitable for part to light shade and is easy to grow in any soil. Prune at any time. Propagate by layering, cuttings, or seeds.

Uses
Edging, massing, hedging.

alpinum p. 122 *Pictured above*
Alpine currant. An ornamental shrub, 5–8 ft. high. Smallish leaves, 1–2 in. long, are alternate, simple, with toothed lobes and early to unfold. Spring flowers small, in 1-in.-long upright clusters, greenish yellow, the male and female on different

plants; both sexes are needed to produce the smooth scarlet midsummer fruits. Europe. Zone 3.

Rudbeckia
Rood-beck′i-a
Compositae. Daisy family

Description
About 25 species of hardy North American annual, biennial, or perennial herbs. Large daisylike flowers, typically yellow with brown or black centers, hence the common name.

How to Grow
The most popular coneflower, black-eyed Susan, is suitable for part to light shade. Plant in well-drained to rich, moist soil. Prefers warm weather and tolerates heat and drought. Sow seeds outdoors after all danger of frost has passed; in areas with a short growing season, start seeds indoors 8–10 weeks before the last spring frost. Move the plants to the garden after frost and set them 18 in. apart. Fertilize at planting time. Often reseed once established.

Uses
Beds, borders, naturalizing, meadows, cut flowers.

hirta 'Gloriosa Daisy' *p. 192*
Black-eyed Susan. These branching plants grow 1–3 ft. high and are covered with short stiff hairs. Simple, rough, hairy leaves are dark green. The summer-blooming flowers reach 2–6 in. across and are yellow, gold, red, or mahogany, with dark centers. Midwestern U.S. Short-lived perennial or biennial, usually grown as a half-hardy annual.

Sabatia
Sab-bay′she-a
Gentianaceae. Gentian family

Description
A genus of 17 species of annual and biennial herbs found in eastern North America and occasionally cultivated.

How to Grow
These plants like part shade, damp soil, and prefer cool weather. Sow seeds in early spring.

Uses
Wild garden.

angularis p. 192   *Pictured above*
Rose gentian. To 3 ft. high, with branching stems and opposite, ovate leaves. Flowers 1½ in. across, pink — sometimes so pale as to appear whitish — with 5 petals and yellow center. Eastern North America. Hardy annual.

Sarcococca
Sar-ko-kok′a. Sweet box
Buxaceae. Box family

Description
A small genus of Asiatic and Malayan evergreen shrubs; 4 of the 14 known species are planted for ornament. The species below has handsome foliage and fragrant flowers.

How to Grow
Sweet box enjoys part to moderately full shade. Though foliage looks good even in deep shade, flowers and fruits do better in light or part shade. In the northern extent of its range, it will need plenty of indirect light, and protection from intense sun in winter as well. It grows best in moist, humus-enriched soil. Slow to establish, the plants spread by suckers. Increase by dividing established clumps.

Uses
Ground cover under high-pruned trees. Also edges and low hedges.

hookerana var. *humilis* p. 237
Sweet box. Low-growing, mounded shrub to 2 ft. high. Leathery, narrow, shiny, dark green leaves, 1–3 in. long. White

flowers in spring are inconspicuous except for their sweet fragrance. Small black berries. Native to western China and especially useful on the West Coast and in the South, with adequate shade. Zone 6.

Sasa
Sa'suh
Gramineae. Grass family

Description
More than 150 species of woody grasses, most native to eastern Asia and Japan. Rhizomatous woody grasses of medium height, with large leaves with prominent midribs.

How to Grow
Performs best in fertile, moist soil and light shade. Enjoys more shade in the South. Spreads rapidly under good conditions, so restrain in the garden. Although evergreen, foliage is frequently shabby by winter's end; cut plants to the ground to groom plantings.

Uses
Screening and ground cover.

palmata p. 266
Palm-leaf bamboo. Slender-stemmed, to 7 ft. high, usually less. Leaves green above, pale bluish green beneath, to 14 in. long, 2½ in. wide, leathery. Zone 6.

veitchii p. 266 *Pictured above*
Kuma bamboo. To 3 ft. high. Canes slender, dull purple at maturity. Leaves 5–8 in. long, 2 in. wide, green above, bluish gray beneath; as season progresses the edges of leaves dry to an attractive parchment color. Zone 6 or 7.

Saxifraga
Sacks-iff'ra-ga
Saxifragaceae. Saxifrage family

Description
About 300 species of mostly perennial herbs, found chiefly in temperate regions of Europe and America. Garden varieties are typically low-growing, spreading by offsets and runners with attractive leaves and clusters of pink, white, purple, or yellow flowers.

How to Grow
The species described below thrives in part to moderate shade in gritty soil with lime. Not suited to hot, dry climates. Propagate from seeds in early spring or division of rootstocks in spring or summer.

Uses
London pride is an excellent ground cover; also useful in rock gardens and borders.

× *urbium* p. 238
London pride. To 6 in. high. Large, toothed leaves form carpets of shiny, dark green rosettes; leaves light green in spring, turning blue-green, then dark with the passing season. Flowers pink, ¼ in. wide, in airy clusters 8–10 in. above the foliage. Also sold as *S. umbrosa*. Zone 5.

Schizanthus
Sky-zan'thus
Solanaceae. Petunia family

Description
About 10 species of showy annuals native to Chile with flowers of many colors growing in abundance in loose clusters. The 5-lobed, somewhat pouched flowers are often streaked, spotted, and shaded.

How to Grow
The species listed below enjoys part to light shade. It prefers cool weather and is best suited to the West Coast. (Elsewhere, it is a subject for the cool greenhouse.) Grown from seed as a winter or spring annual in protected gardens in California. In northern and cool coastal gardens, grow in a cold frame to flower bud stage, then set out in garden as soon as danger of frost is past.

Uses
Luxurious color and soft texture for summer bedding schemes, containers, cutting.

× *wisetonensis* *p. 193* *Pictured above*
Butterfly flower. 1–2 ft. high. Flowers white, blue, pink, yellow, red, magenta, or combined colors, upper lip streaked yellow. Alternate leaves. Hybrid derived from *S. pinnatus* and *S. retusus* 'Grahamii'. Tender annual.

Sedum
See'dum. Stonecrop
Crassulaceae. Orpine family

Description
A large group of succulent plants varying in habit from tiny-leaved mat-forming types to large border plants. Leaves are colorful, thick, and fleshy. Long-lasting flowers are star-shaped, often profuse. A few are suited to dry shade and lean soil.

How to Grow
The species described below is easy to grow in well-drained, average soil and part to light shade. Good drainage is essential, particularly in winter. Propagate by seeds, division, cuttings, or leaves.

Uses
'Dragon's Blood' is an excellent ground cover or wall plant. Worth trying in difficult areas under shallow-rooted trees.

spurium 'Dragon's Blood' *p. 238*
Two-row stonecrop. Species is a strong-growing creeper, to 6 in. high. Foliage 1 in. long or more, opposite, ovalish, coarsely

toothed, the surface roughened. This cultivar has flowers a deep rose-red, to ½ in. wide, in flat clusters, in late summer, and mature foliage tinged bronze-purple on the margins. There is also a white-flowered form. Foliage is long-lasting and the plant is cold-hardy to zone 3; in milder climates, foliage is somewhat evergreen. Zone 3.

Senecio
Sen-ee′si-o
Compositae. Daisy family

Description
More than 2,000 species of perennials, shrubs, vines, and small trees found throughout the world. Some are grown for their daisylike flowers, others for their foliage.

How to Grow
The species listed below prefers cool weather and is best suited to part shade in coastal areas of California. Difficult to grow from seed, so purchase bedding-size plants at the early bloom stage and set out in the garden in light shade and well-drained soil. Plants in full bloom will not adjust.

Uses
Showy summer annual for bedding, filler, containers.

× **hybridus** p. 193
Cineraria. 1–3 ft. high. Flowerheads 2 in. wide, white to reddish pink, blue, or purple, some with contrasting rings. Somewhat stiff in habit, flowers are borne in broad, rounded heads amidst crisp encircling leaves. Variable. Of hybrid origin. Tender perennial grown as tender annual.

Shortia
Short′i-a
Diapensiacea. Galax family

Description
Eight species of low-growing evergreen herbs, native to mountains of eastern Asia and North America.

How to Grow
Adapts to a range of light, from part to full shade, depending on climate, moisture, and exposure. Cool, moist, well-drained, humusy, acid soil in moderate shade is ideal. In clay loam soils,

add peat moss to bring up acidity and improve texture. Propagate by early spring division of established clumps.

Uses
Specimen in wildflower nooks, ground cover, rock gardens.

galacifolia p. 159 Pictured above
Oconee bells. Creeping, 8-in.-high herbaceous perennial which forms rosettes of delightful foliage. Leaves are roundish or heart-shaped, shining green, stalked. In midspring, these are punctuated by a slender flowering stalk bearing a single white bell to 1 in. across, nodding, large in proportion to the plant. Plant is similar and closely related to galax. Mountains from Virginia to Georgia. Zone 5.

Skimmia
Skim'i-a
Rutaceae. Citrus family

Description
Somewhat tender Asiatic evergreen shrubs, several species grown in mild climates for their showy flowers and attractive foliage and fruit.

How to Grow
Both species well suited for part to moderate shade; *S. reevesiana* will adapt to full shade. These shrubs prefer moist, acid soil with plenty of organic matter. Little pruning needed.

Uses
Ground cover and landscaping use in warm climates.

japonica p. 122
Densely branching shrub, to 3–5 ft. high. Yellowish green leaves, 3–5 in. long, more or less crowded at the ends of twigs. Small yellowish white male and female flowers, usually on different plants, in spring. Male flowers are larger and more fragrant. Female plants have small bright red berries. You must have both male and female plants to get berries. Zone 8; zone 7 with protection.

reevesiana p. 239
Low, compact shrub, to 2 ft. high. Leaves dark green, lance-shaped, to 4 in. long. Flowers small, white, in loose clusters at the ends of stems in spring. Fruit is yellow when unripe, matte red when ripe, retained into winter. Self-fertilizing. Zone 7.

Smilacina
Smy-la-see′na. False Solomon's-seal
Liliaceae. Lily family

Description
About 25 species of herbaceous perennials native to North America and temperate Asia. Forms dense stands of medium-high leafy stems.

How to Grow
False Solomon's-seal likes lime-free, humus-rich soil. It needs part to full shade and does not tolerate heat. Do not disturb roots after planting. Propagate older plants by division. Long-lived and trouble-free once established.

Uses
Borders, wild gardens. Berries lend fall interest to woodland borders.

racemosa p. 160
False Solomon's-seal. Arching stems, to 3 ft. high, clothed with long, slender leaves and topped with showy clusters of bright white flowers in spring. Small red berries are showy in fall and popular with birds. Native Canada to Virginia and Tennessee. Zone 4.

Spartina
Spar-tine'a. Cord grass
Gramineae. Grass family

Description
About 15 species of perennial ornamental grasses with showy flowers and seedheads, widely distributed in temperate coastal regions.

How to Grow
Suitable for part to light shade. Grows well in fresh- or salt-water marshes, and in average garden soil. Its spreading roots make it a good soil stabilizer in moist locations; unfortunately, the characteristic may also make it invasive. Increase the cultivar by division. (The species can also be propagated by seed.)

Uses
In the garden, this variety makes a nice group planting or specimen. Suitable for waterside locations if spreading can be controlled.

pectinata 'Aureo-marginata' *p. 267*
Prairie cord grass. Deciduous, of upright open habit, to 6 ft. high, usually less tall in gardens, spreading by rhizomes. This cultivar is a variegated selection, with leaf blades narrow, light green, to 2 ft. long, arching, with rough margins striped yellow. Flowerhead narrow, in late summer. Often listed as *S. michauxiana*. Zone 5.

Spodiopogon
Spoe-dee-o-po'gon. Silver spike grass
Gramineae. Grass family

Description
A deciduous perennial ornamental grass with upright habit, flowering in midsummer. Native to the prairies of Siberia, introduced to the West via Japan.

How to Grow
Performs well in part to light shade and prefers moist or wet soil. Propagate by division or seeds.

Uses
Waterside plantings and damp spots.

sibericus *p. 267   Pictured above*
Foliage to 3 ft. high. Leaves to 12 in. long, dark green, tinged red by midsummer, redder in autumn. Open flowering panicles to 12 in. long, and up to 5 ft. tall. Zone 5.

Stewartia
Stew-ar′tee-uh
Theaceae. Tea family

Description
About 6 species of deciduous shrubs or small trees with showy white flowers, native to the temperate zones of eastern North America and eastern Asia.

How to Grow
Stewartias prefer light or dappled shade. Afternoon shade and soil mulch will help prevent leaf-scorch during summer. The open north side of a house is often a good location. Prefers moist, acid, well-drained soil containing plenty of organic matter. Small trees transplant best. Pruning is seldom necessary or desirable.

Uses
Lawn or border specimen.

pseudocamellia *p. 123   Pictured on p. 453*
Small, slow-growing shrub or tree to 25–30 ft. White flowers, 2 in. across, solitary and showy, with a boss of orange anthers, appear throughout summer. Leaves turn purple in fall; handsome mottled bark adds winter interest. Japan. Zone 6.

Stylophorum
Styl-lof'o-rum
Papaveraceae. Poppy family

Description
A small genus of perennial herbs mostly native to eastern Asia; the single North American member is listed here. Do not confuse this plant with *Chelidonium majus,* also called celandine, which is similar but invasive.

How to Grow
Plant celandine poppy in part to moderate shade. Prefers deep organic soils. Tolerates constantly moist soils if well drained. Sold as seeds and in containers. Where conditions are to its liking, it self-sows and easily naturalizes. Increase in fall or early spring by division or by transplanting seedlings.

Uses
Naturalizing, borders. Combines well with Virginia bluebells, columbine, foamflowers, and creeping phlox.

diphyllum *p. 160*
Celandine poppy. 1–2½ ft. tall and equally wide. Large, deeply cut, light green to blue-green leaves are a focal point all season and make a good foundation for the middle or rear of a spring bed. Bright yellow poppies bloom for much of the spring and sporadically through summer, if season is not too dry. Seedpods are pendulous, plump, and bristly. Zone 5.

Symphoricarpos
Sim-for-i-kar'pos
Caprifoliaceae. Honeysuckle family

Description
A small group of hardy deciduous shrubs, mostly native to North America, planted for their spectacular display of ornamental berries.

How to Grow

Excellent shrubs for part to light shade, and tolerate city conditions far better than most ornamentals. Grow in a variety of soils but prefer slightly alkaline conditions; may be used in plantings around new foundations where masonry rubble might bother acid-loving plants. Prune regularly and heavily in early spring every few years to stimulate growth and remove old wood. Propagated by softwood cuttings.

Uses

Shrub borders, foundation plantings, landscaping.

albus *p. 123* *Pictured above*
Snowberry, waxberry. To 4 ft. high, the branches slender and upright. Leaves ovalish or oblong, 1–2 in. long, blunt. Flowers pinkish, in spring. Conspicuous, waxy white fruit in fall shows up well in shade. Var. *laevigatus* is nearly twice as tall, with larger leaves and fruit. Zone 3.

Symphytum

Sim-fy′tum. Comfrey
Boraginaceae. Borage family

Description

About 25 species of hardy perennial herbs, natives of Eurasia and North Africa. They have large, somewhat coarse leaves and small yellowish, blue, white, rose, or purple flowers in branching clusters.

How to Grow

Comfrey enjoys part to moderate shade, such as the northern side of a house. Easy to grow in average, well-drained soil. Plant in autumn or spring and propagate by seed or division.

May prove invasive in rich, moist soils, but the species listed below is relatively easy to control in the dry shade it tolerates so well.

Uses
Ground cover, among bulbs, front of borders in dry shade.

grandiflorum *p. 239*
Ground-cover comfrey. 8–12 in. high with oblong or oval, hairy leaves. Flowers creamy white to pale yellow, ¾ in. across, tubular, in nodding clusters at the end of the stalk. Cultivars include 'Hidcote Pink', with soft pink flowers; 'Hidcote Blue', with bluish flowers. May be offered as *Pulmonaria lutea*. Caucasus Mountains. Zone 5.

Tanacetum
Tan-a-see'tum. Tansy
Compositae. Daisy family

Description
Some 50 species of herbs or subshrubs, with yellow flowerheads and aromatic leaves, sometimes weedy, from the north temperate zone.

How to Grow
Tansy grows well in part shade and well-drained soil. Tolerant of less than hospitable sites. Easily propagated by division in fall or spring. May self-sow and become invasive, especially in moist, fertile soil.

Uses
Naturalizing; cutting and dried-flower arrangements. The plant has an interesting history as an herb.

vulgare var. ***crispum*** *p. 161*
Tansy. 2–3 ft. high perennial with ferny, much-dissected leaves. Flowers ⅓ in. wide, yellow-gold, in small, buttonlike heads in clusters on branching stalks. This variety has especially fine, crisp foliage. Taller, rangier, darker green, but the shade-gardening equivalent of *Achillea*. Zones 3 or 4.

Taxus
Tacks'us. Yew
Taxaceae. Yew family

Description
A small genus of handsome, slow-growing, coniferous ever-green shrubs and trees. The genus includes upright, mounded, and spreading species whose needles vary in arrangement. All have short, dark green needles that are lighter green under-neath and reddish brown, attractively flaky bark. Female plants produce fleshy scarlet or brown berries, often appealing to children; unfortunately, the seed inside the fleshy pulp, the leaves, and bark of the yew are very toxic.

How to Grow
Yews grow well in part to moderately full shade. They tolerate a wide range of conditions, as long as soil is well-drained and not too acid. Plant yews in an area shielded from winter wind and sun. Prune or shear them at any time to shape the plants and keep them compact if desired. Avoid injuring the bark with lawn mowers, string trimmers, and pruning tools. Prop-agated by seeds, cuttings, and grafts.

Uses
Versatile landscape shrub with suitable varieties for hedging, ground cover, banks, foundation plantings, shrub borders, and dwarf conifer plantings. They can be clipped into formal shapes and topiary.

baccata 'Repandens' *p. 240   Pictured above*
Spreading English yew. English yews have shiny, slightly curved needles that have 2 pale green stripes on the bottom usually arranged in a flat plane. Although most cultivated selections are upright-growing plants reaching 2–12 ft. high, this variety

is an exception, flattish in habit, growing 2 ft. high, spreading to 6 ft. across. Fruit is olive-brown. Old World. Best in zones 6–8.

cuspidata 'Densa' *p. 240*
Cushion Japanese yew. The needles of this species are soft and dull green with 2 yellowish white stripes on the underside. They are usually arranged in a V shape. There are many horticultural forms; most are spreading plants growing 1–12 ft. tall. 'Densa' grows in a dense, round-topped cushion, to 18 in. high, wider than tall, with short side branches. Leaves 1 in. long, tapering to a blunt point. Scarlet berries. Northeastern Asia. Zone 5.

Ternstroemia
Tern-stro'mi-a
Theaceae. Tea family

Description
About 85 species of tropical trees and shrubs, one of which is grown for its ornamental foliage.

How to Grow
This shrub prefers part shade, but can be grown successfully in light to moderate shade, and is tolerant of even more. Provide plenty of moisture and acid soil. Pinch out growing tips to produce compact growth.

Uses
Low-growing landscape shrub for mild climates.

gymnanthera *p. 124*
Low-growing evergreen shrub, 4–10 ft. high. Glossy, oval leaves, to 3 in. long, are purplish with morning sun and afternoon shade, deep green with less light. Small, fragrant, yellowish flowers in summer. Small yellowish or reddish fruit. India to Japan. Reliably hardy to zone 8, may survive in protected spots in warmer half of zone 7.

Thalictrum
Tha-lick'trum. Meadow rue
Ranunculaceae. Buttercup family

Description
A large genus of graceful perennial herbs, most of the 100 species found in the temperate zone. Delicate bluish foliage

and small but numerous flowers make them splendid border plants for shade.

How to Grow
Easy to grow in moist, well-drained, humusy soil, in part to light shade. Divide in spring. This species often needs staking; plant at the back of the border or next to a fence it can lean on. Not well suited for hot climates.

Uses
Borders, naturalizing, rock gardens.

***rochebrunianum** p. 161   Pictured above*
Meadow rue. Perennial, 3–5 ft. high. Leaves divided into segments suggesting maidenhair fern's. Flowers ½ in. across, in loose, airy clusters, purple, lavender, and mauve, for a long stretch in summer. Japan. Zone 5.

Tiarella
Ty-a-rell′a
Saxifragaceae. Saxifrage family

Description
A small genus of low-growing spring woodlanders with long-lasting foliage.

How to Grow
Foamflower grows best in woodland conditions: moist, well-drained, humus-rich soil and light shade. It will not make a dense cover in deep shade. Propagate by seed or division in the fall. Susceptible to disease in wet springs in warmer climates.

Uses
Ground cover, wildflower and fern plantings, edging, rockeries, light woods.

cordifolia *p. 241   Pictured above*
Foamflower, false miterwort. Deciduous perennial (almost evergreen in the South), to 6 in. high. Leaves broadly heart-shaped, 3–4 in. wide, the margins lobed and toothed. Flowers small, 5-petaled, white, in dense narrow spikes 8 in. high in spring. Colonies in bloom lend a foamy texture to woodland. Zone 5.

Torenia
Tor-ren′i-a. Wishbone flower
Scrophulariaceae. Snapdragon family

Description
African and Asiatic annual or perennial herbs comprising more than 40 species and related to *Mimulus*. Richly ornamental pouch-shaped flowers, velvety in appearance, faintly 5-petaled, irregular with yellow markings.

How to Grow
Prefers part to light shade; colors are richer with afternoon shade. To grow the tender annual described below, start seeds indoors 8–10 weeks before last spring frost. Transplant after danger of frost is past. Prefers warm weather.

Uses
Borders, edges, rock gardens, hanging baskets. This species is often planted beneath dripline of live oak trees in the South.

fournieri p. 194
Wishbone flower. 10–12 in. high, upright. Branching, 4-angled stems, opposite, ovalish leaves. Flowers 1 in. long, 2-toned purplish blue, white with purplish blue spots, or pink and white, with yellow throats in clusters. Many cultivars are available, including compact and large-flowered types. Vietnam. Tender annual.

Trachelium
Tra-kee'li-um
Campanulaceae. Bellflower family

Description
Widely grown perennial herbs comprising about half a dozen species from the Mediterranean region. Closely related to *Campanula,* and cultivated for its dense clusters of flowers.

How to Grow
Enjoys part to light shade. In the Deep South, sow seeds outdoors in the early spring. Elsewhere, start seeds indoors 8–10 weeks before the last spring frost. Plant in the garden when danger of frost is past. For first-year bloom, plants must be started early. Prefers warm weather.

Uses
Blue flower for summer beds and borders.

caeruleum p. 194
Throatwort. 1–4 ft. high, with alternate, ovalish leaves, unequally toothed. Flowers blue or rarely white, in 3–5 in. wide heads; individual florets are tubular, with 5 narrow lobes. Hardy in zone 8; in colder climates, treat as a tender annual.

Tradescantia
Tray-des-kan'ti-a. Spiderwort
Commelinaceae. Dayflower family

Description
About 65 herbaceous species, native to North and Central America. Foliage is grasslike. The 3-petaled flowers are white, blue, purple, or pink, and last only a day over a long period in early summer.

How to Grow
Spiderwort needs well-drained soil and part to light shade.
Easy to increase by division in spring, from stem cuttings
separated at a joint, or from seeds. Space new plants 12 in.
apart.

Uses
Borders, containers, wildflower gardens, or under trees and
shrubs. Tolerates urban conditions.

× *andersoniana* 'Pauline' *p. 162   Pictured above*
Spiderwort. Dense, grasslike foliage, 12–24 in. high. Smallish
3-petaled pink flowers, but many are produced over a long
period in late spring or early summer. After flowering, cut
foliage back; it dies back on its own and reappears in the fall,
but gone-by leaves may look rather messy. The species tends
to have blue to purple blossoms. Other cultivars include
'Zwaanenberg Blue' and white 'Snowcap'. Often listed as *T.
virginiana*. Zone 5.

Tricyrtis
Try-sir′tis
Lilaceae. Lily family

Description
Half-hardy perennial herbs comprising about 12 species, natives of Japan and Taiwan. Linear foliage and orchidlike flowers.

How to Grow
The species below needs part, light, to moderately full shade
and moist, fertile, slightly acid soil. Propagate by division.

Uses
Wildflower nooks, rockeries, among ferns.

hirta p. 162
Toad lily. To 3 ft. high. Flowers 1 in. long, somewhat bell-
shaped, whitish, waxy, heavily spotted with purple and black
on the inside. Leaves are arranged formally, in symmetrical
pairs on long, leaning stems with the flowers appearing between each pair of leaves. Zone 6.

Trillium
Trill′i-um
Liliaceae. Lily family

Description
About 30 species of hardy perennial herbs, natives of North
America and Asia. Thick, short rootstocks send up flowering
stalks, bearing a flat ruff of 3 oval leaves below a showy, pink,
white, greenish, purplish, red, or yellow tripartite flower.

How to Grow
Well-adapted for part to moderately full shade. Trilliums prefer woodland conditions: a deep, rich, moist, acid soil with
plenty of humus. Propagate by fall or early spring division.

Uses
Wildflower nooks and woodland. Lovely in colonies at the
foot of rocks and with ferns.

grandiflorum p. 163   *Pictured above*
Snow trillium. 12–18 in. high. Flowers face up, 2–3 in. wide,
on stalks 3 in. long, waxy white fading to pink. Native Quebec
to North Carolina, west to Minnesota. There are double
forms. Zone 5.

Tsuga
Soo'ga. Hemlock
Pinaceae. Pine family

Description
About 10 species of beautiful evergreen conifers, chiefly from
North America and East Asia.

How to Grow
Hemlocks need cool, well-drained, acid soil and adequate
moisture. They will grow in part to full shade, eventually
adjusting to full sun as they grow. Usually sold in containers
or balled and burlapped; space 25 ft. apart to allow for ultimate growth. A cooling mulch is helpful in establishing young
trees. Avoid planting in the path of harsh and drying winds
or in dry or alkaline soils. Hemlocks cast a dense shade; few
plants will grow underneath them. While plants tolerate shearing and heading back better than most needled conifers, do
not limb up trees from below, which creates an awkward
naked-leg look.

Uses
The species listed below is a versatile evergreen, bringing a
softer, more relaxed feel in hedges, screen, or as a specimen.
Good cover for songbirds.

canadensis p. 87   *Pictured above*
Canada hemlock, eastern hemlock. Magnificent tree, ultimately 90 ft. tall in its natural state, though usually shorter.
Branches droop gracefully with age. Small needles, lustrous
green above, bluish beneath. Small larchlike ornamental cones.
'Pendula' or 'Sargentii' is compact, bushy, usually more broad
than high, with pendulous branches, highly variable in habit
and potentially the most graceful of evergreens. Native Canada
to Alabama, and best suited for gardens in zones 4–7, though

suitable niches may be found in protected sites in zone 3 and cooler locations in the northern half of zone 8.

Uvularia
You-vew-lair'i-a. Bellwort
Liliaceae. Lily family

Description
A small genus of hardy North American perennials. Planted for its large bell-like flowers.

How to Grow
Shade-loving, uvularia enjoys light to full shade. Easy to grow in moist, fertile, slightly acid soil rich in organic matter. Propagate by division in fall.

Uses
Delicate filler in woodland and wildflower gardens, or for massing under shrubs with ferns.

grandiflora p. 163
Big merrybells. To 30 in. high. Thick creeping rootstocks send up branching stems with clasping, alternate, lance-shaped leaves. Flowers yellow, bell-shaped, to 2 in. long, drooping at the ends of the stalks, in spring. Zone 5.

Vaccinium
Vak-sin'i-um
Ericaceae. Heath family

Description
More than 150 species of woody plants, including blueberries, cranberries, and huckleberries. Varying in habit from creeping ground covers to tall shrubs. Most have small, waxy urns for flowers, finely branched twigs, and narrow leaves. Berries edible, though not all are palatable. Native from the Arctic Circle to the summits of tropical mountains.

How to Grow
Plant highbush blueberries in moist, acid soil. Usually available as container-grown or balled-and-burlapped plants. This species is suitable for part to light shade, although fruiting and autumn color will not be as full without adequate light. Like other ericaceous shrubs, blueberries are particular about pH.

Use ammonium sulfate fertilizers, not those containing ammonium nitrate. Add sulfur to bring up acidity. Use mulch to control weeds; cultivation can damage roots that are close to the surface. Prune plants lightly after fruiting. Usually propagated by seed or softwood cuttings in late spring.

Uses
Informal hedgerows, shrubbery, thickets for wildlife. Good for edging and screening kitchen gardens from more ornamental areas. You can eat the late-summer berries if the birds don't get them first.

corymbosum p. 124
Highbush blueberry. Spreading, bushy shrub, 8–12 ft. high. Oval leaves, 2–3 in. long, turn yellow or red in fall. Small white or pinkish flowers in spring and plump blue berries in summer. Plant several varieties together for best fruit production. Eastern North America. Zone 4.

Veronica
Ver-on′i-ka. Speedwell
Scrophulariaceae. Snapdragon family

Description
More than 250 species of herbaceous perennials, many popular for borders or rock gardens. Some species are upright, others are prostrate and more suited to ground covers and edging.

How to Grow
Suitable for part to light shade. Easy to grow in average well-drained soil. Increase by division after flowering.

Uses
Reliable blue flower for midsummer beds and borders.

latifolium 'Crater Lake Blue' p. 164
This cultivar is more compact than the species, with especially bright blue flowers. Species is 12–18 in. high, with fine, narrow foliage. Flowers blue, ½ in. across, in loose, spiky clusters. Zone 4.

Viburnum
Vy-bur'num
Caprifoliaceae. Honeysuckle family

Description
About 150 species of chiefly deciduous shrubs and small trees of the north temperate zone. Many are cultivated for their attractive clusters of fragrant white spring flowers, their often showy fruits, autumn foliage, and handsome form.

How to Grow
Viburnums are easy to grow and enjoy part to light shade. They prefer moist, well-drained, slightly acid soil. Prune plants after they flower, but lightly — to shape and remove awkward limbs. Propagated from seeds or cuttings or by layering. To ensure heavy berry production, plant at least 2 plants of the same species.

Uses
Versatile landscape shrubs; the 2 species described below could happily find their way into mixed borders, shrubberies, wildlife thickets, in pairs or rows in more formal schemes. Berries are much enjoyed by songbirds.

× *carlcephalum* *p. 125   Pictured above*
Rounded, deciduous shrub, 6–10 ft. high and wide. Oval, hairy, dark green leaves, to 4 in. long, turn reddish purple in fall. Very fragrant white flowers in 5-in.-wide clusters in late spring. Berries are red, changing to black. One of the latest viburnums to flower. Hybrid of Asian origins. Zone 5.

dilatatum *p. 125*
Deciduous shrub, 6–10 ft. high. Leaves nearly round, 4–5 in. wide, hairy on both sides and coarsely toothed. Flower clusters

5 in. wide. Fruit showy, scarlet. An attractive shrub in the fall, for the fruit is persistent and foliage turns orange-red. Japan. Blooms in late spring. Best in zones 5–8.

Vinca
Vin′ka.
Apocynaceae. Dogbane family

Description
About 12 species of evergreen, erect, or trailing perennial herbs or vinelike shrubs, natives of the Old World. Two are widely planted as ground cover.

How to Grow
Vinca makes a thick carpet in moderately fertile garden soil. It grows best in light or partial shade but tolerates even more shade. May be sheared annually to encourage denser growth. Easy to propagate by cuttings or division.

Uses
Versatile ground cover and trailer over walls, rocks, terraces.

minor *p. 241   Pictured above*
Myrtle. Trailing, hardy, to 10 in. high, the rooting stems thin and wiry. Leaves broadly lance-shaped, to 2 in. long, dark, glossy, green, and graceful. Flowers small, typically light blue. There are forms with white or double flowers and variegated foliage. Zone 5.

Viola
Vy-o'la. Violet
Violaceae. Violet family

Description
About 500 species of hardy perennial herbs and a few annuals, distributed throughout temperate regions and including the violet and the pansy. Low plants heart-shaped or oval, ruffled leaves often growing in crisp rosettes. 5-petaled, slightly irregular flowers are stalked, solitary, sometimes nodding. Colors include dark violet, blue, reddish purple, lilac, yellow, orange, white, and combinations thereof. They are showy and typically marked with nectar guides in the form of spots, lines, or blotches, often suggesting a human face.

How to Grow
Pansies and violas, usually grown as annual bedding plants, thrive in part or light shade, but the perennial species, usually called violets, perform well in more shade and rich, moist soil. An organic mulch will help maintain soil moisture. Many are short-lived or tender but self-seed successfully or are easily grown as annuals. Propagated by division, rooted runners, or seed. Some are invasive.

Uses
Border edgings, naturalizing, among spring bulbs and ferns, raised beds, children's gardens. Choicer perennials are suited to rockeries if you don't mind their spreading.

cornuta p. 164
Horned violet, bedding pansy. Perennial, 5–8 in. high. Flowers violet, white, apricot, red, or yellow, 1½ in. across, solitary, stalked, and nodding. Where summers are cool and moist, this species blooms all season. Spain and the Pyrenees. Hardy to zone 5, and also treated as an annual bedding plant.

odorata 'Royal Robe' p. 165
Sweet violet. Clump-forming perennial to 6 in. high, with long runners. Heart-shaped basal leaves to 3 in. wide. Sweet-scented flowers open from fall to spring. Spreads to form ground cover. This cultivar has purple flowers; other named varieties include pink 'Rosina' and 'White Czar'. There are also double forms. Native to Europe, Africa, and Asia. Suitable for the South, north to zone 6.

striata p. 165
Striped violet. 4–12-in.-high perennial. Flowers small, frag-

rant, ivory-white but veined brown-purple. Likes a moist, well-drained spot. U.S. zone 5.

tricolor p. 195
Johnny-jump-up. To 12 in. high. Flowers tricolored, purple, white, and yellow, solitary, ¾ in. long, like a tiny pansy. Arguably the most popular spring bedding plant in much of the country, Johnny-jump-ups are a favorite for planting over tulip and daffodil beds. If plants are sheared back, a second more subdued flowering may appear with the return of cool, moist weather in the fall. Europe, naturalized in North America. Perennial to zone 4, usually grown as a hardy annual.

× *wittrockiana* p. 195
Pansy. To 9 in. high. Flowers flat, 2–5 in. wide. Solid colors and combinations ranging from purple, blue, maroon, and red to yellow, orange, and white, some with 3 colors, most with some kind of "face" pattern. Numerous cultivars available, including winter-blooming kinds. This hybrid derives from *V. tricolor, V. lutea, V. altaica,* and possibly other species. Biennial or short-lived perennial usually grown as a hardy annual.

Vitis
Vy′tis. Grape
Vitaceae. Grape family

Description
About 60 species of woody vines native to the north temperate zone. They climb by means of tendrils and produce handsome, large, usually deciduous leaves, muscular vines, and exfoliating bark. The genus includes all the edible grapes, but the species below is grown for bright, ornamental autumn leaves, not its fruit.

How to Grow
Crimson glory vine is suitable for part to light shade and prefers well-drained, fertile soil. A vigorous grower, it should be pruned to desired size and shape at least once every spring. Propagate by seeds or cuttings.

Uses
Excellent climber for adding autumn brilliance to a trellis, tree, or fence.

coignetiae *p. 251*
Crimson glory vine. Strong-growing, to 50 ft. high. Leaves roundish or ovalish, 4–12 in. wide, deeply heart-shaped at base, grayish or rusty beneath. Leaves turn bright crimson in fall. Zone 5.

Appendix

Organic Control of Pests and Diseases in Shade Gardens

NANCY BEAUBAIRE

Shade offers you an opportunity to grow a rich palette of plants that those who garden in the sun must forgo. But whether you garden in shade or in sun, you're likely to find pest and disease problems with your plants from time to time. In fact, with the diversity of plants that can be grown in shade gardens and the varying degrees of light found there, shade plants are subject to as many different kinds of pests and diseases as are sun-loving plants.

Many pests and diseases, such as aphids and powdery mildew, are equally content to feed on susceptible plants whether they grow in shade or sun. Other culprits, notably slugs and snails, favor the cool, dark, damp habitat that shade gardens often provide, though these pests will also foray out into more exposed parts of the garden under cover of night. In woodland settings, deer often become a serious problem.

Shade in a garden is only one of many influences affecting whether plants are attacked by certain pests or diseases. Climate, weather conditions, availability of food, a suitable habitat, and the number of beneficial insects all contribute to the severity and frequency of pest or disease problems. And even if a shade plant is attractive to particular pests or diseases, there's no guarantee they'll appear, or if they do that they'll cause much damage. Plants might be seriously damaged one year, but not the next. Or your neighbor's plants can be de-

cimated by a pest or disease while your garden remains un-
scathed. In part, these differences exist because populations
of pests and disease-causing organisms fluctuate in the garden,
as they do in nature.

The more your landscape resembles a natural ecosystem, the
more likely it is that natural controls, of which there are many,
will kick in. Over the centuries, gardeners who were keenly
aware of the connection between their gardens and the surrounding environment took a cue from nature and developed
environmentally sound tactics for managing pests and diseases.
If, like an increasing number of today's gardeners, you are also
concerned about the environmental liabilities of many synthetic chemical pesticides, you can use these less toxic methods
with great success in your shade garden.

Pest and Disease Control: Environmentally Sound Approaches

To better understand the organic approach to pest and disease
control, it will help to take a look at another environmentally
safe approach to pest control practiced today: integrated pest
management (called IPM).

IPM (also known as least-toxic pest management) is a sys-
tematic approach that relies on regular monitoring of pest
populations to decide if and when to take action. If pests are
causing intolerable damage, nontoxic control strategies are
implemented first, including physical, mechanical, cultural,
and biological methods. When all else fails, pesticides with the
least toxicity, including synthetic chemicals, are selectively applied.

By focusing on a pest in the context of the garden ecosystem,
rather than just as an isolated nuisance to be eliminated, IPM
gives you a method for carefully targeting your control efforts.
This increases the chances that the actions you do take will
be effective. The infrequent use of synthetic pesticides reduces
the potential for harming people and the environment, but still
enables you to take advantage of these products if necessary.
IPM, however, is not a quick fix. It requires more careful
planning and observation, and often more time and effort up
front than synthetic chemicals, but offers the potential of less
work over the long haul.

Organic Gardening: Basic Principles

An organic approach like IPM emphasizes prevention of
problems through careful garden design, sound horticultural

practices, and an understanding of pest and disease life cycles. Organic gardeners rely on many of the same tactics employed in IPM, with the exception of synthetic pesticides. Instead, organic gardeners only use naturally occurring or naturally derived materials or organisms for pest control, such as insecticidal soaps, sulfur dust, or beneficial insects. (According to a chemist's definition of organic, a carbon-containing compound, some of the accepted organic controls, such as sulfur, would be considered inorganic. But in popular usage, organic encompasses a broader view, including where materials come from and how they break down.) Compared to synthetic chemicals, most organic controls pose little or no risk to you, other creatures, or the environment. This makes it easier for existing predators and parasites to come to your aid. Some pesticides that are derived from plants are highly toxic to mammals or to some beneficial organisms, but they all tend to break down quickly into harmless compounds. (Many organic gardeners, in fact, try to minimize use of the more toxic botanical pesticides.) Naturally derived pesticides do have a few disadvantages. They are sometimes slow-acting, and those that break down quickly may require frequent application. As with IPM, your extra work is likely to be rewarded as your garden becomes a more balanced ecosystem.

Organic pest control involves much more than a bagful of environmentally safe remedies. Instead, it's just one part of an overall approach to gardening. Simply put, organic gardeners view the garden as a whole system, they model its design and care on natural processes and they take action only if it's needed. A myriad of gardening practices, from the simple to the sophisticated, continue to evolve from these principles.

This approach, often called "holistic," is more than a philosophical preference, it's based on a biological reality. Everything in your garden is interrelated in one way or another — a fact that's difficult to appreciate when an infestation of bugs on your favorite flowers is as welcome as an invasion from another planet. Nonetheless, all the living and nonliving components of your garden — bugs and blight, roots and shoots, sun and soil, water and wind — make up an ecosystem, which is part of still larger ecosystems around it.

Almost anything you do with one part of your garden will eventually cause something to happen in another part of it, for better or worse. Sometimes the connection is simple; in some regions, if you mulch deeply with leaves during the rainy season, you're likely to create a slug and snail haven. Other times, cause and effect may be very difficult or nearly impossible to pinpoint. In a side-by-side planting of two viburnums of the same species, for example, one shrub may be heavily infested with aphids while the other remains untouched. But in either case, the more you try to understand how each aspect of your garden fits into the big picture, the better you'll know when to take action and when to sit back and let nature take its course.

Learning from Nature

Natural systems provide a sound guide for maintaining your landscape organically, as well as offering inspiring ideas for design. Time spent in woodlands and other naturally shaded environments can provide you with a better understanding of how to care for your garden. With nature as a model, you can design potential pest and disease problems out of your landscape and design in buffers against future problems, all before you ever put spade to soil. The following practices, basic to an organic approach, will prevent many pest and disease problems and help you establish a landscape that's easier to maintain naturally.

Match plants to your site

For starters, grow plants that are suited to the amount of shade you have in your garden. Keep in mind that not all shade is alike; it can range from the deep shade of a mature woodland to partial shade on the north side of a house to seasonal shade beneath a deciduous tree. And shade at higher elevations can provide more light than equivalent hours of shade farther south.

A mismatch between a plant's tolerance of shade and the location where you place it can increase the likelihood of pest or disease problems. For example, pachysandra, which does best in part shade, is more likely to be infested by spider mites and scale when it's grown in full sun. English ivy grows well in shade or sun, but it's more prone to leaf spot (a fungal disease) in sunny locations. Lace bug populations will generally be lower on rhododendrons and azaleas grown in the shade than those in the sun. Many plants that perform well in either sun or shade aren't as susceptible to Japanese beetles when they're grown in the shade.

Susceptibility of shade plants to insects and diseases also can depend on where you garden. Part shade in the South, coupled with intense heat and humidity, can provide a more favorable environment for pests or diseases than the same degree of shade in cooler, drier climates. Warm, moist nighttime temperatures in parts of the South, for example, contribute to fungal diseases on rhododendrons. Azaleas planted in full sun in southern gardens fall prey to spider mites more than those planted in part shade. Farther north, research in

Massachusetts suggests that anthracnose (a fungal disease), is more severe on dogwoods planted in heavy shade near wet-lands or on north-facing slopes, but in the South this disease is more severe on dogwoods planted in the sun.

Choose plants that are well-adapted to your soil, climate, and other characteristics of your site's topography or micro-climate, such as a steep hillside, high winds, early frosts, or reflected heat from nearby paving. Select disease and/or pest resistant varieties or cultivars if they are available.

Provide good growing conditions

Providing optimum conditions for shade plants can go a long way toward preventing pest and disease problems. Learn about the growing environment preferred by the plants you've chosen, and use that as a guide for planting and caring for them. Group together plants that prefer similar conditions. If you are growing annuals, consider planting them in different locations each year to avoid potential build-up of pests and pathogens (disease-causing organisms).

Gear your soil improvement toward meeting the needs of the specific plants you're growing. Cultivate as little as pos-sible, except to work up new areas or control weeds or dis-eases. Enrich the soil with organic matter, such as compost or cover crops, and naturally derived mineral fertilizers. This is always a good practice, but especially important with many shade plants, which thrive in soils rich in organic matter. Com-post your plant debris.

Mulch can be a double-edged sword in a shade garden. It helps create the look of a natural woodland, protects the soil and conserves water, but mulch also can be an irresistible hangout for slugs and snails, who use it as a hiding place. (They also love the big, soft leaves characteristic of many shade plants.) On the other hand, mulch can provide a habitat for snakes that prey on slugs and snails but are harmless to people. If you can't control slugs and snails by nontoxic means, elim-inate the mulch or mulch with a fine material that will be a less suitable habitat for them.

All of these practices will help build friable, nutritionally balanced soil, encourage an active soil life and provide growing conditions that will foster stronger, healthier plants. Healthy plants aren't necessarily less appealing to pests and pathogens, but they are usually better able to tolerate the damage.

Encourage diversity

Nature abhors a monoculture and so should you. By in-cluding many different species and avoiding planting all of one kind together, you're more likely to create a stable eco-system with plenty of beneficial organisms that will help keep problems in check. A mixture of plants also greatly reduces the chance that your entire garden will be wiped out by one particular pest. Plant plenty of flowering plants, especially those in the parsley and sunflower family; they'll provide food for beneficial insects. Create habitats for other natural predators, such as toads, frogs, and birds.

Diagnosing Pest and Disease Problems

The practices outlined above will give you a head start toward creating a balanced garden system. Even so, you're likely to eventually encounter some kind of pest problem that requires additional action. To prepare yourself, find out as much as you can about the pests and diseases that are most common in your area. Learn their symptoms, when they're likely to appear, and which plants are susceptible. Your nursery supplier, a local plant society, arboretum, or botanical garden may be able to help out.

Once you see damage to a plant, the first task is to identify the culprit. This step is easier said than done, but essential if you want to solve the problem with the most environmentally safe and effective techniques. Not every problem on your plants is caused by an insect or other pest organism — damage also can be caused by cold, heat, wind, air pollution, too much or too little water or fertilizer, or other environmental and cultural factors. To make matters more confusing, sometimes this damage looks similar to that caused by pests.

When pests or diseases are the problem, they often are misidentified. Many insects look similar to the nonexpert eye. Sometimes the perpetrator has left the scene before you arrive, and whatever insect is present is blamed. Pests also sometimes hide within the plant or operate underground. Applying controls for the wrong pest often fails to solve the problem or, even worse, aggravates it. Here are some activities to help you figure out whodunit.

Be vigilant
Regularly check your garden for damaged plants and insects and other organisms. Over time, careful observation will help you recognize when something's gone awry with your plants and give you a better sense of local pest and disease cycles. Take an up-close look: check the top and underside of the leaves, along the stems, where the branches meet the stem, buds and flowers, the base of the plant, and the surrounding soil surface. Note leaves that are munched, covered with webbing, or abnormal in shape and color. Pay attention to whether the damage occurs along the leaf margin, the veins, or through-

out the leaf, and whether holes or discolored areas are regular or irregular in shape. Look for wilted, blackened, or chewed stems, sticky exudate on branches, withered or browned flower buds, or loose mounds of soil near the plant.

Look for insects — a 10× hand lens will help you see tiny ones or those not visible to the naked eye. Check for egg masses on or near the plants. Also take a look at plants in nearby wild areas, where pest species may find a habitat to their liking. Occasional nighttime forays into the garden with a flashlight might reveal critters that are hidden from view in the day. Collect samples of any insects or damage that you want to identify.

Take notes

Sometimes, casual observation of your plants will give you all the information you need; other times more serious and regular inspection is in order. In either case, you might find it helpful to carry a notebook with you and record damage or anything else unusual that you observe on your plants. Also record the date you first notice the problem and how it changes over time. Keep track of your garden activities and the environmental conditions. Outbreaks of many pests and pathogens are triggered by changing weather conditions. Warm, wet winters are harbingers of spring outbreaks of slugs and snails; weeks of rainy weather anytime may encourage fungal outbreaks. This record-keeping may seem like a lot of trouble, but the information will provide invaluable clues for tracking down the cause of the problem.

Identification

One of the best clues to the identity of a pest is the damage it causes. Chewing insects, such as beetles, caterpillars, and grasshoppers, eat holes in leaves or munch away surface leaf tissue, leaving a sort of leaf skeleton. Cutworms often nip off seedlings at ground level. White, irregular-shaped pathways on the surface of a leaf mark the trails of leaf miners, which tunnel their way between the layers of leaves. Borers burrow into stems and branches, sometimes leaving oozing, sticky sap or sawdust in their wake. Slugs and snails also chomp leaves.

Aphids, mealybugs, scale insects, whiteflies, and mites (which are more closely related to spiders than insects), all suck the sap from plants. This disruption of normal plant growth causes a variety of symptoms, ranging from wilted, twisted, yellowed, spotted, or curled leaves to stunted or dead plant parts. If aphids or scale insects are causing the damage, they will often leave behind an accumulation of honeydew, a sticky, shiny substance, on leaf surfaces, as well.

Plant diseases are most often caused by fungi, bacteria, or

viruses. But pathogens are more elusive than insect pests. Most are microscopic, so your best bet is to try to identify them by their typical symptoms or signs. Mildews are recognized by a gray-white powdery coating on leaf surfaces, stems, or fruit, sometimes with yellowed or dead areas beneath. Leaf spots, which can result from fungi or bacteria, appear as discolored lesions on the leaves — yellow, red, brown, tan, gray, or black spots. Sometimes the infected leaves wilt and rot. Blights cause leaves, branches, twigs, or flowers to suddenly wilt or become brown and die. Often, the stem appears water-soaked and blackens at the soil line. Rots, caused by fungi or bacteria, can cause similar decay of roots, of the lower part of the stem, or of other succulent plant tissue. Viruses can produce white, yellow, or pale green discolored patterned or spotted areas on leaves, and less commonly on stems, fruit, or roots. Virus-infected plants often become stunted. While these symptoms are generalizations at best, they should point you in the right direction.

For help in identifying the insects, other organisms, or symptoms you encounter, refer to books on the subject. Those with good color photos and/or diagnostic keys are likely to be the most helpful for beginners. Reliable diagnosis of plant problems is often tricky business, so you shouldn't feel reluctant to turn to an expert for assistance. Your Cooperative Extension Service (listed under government offices in the phone book) or a local nursery or garden center may be able to help or refer you to someone who can.

Before you take action
Learn as much as you can about the pest's life cycle and preferred environment before you take action. Find out at which stage in its life cycle the damage has occurred — if a caterpillar is chomping your leaves, you'll need to control it, not the adult butterfly or moth it will become. Monitor pest populations to see if their numbers are increasing, decreasing, or holding steady. Check for beneficial insects or other organisms that prey on the pest; given time, they may provide adequate control. Even an ill-timed spray of an apparently harmless substance like water can wash off beneficial insects.

Decide if you and your plants can live with the damage. Specific guidelines have been developed to help large-scale growers of commercial crops figure out just how many of a particular insect pest are too many, but home gardeners are left to their own judgment. Keep in mind that beneficial insects need a supply of pests to maintain their populations. If a pest-covered plant is seriously damaged and going downhill fast, and there are no natural enemies in sight, you need to seriously think about taking action. On the other hand, if you spot a few pests here and there, but they aren't causing much harm, and they aren't on the increase, then you might take a wait and see attitude. You'll also need to think about your aesthetic standards and decide just how much damage is acceptable to your eye.

Organic Controls

It is impossible here to address individually the many pests and the controls for each one. Instead, we offer an overview of the types of organic controls available. Each particular problem will require some research on your part — consulting a neighbor experienced in organic practices, a local professional, or detailed reference books. This research can be interesting and, with experience, you'll become an expert yourself.

To choose the most appropriate, safest organic control, ask yourself the following questions. Do I need a control with immediate impact or can I wait for a long-term control to take effect? Is this the right time to take this action? Is this control the least disruptive to beneficial insects and the safest for humans, other animals, and the environment? If the control requires me repeatedly to do something, such as handpicking insects off plants, do I have the time and patience to follow through?

Once you decide to take action, start with the most benign controls, ones that you can accomplish with just your own hands (or feet), and move on to other tactics as needed. In the end, a combination of strategies often proves most successful.

Cultural controls

First, change any cultural practices that might make your plants more susceptible to a particular pest. For example, planting earlier might give your plants a chance to establish themselves before the pests that attack them are up and running. Another strategy is to modify the pest's habitat in a way that discourages its survival. For instance, you might remove a thick mulch or clear out adjacent weedy areas where the pests hide when they're not feeding in your garden.

Mechanical and physical controls

Traps, barriers, cages, row covers, and other mechanical devices are an excellent way to exclude pests before they arrive and create a pest-free zone once you've rid your plants of existing pests. Physical controls, such as handpicking pests or crushing them underfoot, are particularly successful for larger critters such as beetles, snails, and slugs. Strong water sprays can physically dislodge certain insects. (To avoid potential disease problems, hose off the plants early in the day so the leaves dry before night.) None of the above methods of control pose any risk to people or the environment.

Biological controls

Increasingly, gardeners are making use of their pests' naturally occurring enemies: predators, free-living organisms that feed on other organisms; parasitoides, which kill their hosts; and pathogens, microorganisms that release toxins into the insects that ingest them. These beneficial insects, mites, nematodes, and microorganisms are probably already at work naturally in your garden. Under the best of circumstances, you can just sit back and enjoy the fruits of their labor.

If, however, these beneficial organisms haven't appeared yet or their numbers are too small to provide control, you can purchase laboratory-reared beneficials to release in your garden. There are commercially available beneficials that control pest insects, mites, or snails. Some, like the larvae of the green lacewing, can be quite effective, while others, like the convergent lady beetle, often fly away before they've adequately controlled their prey. Sometimes the introduced beneficials will establish large enough populations in your garden to provide ongoing control, other times you'll need to release more periodically.

Microbial insecticides are commercially available, as well. These pathogens include bacteria, fungi, and viruses that are effective against insects and, in some cases, against other plant diseases. One of the most common microbial pesticides, *Bacillus thuringiensis* (commonly called Bt), is a toxin-producing bacteria that kills caterpillars and insect larvae after these pests eat leaves or stems sprayed with it. Bt breaks down quickly in sunlight and is heat-sensitive, so it may require reapplication and must be stored in cool conditions. Depending on the particular pest you want to control, you can choose among several species and varieties of Bt.

Naturally derived pesticides

A wide range of compounds derived from natural sources are sprayed or dusted on plants to control pests and diseases.

Insecticidal soaps. Made of fatty acids, these compounds penetrate the coating of susceptible insects and dissolve their cell membranes, causing death. They are most effective against soft-bodied insects with sucking mouthparts, such as aphids, mites, whiteflies, and thrips. Fungicidal soap formulations, made of sulfur and fatty acids, are used to control diseases such as mildews, rots, leaf spots, and rust. These soaps, sold as liquid formulations, are sprayed on affected plants. They are very safe to use and break down rapidly in the soil, but they can be poisonous to plants (phytotoxic). Test them on a small portion of the plant first. Thorough coverage and periodic reapplication is needed for good control.

Horticultural oils. Oils are used to smother the adults and eggs of a wide range of pests, including certain aphids, scale insects, caterpillars, and mites. Traditionally sprayed when the plant is dormant, newer formulations are safe for spraying on leafed-out plants as well. Follow label precautions to avoid potential phytotoxicity and wear protective clothing to prevent eye and skin irritation during application. Most of the horticultural oils are derived from petroleum; those extracted from vegetables or animals are preferable for an organic approach. The oils have a low toxicity to humans and wildlife and biodegrade rapidly.

Diatomaceous earth. An abrasive dust composed of the skeletal remains of microscopic marine creatures, diatomaceous earth is sometimes sprinkled on the ground as a barrier to protect plants from snails and slugs — with varying results. Diatomaceous earth is nontoxic to mammals but can irritate eyes and lungs, so wear goggles and a dust mask when you're applying it.

Botanical pesticides. These are derived from plants that contain active ingredients toxic to insects. Some botanicals, such as pyrethrin or neem, are effective against a wide variety of pests (they're called broad-spectrum pesticides), while others, such as sabadilla, kill a more limited range of pests. Botanicals also vary widely in their toxicity to humans, other mammals, and insects — pyrethrin, sabadilla, and neem have low mammalian toxicity, while nicotine and rotenone are highly toxic. On the other hand, rotenone is not toxic to honeybees, but sabadilla is highly toxic to them. Regardless of their toxicity, botanicals quickly break down into nontoxic compounds in the presence of sunlight or in the soil. They may require frequent reapplication, but their short period of toxicity minimizes their potential to harm organisms other than the targeted pests.

Minerals. Sulfur, copper, and lime are primarily used to control fungal and bacterial diseases, including mildews, rots, leaf spots, and blights. Sometimes these minerals are sold in a combined formulation, such as copper sulfate or Bordeaux mix, a mix of copper sulfate and hydrated lime. Sulfur dust, lime, and lime sulfur control some plant-sucking insects, as well. Both sulfur and copper disrupt the metabolic processes of targeted pathogens and insect pests. Sulfur is relatively nontoxic to humans; the toxicity of copper varies depending on the formulation. Whether you apply minerals as a dust or a spray, protect your eyes, lungs, and skin to avoid irritation.

Safety. It's wise to wear protective clothing when you apply any of the naturally derived pesticides. This includes a long-sleeved shirt and long pants, rubber gloves, boots, goggles, and a mask. Always follow label directions for use, storage, and disposal. Don't spray on windy days.

A Note on Diseases

Diseases can be transmitted to your plants quite rapidly by a variety of means — air, soil, water, insects, humans, and propagation tools. They can be carried in seed, in cuttings, and divisions. Since pathogens are rarely visible, it's hard to control them by mechanical or physical means.

Prevention plays a more important role in controlling disease pathogens than in controlling insect or animal pests. It's much easier to protect a plant from disease than to cure it. To minimize disease problems in your garden buy healthy plants, choosing disease-resistant varieties if available.

Good air circulation is especially important in a shade garden, where air penetration is often blocked by a dense tree canopy, adjacent walls and buildings, or low-growing, lush carpets of foliage. Whenever possible, choose a site with good air movement, which can reduce disease problems. Space plants far enough apart — crowded plants are a sure invitation for fungal diseases. As the plantings mature, prune or thin the taller, overstory plants to let more air in; if necessary, thin the plants beneath as well.

Other cultural practices can create unfavorable conditions for many pathogens and minimize the spread of existing ones. Don't overwater. Provide adequate drainage by planting in raised beds or amending the soil with fast-draining material. Don't overfertilize, especially with nitrogen. Avoid mechanical damage to your plants — lawn mowers are so frequently rammed into trees that the aftermath has been dubbed "lawn mower blight." Prune out diseased or dead plants and discard them. Debris from healthy plants, which you should also remove from the garden, can be composted. Don't leave long stubs of pruned branches or stems, which can serve as a conduit for disease organisms.

Photo Credits

Gillian Beckett: 80B, 99B, 169A, 175A, 202B, 218A. John E. Bryan: 85A. Bullaty/Lomeo: 140A, 185B. Monika Burwell: 263A. Al Bussewitz/ PHOTO NATS, INC.: 80A, 88–89, 93B, 109B. Ornamental Horticulture Dept., Calif. Polytechnic State Univ.: 256B. David Cavagnaro: 212–213, 220B, 270B. John E. Elsley: 237A, 251B. Thomas E. Eltzroth: 166–167, 169B, 173A, 181B, 186A, 188B, 190A,B, 191A, 192A, 218B, 231A, 242– 243, 248B, 251A. Derek Fell: 83A, 91A, 94B, 106A, 108B, 109A, 112A, 114A, 117A, 119B, 120A,B, 121A, 184A, 187A, 198A,B, 204A, 206A, 219A, 220A, 232A,B, 240A,B, 254A, 259A,B. Charles Marden Fitch: 84B, 97B, 103B, 248A. Judy Glattstein: 173B, 180A. Pamela Harper: 92B, 94A, 95B, 96A, 97A, 98A, 100A, 101A, 102B, 104B, 105A, 107A,B, 110B, 111B, 115B, 116A,B, 118A,B, 121B, 123A, 124A, 125A, 126–127, 128A,B, 129A,B, 130B, 131B, 132B, 133A,B, 134A,B, 135A,B, 136A,B, 137A,B, 139A, 141A,B, 142A,B, 143A,B, 144A, 145A,B, 146B, 147A,B, 149A,B, 150A,B, 151B, 153A, 154B, 155A,B, 156A,B, 157A, 158A,B, 159A, 160A,B, 161A,B, 162B, 163B, 165A, 168A,B, 170B, 172A, 174B, 175B, 178B, 180B, 181A, 182A, 183B, 185A, 188A, 192B, 193A, 196–197, 199A,B, 200A, 203A,B, 204B, 208A, 209B, 210B, 215A,B, 216B, 217A,B, 221A,B, 222A,B, 223A,B, 224A, 227A,B, 228A,B, 230A, 231B, 233A,B, 234A, 235A, 236A,B, 237B, 238A, 239B, 241A,B, 244A, 245B, 246B, 247A,B, 256A, 257A, 260B, 261B, 262A,B, 263B, 271B, 272B, 273A. Walter H. Hodge: 102A, 103A, 111A, 113A,B, 122B, 139B, 178A, 182B, 189A, 193B, 201A, 258B, 266B. Sam Jones: 91B, 268–269, 270A, 271A, 272A, 273B. P. E. Keenan Photo Library: 86A. Helen Kittinger: 230B. Peter Loewer: 172B, 177A. Dorothy Long/PHOTO NATS, INC.: 199A. John A. Lynch: 82B, 159B, 163A, 165B, 224B, 245A. Robert E. Lyons/PHOTO NATS, INC.: 78–79, 87B, 239A. Frederick McGourty: 205B, 216A, 252–253, 261A, 265A. Edward A. McRae: 207A, 208B. Richard A. Simon: 255B, 257B, 260A, 266A, 267A,B. Joy Spurr: 90A, 123B, 140B, 144B, 148A, 174A, 184B, 191B, 211B. Alvin E. Staffan: 124B, 211A. Steven Still: 81A,B, 82A, 83B, 86B, 87A, 90B, 93A, 95A, 96B, 98B, 99A, 104A, 105B, 106B, 108A, 110A, 112B, 115A, 117B, 122A, 125B, 130A, 131A, 132A, 138A,B, 146A, 148B, 151A, 152A,B, 153B, 154A, 162A, 164A,B, 170A, 171A,B, 176A,B, 179A, 186B, 187B, 189B, 194A, 195A,B, 200B, 201B, 202A, 214A,B, 219B, 225A,B, 226A,B, 229A,B, 234B, 235B, 238B, 244B, 246A, 249A,B, 250A,B, 254B, 258A, 264A,B, 265B. David M. Stone/PHOTO NATS, INC.: 84A, 101B, 177B, 194B, 205A. George Taloumis: 85B, 92A, 100B, 114B, 255A. T. K. Todsen: 183A, 210A. Herman V. Wall: 206B, 207B, 209A.

Index

Titles available in the Taylor's Guide series:

At your bookstore or by calling 1-800-225-3362